The Spiral Road

Change in a Chinese Village
Through the Eyes of a
Communist Party Leader

Development, Conflict, and Social Change Series

Series Editors
Scott Whiteford and William Derman
Michigan State University

The Spiral Road

Change in a Chinese Village Through the Eyes of a Communist Party Leader

Huang Shu-min

Iowa State University

Foreword by Bernard Gallin

Westview Press
BOULDER, SAN FRANCISCO, AND LONDON

Development, Conflict, and Social Change Series

Copyright © 1989 by Westview Press, Inc.

Published in 1989 in the United States of America by Westview Press, Inc., 5500 Central Avenue, Boulder, Colorado 80301, and in the United Kingdom by Westview Press, Inc., 13 Brunswick Centre, London WC1N 1AF, England

Library of Congress Cataloging-in-Publication Data
Huang, Shu-min
    The spiral road: change in a Chinese village through the eyes of
a Communist Party leader / by Huang Shu-min.
        p.   cm.—(Development, conflict, and social change series)
    Includes index.
    Bibliography: p.
    ISBN 0-8133-7637-8
    ISBN 0-8133-0938-7 (if published as a paperback)
    1. Villages—China—Lin Village (Fukien Province)—Case Studies.
    2. Fukien Province—(China)—Rural conditions—Case Studies.
    3. Communism—China—Fukien Province—Case Studies. I. Title.
    II. Series.
    HN733.5.H84   1989   88-17596
    307.7′62′0951—dc19   CIP

Printed and bound in the United States of America

    The paper used in this publication meets the requirements of the American
(∞) National Standard for Permanence of Paper for Printed Library Materials
    Z39.48-1984.

10   9   8   7   6   5   4   3   2   1

Contents

Illustrations

Foreword

My involvement in this book and its Foreword has personal as well as professional roots. I first met Professor Huang Shu-min in 1969 when I traveled to Taiwan to continue my anthropological study of Chinese culture and society. Huang was a graduate in anthropology from National Taiwan University and a junior scholar at the Institute of Ethnology, Academia Sinica. I was delighted when he agreed to work with me as my research assistant, and his help in no small way was responsible for the success of my field study. In the years since that work, we have maintained our relationship, first as teacher-student, when Huang came to Michigan State University in 1970 for his doctorate in anthropology, and then as colleagues in the field of China studies.

In November 1984, soon after Professor Huang began his research in Fujian, I visited him in the field. My visit was brief, but I gained an intimate and invaluable view of rural life in China. Huang introduced me to his village and villagers and, through his insights, illuminated the impact of the recent economic reforms on the countryside and their relationship to Taiwan's socioeconomic development and change.

Most researchers as well as the government of the People's Republic of China (PRC) had long held the view that the Taiwan experience was irrelevant to the PRC. The political and economic systems of the two Chinese areas were so different that comparison was considered pointless. Introduction of economic reforms and the "opening" of the PRC in the late 1970s, however, were accompanied by the recognition that the reorganization of the economy, particularly in the rural area, was producing changes that paralleled those that had occurred during the process of Taiwan's development. The comparison, it was realized, held promise both as a guide to interpreting change in the PRC and as a key to understanding Chinese society.

Professor Huang's work establishes an important base for the construction of such a comparison. His earlier, extensive research on Taiwan (Huang 1981) documented the way the government's policies led to the "degradation of agriculture" and the undermining of community solidarity. His current study shows how different state policies operate in a similar cultural context. Through his Fujian village research, he enlightens us on the link between government policy and rural change and on a number of long-standing concerns in the study of Chinese society—for example, the nature of the government's involvement in local-level village life and issues of grass-roots rural organization and control; the structure of local leadership and the buffer role it plays between government and peasantry; the role of family, kinship, and non-kin social relationships in rural life; and the nature and role of China's peasantry in the country's economy and development process.

Huang's analysis of peasantry is particularly illuminating for its contribution to both definition of this social category and understanding of "twists and turns" in China's policies. There has been long-standing debate over whether peasants are non-capitalist subsistence producers or capitalist entrepreneurs. These opposing views have been reflected in the state's position toward the Chinese peasantry as it has grappled with the question of how to modernize the country. Fearing that following a capitalist, rather than a socialist, road would lead to "capitalist restoration" (Hinton 1972:9–22), the government has taken different, and seemingly contradictory, positions on China's mass of rural residents.

For most of their years in power, China's leaders viewed peasants, in the words of Hinton, "as petty owners of productive property, [who] were carriers of bourgeois ideology" (1972:25), and individualists who wished to "enlarge private plots . . . expand free markets, reduce planning to the family level, and base production on the family as a unit" (1972:42). From the perspective of the government, this "bourgeois ideology" was a barrier to China's progress. The state thus sought to modify the "short-sighted," "backward," and "superstitious" mentality of the rural population. The first three decades of the PRC's existence were marked by programs implemented to transform "the ideology, culture, customs, and habits [of the peasantry] . . . along with all the institutions that reflect and perpetuate them . . ." (Hinton 1972:19).

Huang's Fujian village study provides valuable insights into the how and why of this transformative effort. In this book we see how the government attempted to change the peasant mentality and to modernize the country through collectivization of the land and the economy and why it abandoned the effort in the late 1970s and replaced its failed policy with the Responsibility System that reinstituted family farming. The book demonstrates well how entrepreneurial, "bourgeois," Chinese peasant values—originally viewed as the root of China's backwardness—came to be accepted as the answer to China's rural economic problems.

Other scholars working on the PRC as well as on traditional and pre-revolutionary China have long shared a concern with issues such as peasantry, development, and the character of and way in which Chinese rural society interacts with the market and the state. But, unfortunately, until the end of the Cultural Revolution and the death of Mao Zedong, our understanding of these issues in contemporary China was limited. The country was relatively inaccessible, and most of our knowledge was obtained from the frequently distorted picture the government presented of its achievements and problems and the reports of those allowed to visit the PRC, most of whom were people ideologically predisposed to accept the means deemed necessary to achieve the revolution's ends. Some more pragmatically oriented "China Watchers" were permitted to enter the country. But their ability to observe and document the Chinese situation was hampered by the fact that they could travel only in certain approved areas and primarily were dependent on information selectively made available by their hosts. Even researchers allowed to conduct studies were restricted in the areas where they could work, and they usually could remain in any one rural village for no more than a few weeks at a time.

In the post-Mao period and, more specifically, in the period of the economic reforms, the government has begun to permit foreign scholars to conduct long-term research in China. As a result, our knowledge of the PRC increasingly is based on data collection through extensive fieldwork. Western scholars, often working in cooperation with their Chinese counterparts, are conducting field research in China in a single place and, frequently, over relatively long time periods. Such research conditions are essential for observation and data collection if adequate analyses are to be made of economic, political, and cultural change in China.

Huang Shu-min's work in the PRC has benefited from the government's new stance toward research in the country. It has enabled him to produce an objective and diachronic picture of one rural village. Huang's work also has benefited from the qualifications he brings to the study of China. He was born on the mainland, raised and educated in Taiwan, and trained as an anthropologist in Taiwan and the United States; he has a native fluency in Mandarin and in the language (known as Hokkien, Amoy, or Minnan) of his Fujian research area. These qualifications facilitated his fieldwork and have been invaluable in the development of his insightful analysis of the village.

In this book, Huang provides a detailed life history of the village's most important official. But he also incorporates intensive enthnographic work and interviews with others in the village and larger area into his narrative. Through the dual approaches of ethnography and life history, he presents and analyzes his informants' own perceptions and interpretations of changing social life as they lived through the various phases of China's revolution. Huang also provides insights into the continuing problems of fieldwork in China and of anthropological fieldwork in general. By presenting his personal thoughts during give-and-take discussions with informants, he helps the reader experience a fieldworker's interview strategies, fears, tensions, and need for self-assurance throughout the interview process. The reader is thus afforded the opportunity to understand how the very process of fieldwork plays a determinant role in ultimate findings.

As Professor Huang moves to other areas of China for fieldwork—he now is conducting research in the northern province of Shandong—we can look forward to additional material that will contribute to our understanding of China's peasants and their role in the PRC's development and change. At this point, we need comparative studies that highlight the significance of China's regional differences. The work of scholars such as Professor Huang is building the data base necessary for understanding the diverse nature of Chinese society. His book represents a major contribution to our knowledge of change in one province of China and will serve as a classic source for future comparative work.

Bernard Gallin
Michigan State University

References

Hinton, William (1972). Turning Point in China: An Essay on the Cultural Revolution. N.Y.: Monthly Review Press.

Huang Shu-min (1981). Agricultural Degradation: Changing Community Systems in Rural Taiwan. Washington, D.C.: University Press of America.

Acknowledgments

This book is a spin-off of my several years of research involvement in southern Fujian Province in southeast China. Financial support was provided by several organizations and included an international conference travel grant from the American Council of Learned Societies in 1981 for a trip to Xiamen City, an Iowa State University (ISU) summer research grant for a one-month visit to Harvard University's East Asian Studies Center for library research in 1981, a grant from the National Science Foundation, and a fellowship from the Committee on Scholarly Communication with the People's Republic of China (under the auspices of the National Academy of Sciences) in 1984–1985 for the actual field project in Fujian. I am grateful to all these organizations for their support of my research.

In fall 1985 I received a one-semester Faculty Improvement Leave from Iowa State University to work on this manuscript. Dr. George Christensen, then vice president of academic affairs and Dr. Gerald Klonglan, chairman of the Department of Sociology and Anthropology, made this leave possible. In 1985–1986 and 1986–1987 I received research assistantships for two graduate students: one assistantship from ISU's World Food Institute (then headed by Dr. Charlotte Roderuck) and one from the Technology and Social Change Program (now headed by Dr. Dennis M. Warren but at that time by Dr. Edwin Jones). Their generous financial support and faith in my work are deeply appreciated. Dr. Roderuck also provided funds for editorial assistance to prepare this manuscript.

Many people have influenced me throughout my career. Because of their teaching, friendship, and encouragement, I have been able to develop my appreciation for anthropology through my research in rural China. Professor Li Yih-yuan, dean of the College of Humanities and Social Sciences, Tsing Hwa University, Taiwan, and Professor Wang Sung-hsing, chairman of Comparative Cultures, Chubu University, Japan, first introduced me to fieldwork in rural Han Chinese society in Taiwan. Their dedication to learning and their unyielding moral integrity despite political pressure have been important influences in my career. Professors Bernard and Rita Gallin of Michigan State University not only took me in as part of their family during my graduate school years there but also provided guidance, encouragement, and intellectual exchanges since then. Through many years of close collaboration with them I have been able to look at subjects with a new perspective.

My year in Fujian was made possible by Professor Chen Bisheng, former director of the Taiwan Research Institute, Xiamen University. He also provided four graduate students from Xiamen University to assist with my field project: Ge Xiaojia and Su Weimin of the Taiwan Research Institute and Shi Yulong and Guo Zhichao of the Anthropology Program. Without Professor Chen Bisheng's continuous support and timely advice, this project would not have been possible. Party Secretary Ye and the villagers in Lin Village did their best to make my stay among them an experience in family living. Words alone cannot fully convey my most sincere gratitude to them.

Several people have read and commented on earlier drafts of this book. Professor Bernard Gallin first suggested the book's present format and later read the manuscript thoroughly and offered most insightful comments and suggestions for revision. Kathy Gardner of Ames, Iowa, provided expert editorial assistance in the final draft and made valuable additions to its contents. Professors Scott Whiteford and William Derman, Department of Anthropology, Michigan State University, and Dean Birkenkamp, vice president of Westview Press, also discussed with me necessary revisions to make this book acceptable to a broad audience rather than to only a few China scholars.

My final words of appreciation go to my wife, Anne, and my children, Wendy and Winston. Their willingness to accept my long absences and their continuous emotional support have made my fieldwork possible.

Huang Shu-min

The Spiral Road

Change in a Chinese Village
Through the Eyes of a
Communist Party Leader

Introduction

China has one of the oldest riverine civilizations in the world. In the north, where agriculture first developed in China, fertile river valleys and alluvial plains along the Yellow River, plus hardworking and creative peasants, produced a stable agrarian society that continued uninterrupted for several millennia and expanded to cover the entire eastern rim of the Asiatic continent (Anderson 1988).

The Chinese Peasantry in Historical Context

Peasants in traditional China laid the economic basis of the society; yet their status in society can be described at best as ambivalent. On the one hand, traditional Confucian scholars and officials, recognizing the important role of peasants in an agrarian economy, lavishly enshrined them as a quasi-nobility second only to the scholar-officials themselves in social standing. In the idealized Confucian world, these humble, frugal, and industrious peasants shared with the scholar-officials respect for tradition and universal harmony and unquestioning loyalty to the ruling regime. It was among these bucolic, down-to-earth country folk that the Confucian scholars first acquired their knowledge about human society and further nourished their political ambition to serve.

This official orthodoxy, however, was probably more valid in theory than in reality and was rarely practiced. Peasants were accorded nothing like the status that Confucian scholars ascribed to them. In fact, the opposite seemed to be true. Mencius (circa 390–305 BC), in his dialogues with petty kings and nobility of his time, commented on the peasants' suffering at the hands of despotic rulers:

> In calamitous years and years of famine, the old and the weak of your people, who have been found lying in the ditches and water channels, and the able-bodied who have been scattered about to the four quarters, have amounted to several thousand (Legge, n.d., *Mencius*, Chapter XII, Entry 2, p. 503).

> Now, the livelihood of the people is so regulated, that, above, they have not sufficient wherewith to serve their parents, and below, they have not sufficient wherewith to support their wives and children. Notwithstanding good years, their lives are continually embittered, and in bad years, they do not escape perishing.

1

In such circumstances they only try to save themselves from death, and are afraid they will not succeed (Legge, n.d., *Mencius*, Chapter VII, Entry 22, p. 464).

Along with merchants, landlords, and usurers, who typically lived in towns and cities and who preyed on peasants' ignorance or misfortunes, even the scholar-officials frequently wrested from the peasants their last handfuls of grain, their only source of revenue to cope with natural disasters, foreign invasion, or any other crisis. Pearl Buck's keen observation succinctly pointed out the powerlessness of Chinese peasantry: "They were the voiceless ones, though they and their kind made four fifths of all China's people. They were the ones . . .abused by overlords and taxed by governments. They were the ones who were at the mercy of famine and flood" (Buck 1949, p. vi). Things seemed to have changed little between Mencius's time and that of Buck.

Besides their ambivalent social position, the real enemy Chinese peasants had to deal with throughout history was probably nature itself. There was only a limited amount of arable land the peasants could expand into before they confronted barren deserts, forbidding hills, hostile nomads, or ultimately, the ocean. In the meantime, the number of children produced in peasant families multiplied. Inevitably, the clash between a burgeoning peasant population and a limited ecosystem produced the classic example of human miseries that Thomas Malthus had gloomily predicted in his population theory.

This human-nature conflict was most clearly embodied in the dynastic cycles that scholars, both Chinese and Western, have long recognized as the most distinct attribute of Chinese history (e.g., Owen and Eleanor Lattimore 1944; Elvin 1973; Perkins 1969). The cycle was characterized by a period of stability and prosperity at the beginning of a dynasty, gradually turning into disunity and disintegration, and ultimately chaos and warfare, until the old regime was toppled and replaced by a new one. During this turbulent finale, a large segment of the population would be eliminated through war, famine, dislocation, and pestilence, until a new equilibrium between humankind and land could be re-established and a new cycle begun.

Occasionally, there were major innovations and breakthroughs in China's pre-modern technology that lifted the ceiling on agricultural production and hence temporarily postponed this inevitable clash between humans and nature. Technological developments such as the iron plow, sluice gate, and inter-cropping belong to this category. The introduction of New World crops to China after the sixteenth century also contributed significantly to population growth in subsequent centuries (Ho 1955). Likewise, territorial expansion of the Chinese peasant population to the southwest in the seventeenth and eighteenth centuries, and to Manchuria in the nineteenth century, also reduced some of the potentially disruptive factors that ultimately exploded in the twentieth century.

Despite all the hardships traditional Chinese peasants endured, they led a life that appeared to be useful and gratifying, and established a society that seemed to be durable and resilient. Soon after a major dynastic disruption, the peasants settled back quietly to rebuild their adobe huts and arduously toiled the field for the promised foods. The peasants' relentless efforts and creative ingenuity notwithstanding, a new social order was established in which they were the perennial underdogs. The question one may ask is, What contributed to this durability and stability? What made the Chinese peasants susceptible to all those tyrannical rulers and abusive overlords? Some of the possible factors are identifiable.

The most stabilizing factor in Chinese peasant social life was concern for the family. A family, in the traditional peasant world, implied not just a homestead in a materialistic or economic sense in which one found food, comfort, protection, security, and old age support. The family was even more important: It was the social, ideological, and ritual entity in which the peasants found continuity in time and a place for self in the afterlife. A family in this sense was more than the sum total of all its living members. A family was the converging point in the temporal sense where the ancestors, who begot the living members, and the offspring, who were yet to be conceived and raised, interfaced. A man's place in the universe was thus defined by his ability to provide the proper linkage between the past and future. For his ancestors, he should provide proper burial and ceremonial sacrifices to appease them. For his descendants, he was obliged to ensure them a place to live and a proper marriage to produce sons.

This family concern, as many scholars have pointed out (e.g., Harrell 1985; Hsu 1948; and Nee 1985), motivated traditional Chinese peasants to work hard, to compete relentlessly, and to defer immediate consumption needs for long-term interests. Each family acted as a collective entity in which all individual capabilities were carefully measured, weighed, and prioritized, and a long-term strategy was charted out to maximize this shared potential. The success of a family gave the members both security in this life and definable positions in the spiritual world. This concern for family continuity motivated traditional Chinese peasants to be ready to settle down, build a homestead, toil in the meager fields, and accumulate whatever possible for long-term needs.

The second factor that contributed to stability in traditional Chinese social life can be seen in its relatively flexible class system. Even though the peasants traditionally occupied the bottom layer of the social hierarchy, this class division was never rigid. Through careful planning and shrewd management of the available resources, a peasant family might successfully push one of its more talented sons to become a merchant, a handyman, or even an official. Since the peasants were not excluded from acceptable avenues of upward social mobility, their aspiration was first and utmost to achieve success *within* the established social order. Antiestablishment sentiment was generally not a part of the peasant mentality, as the Confucian scholars correctly stated.

Nor was the traditional Chinese peasant always governed by a tyrannical, coercive, and abusive regime. The meritocracy promoted by Confucius did indeed incorporate many capable and conscientious scholars into the officialdom. Even more important, as many scholars have pointed out before (Fairbank 1979; Hsiao 1960), the imperial Chinese bureaucracy was really too small for it to be an effective and ubiquitous governing body. Court rulings, at best, reached the county level, and below that there was something more like local autonomy. Local gentry or powerful families might serve as intermediaries between the central government and the masses in fulfilling taxation quotas and military conscriptions. They thus occupied a pivotal position for potential abuse. But as these local elite were constantly under the close watchful eyes of the central government, and as they had multiple kinship ties with the local peasants, the extent of their abuse was limited. There were acknowledged legalities that all involved parties had to respect, such as rent for tenant land or usury rates for money borrowed. These contractual obligations were established through mutual consent, and in an open market both parties could make their own choices in an agreement. A peasant family might be exploited by the landlord or the usurer. But there was always the possibility, through thrift and hard work, that the family could rid itself of all debts or loans and, ultimately, put itself in a position to collect rent or interest.

It is under this cultural ethos that we find the tenacity, continuity, and creativity of traditional Chinese peasant society. This system seemed to function smoothly during the pre-modern era when China was more or less isolated from other major civilizations of the world, and when there were few challenges from neighboring political entities. The perpetual cycle of growth, decline, decay, and regeneration that characterized the dynastic processes testifies to the wisdom and utility of established cultural tradition. Conservatism rather than innovation became the rule of conduct in intellectual pursuits.

The conditions changed, however, after China was brought to the modern world in the mid-nineteenth century by invading European colonial powers equipped with armored gunboats and fast and accurate rifles. Continual defeats at the hands of invading foreign armies throughout the second half of that century first enticed the traditional elite to imitate and duplicate whatever made the "barbarians" tick. But when even the weapons that most cleverly imitated those of the foreigners failed to resist the encroaching colonial powers, the most radical and impatient intellectuals began to question the value and validity of their traditional culture. They proposed to re-evaluate and reject some of the most repugnant traditional practices, and thousands of students demonstrated during the May Fourth Movement in 1919.

Because this gradual, reformist approach failed to stop an aggressive fascist Japan from nibbling more and more territories from China throughout the 1920s and 1930s, the call for a complete, revolutionary change to sever China from its rather inglorious past, the theme of the Communists, gained increasingly wide popularity. With the success of the Chinese Communist Revolution in 1949, the human versus land conflict was redefined and China stepped from its past into an unknown future. Overnight, the pre-modern, conservative peasants were hurled by the Party into the brave new world.

About This Book

I will present in this book a historically oriented case study of changing peasant life in a village in southeast China after the Communist Revolution in 1949. Southeastern China, especially the area along the coastal regions of Guangdong and Fujian provinces, was relatively well developed economically prior to the Communist Revolution. Throughout much of the pre-modern period this area was already known for experimentation with new crop varieties and intensive use of rice paddies, yielding sometimes up to three crops per year. Commercialization of agriculture in this region supported an active, cash-based market economy. Maritime trade also made several of the cities along the coast, such as Canton, Zaitong, and Fuzhou, internationally known throughout the dynastic period.

Despite all of these developments, this region was consistently under the dual pressures of insufficient farmland and overpopulation. High population density and insufficient land resources brought to this region two interrelated developments. The first one was an intricate land tenancy system, which often involved more than half of the farm population. The second one was massive out-migration of the rural poor from this region to Southeast Asia, North America, and Taiwan throughout much of the late imperial period. Successful overseas Chinese funneled back their savings to purchase farmland for their family estates, thus further aggravating the land tenancy problems.

The successful Communist Revolution changed all this. Land tenancy was abolished, and Land Reform (1950–1951) gave to many poor tenants their privately owned land. But before the peasants had the opportunity to enjoy the fruits of the revolution, they began to experience setbacks. The rural masses were restricted in their geographic movement not only across international boundaries but also domestically. Suddenly, the peasants became a land-bound underclass, with little opportunity for either social or geographic mobility (Potter 1983).

In the meantime, a new and more penetrating administrative system was established to promote development. Not only was the formal administration system extended to the countryside, the Party itself also established a parallel network to ensure that Party decisions were faithfully executed at the grass-roots level. The establishment of the communes in 1958 further integrated all peasants into a comprehensive organization that was at once administrative, economical, educational, and medical. Never before in Chinese history had the national government had so much control in peasants' day-to-day life.

Effective political control permitted the government to deal with this perennial human-land conflict with modern, innovative measures. Successive mass campaigns engineered by the government, such as the collectivization of agriculture and the birth control campaign, were partially designed to break away from this old dynastic cycle.

Since rural China has been virtually off-limits to foreigners since 1949, very little was known to the outside world about what had happened there and how much was accomplished by the Communist government. The opportunity to conduct intensive fieldwork in rural China in recent years is thus important in providing essential information to fill the void of knowledge.

In this study I use the life-history approach to illustrate changes in Lin Village during the past three-and-one-half decades. By focusing on the experiences of Ye Wende, who grew up in Lin Village and become Party Secretary there, this book sheds light on the turbulent events that compose an important chapter in modern Chinese history.

Although in this dramatic story Ye is the protagonist through whom we learn how this new government affected the villagers and their ethos, I want to point out that the picture I present here is by no means a single-dimensional, personal account of Ye. Despite his penetrating observations and provocative thoughts, Party Secretary Ye is the same as any other human being, who can be biased, contradictory, and self-serving. As a dedicated Communist, he is supposed to be unselfish. And as a leading cadre in this village, he is supposed to be fair and open. Even though he professed to believe in these tenets and tried hard to live up to them, he often failed without even realizing the contradiction.

As readers will find in the following chapters, Ye, in his handling of village affairs, could be very inconsistent in dispensing justice. Through his shrewd manipulation of personal connections and traditional symbols, Ye became the most successful village administrator in the entire township. While Ye was unembarrassed to tell how he had effectively extended his personal connections into various levels of the bureaucracy and utilized them for his personal successes, his kind of conduct constitutes the most serious obstacle for the government's current effort to accomplish legal and political reforms. I have thus purposely included several episodes from which readers can clearly see the discrepancies between Ye's ideals and his behavior.

In this book I use Ye's personal account to depict the changes and developments in Lin Village, but the picture presented here is not solely based on the information provided by Ye. I did rely on Ye as my key informant. But during my seven-month stay in this village I also conducted in-depth interviews with numerous villagers from all sectors of this community to learn about their family history, personal life, economic activities, and religious practices.

Based on participation and observation, the principal research instrument of anthropology, I was able to collect a substantial amount of information concerning the village history, customs, internal frictions, religious practices, and current developments. All this information was used to corroborate and supplement Ye's story. In doing so I hope to achieve a certain level of objectivity that may otherwise have been lost in a biography.

Significance of the Book

Even though the rural population constitutes the most predominant sector in Chinese society—according to the government classification system it includes about 80 percent of the national population—it was not until quite recently that outsiders were able to take a direct, close look at the magnitude of change that has taken place since the revolution. What have studies like this one revealed about rural China? Several salient characteristics are readily definable.

The first one is without a doubt the tremendous progress that has been accomplished in the people's daily life. Significant improvements in agricultural production, education, and public health have eradicated many social problems that menaced the Chinese peasantry throughout much of their history. Education, food, medical facilities, and work assignments have been available to most rural residents. The pre-condition for all these accomplishments, without a doubt, is the effective political control that penetrates every corner. of the Chinese society. All these improvements, plus a relatively peaceful period without large-scale warfare since 1949, have contributed to a significant population increase. Lin Village's population increased by a factor of 2.5, from 400 in 1949 to slightly more than 1,000 in 1985.

The second characteristic of rural China that this study implies is the apparent emergence of a national culture. Traditional small, semi-autonomous, and cellular village communities have gradually been replaced by a mass culture centering around the national government. Policies formulated at the top are being effectively pushed down, with minor modifications, to the grass-roots level. The political apparatus established at the village level, the jargon used by cadres in day-to-day activities, the restrictions imposed on the peasantry, and the limited opportunities reserved for peasants in social mobility all seem to have cut across traditional geographic and social boundaries to create a somewhat uniform national culture. Most of all, the villagers seem to have become very politicized and well integrated into the national political arena.

Against these dynamic changes are the less observable but more important aspects of rural life that I want to underscore: the persistence of certain traditional beliefs and values, such as filial piety, the ideal extended family, geomancy, ancestral worship, preference for sons over daughters, and so on. All these are important to villagers in their day-to-day considerations. Government attempts to change these traditional beliefs and practices, using coercion, have been successful only during certain periods of the Communist rule. But once these heavy-handed policies were relaxed, the peasants quickly reverted back to their centuries-old practices.

The preservation of these traditional beliefs and practices, which the present Chinese government considered less than desirable and has made repeated attempts to eradicate, poses an interesting dilemma for development thinkers. For societies employing revolutionary means to achieve development, the critical question is where will the proper line be drawn between objective policy goals and the people's subjective needs. Revolution, by definition, is a dramatic and forcible procedure aimed at overthrowing the existing social order. Revolutionary governments often mobilize the masses to achieve visionary goals. Traditional practices and values are often criticized and even rejected as true obstacles for realizing these goals. New practices and values, based on the vision of the ruling elite, are imposed from the top on the people. In the name of revolution, the masses are forced to conform to these new social blueprints. In the name of revolution, personal dignity and integrity are easily brushed aside and replaced by submission to power. In the end, even though actual and tangible progress might be accomplished, what is lost in the process is the confidence and identity of the masses toward the revolution and the government. The study in Lin Village thus shows a society full of internal hatred and bitter factional conflicts, especially during its more radical periods of revolutionary change.

The last point I want to discuss in this context is the status of the peasantry in contemporary Chinese society. Peasants are anomalies to Communist revolutions. Marx is known to have been openly contemptuous toward peasants, as the following remarks testify. Peasants, according to Marx, are "barbarians in civilizations," or "anachronism in history," or "potatoes in a sack that form a sack of potatoes," or "they can not represent themselves, they must be represented." This orthodox view was adroitly downplayed by leaders of the Chinese Communists, for much of their revolutionary success depended upon the unwavering support of the peasants (Bianco 1971; Chesneaux 1973).

What has happened to Chinese peasants since the founding of the People's Republic? Have the peasants enjoyed the fruits of the revolution? Have they been truly "liberated" from their feudalistic yoke of the past? The answer, unfortunately, appears to be a negative one. What we learn from Ye's life and others in Lin Village is that Chinese peasants today still stand at the very bottom of the social hierarchy. Public glorification of the peasantry by government officials today is not much different from that of the Confucian scholars in the past: It is merely lip service without substance. Compared with city dwellers, who work in factories, service establishments, and government offices, the peasants of China have been carrying the main burden of financing the national budget while enjoying the least amount of benefit. Right up to the current reform that began in the late 1970s, peasants were forced to sell most of their products to the government through various procurement programs at artificially low price levels. They in turn had to purchase industrial products at artificially high prices to subsidize the industries. Thus, the "price-scissors," as Chinese officials call them, cut both ways against the peasants.

The most controversial practice the Chinese government attempted in modern China was to remake the peasant family into a simple economic and social unit, depriving it of its traditional ideological, spiritual, and ritual significance. The attacks waged by the government against ancestral worship, lineage organization, geomancy, and patriarchal authorities, all lumped together as "feudalistic practices," represent such efforts. Most of these policies have been successful only superficially and have merely driven these traditional practices underground. The family and its continuity still occupy the focal point of peasant life.

The real challenge imposed by the government, which may ultimately weaken or even fundamentally change the traditional peasant family, has been the birth control campaign implemented under the one-child-per-family policy in rural areas since the early 1980s. Since each family was allowed to have only one child, regardless of sex, most peasants immediately recognized the threat this policy posed to them. Socially and economically, the well-being of a couple with only a daughter, who typically moves out to live with her husband after marriage, would be endangered when they could no longer carry out manual labor on their farm. Without adequate retirement pension or old-age welfare programs, the best insurance aging peasants have is still a filial son with two economically productive hands.

Similarly, in the spiritual sense, a family without male issue would be terminating the family line that stretches back to time immemorial. Without descendants to continue ancestral worship, a man's place in the universe would be permanently lost. Worse still, all the ancestral spirits that previously were attached to this family line would be turned loose and become unattended, unfed, and wandering ghosts.

These concerns explain the vehement resistance of the peasants to this one-child-per-family policy. From the government's perspective, as an attempt to reduce the population growth rate and hence to postpone the potential human-land collision, it was necessary to ensure this policy's success through whatever stern measures were required. Thus a perplexing situation developed. Although the overall trend under the current rural reform has been toward decentralization and relaxation of control in people's day-to-day lives, the severity of the birth control campaign appeared to be astonishing. Tragically, female infanticide was practiced widely by peasants to solve their problems. Naturally the government could not escape from its share of the blame for imposing this policy so drastically.

With increased geographic mobility and wealth in rural China now, the peasants will be more capable of resisting government pressures to conform with this policy. A new round of human-land conflict may develop, but it will be under modern social, technological, and international contexts. How this new drama unfolds could have significant impact on China and the world in the next century. No matter what the outcome will be, the seeds of change have already been sown today. What we see in Lin Village now permits us to have a better understanding of rural China today and into the future.

Prologue

1 It was almost unthinkable that my perception of Party Secretary Ye of Lin Village could change so dramatically within such a short time. It was even more unthinkable that my initial hostility toward him would dissolve so quickly and completely that I could later sit in front of my typewriter to record his life history.

I still remember vividly my arrival in Lin Village and my first face-to-face encounter with Party Secretary (P.S.) Ye, about the rental I should pay for a flat in the village. It was a dusty, hot, humid afternoon in mid-November 1984. In Iowa where my family lived it was late fall, with frosty, chilly nights. But here in this subtropical area of southern Fujian Province in China the sun mercilessly scorched the fields and the stifling air was mixed with the stench of public outhouses, mildewed plaster on walls, and animal droppings. I sat in a bamboo chair, sweating not only all over my back but also along my legs. I could feel the sweat running down my thighs to my calves and then to the ground. I felt a bit dizzy from the heat and humidity and yet kept waving my arms to ward off the flies that swarmed over a plate of cane-sugar-preserved dried fruit provided by my prospective landlord, Mr. Lin Qishan.

Sitting across the table from me was Party Secretary Ye, the head of the Communist Party branch in the village. The village had its nominal, publicly elected mayor, a Mr. Lin, but everyone in China knows that it is the Party secretary who is the de facto village ruler. Ye sat motionless in his chair and said nothing about my futile attempt to keep the flies off the food on the table.

P.S. Ye is relatively short, about five foot three. Even though the day was hot and humid, he already had on his long sleeved, drab Mao jacket. He looked official. He seemed to have just had a haircut, the kind of short crewcut that exposes the light skin around the lower part of the scalp. He chain-smoked, and his face was often hidden behind the smoke that puffed out of his mouth. But from my first glimpse of his face, I knew immediately from his glittering, penetrating eyes that he was a shrewd, strong-willed, cunning person.

In his high-pitched staccato voice he calmly spelled out the demands that he considered reasonable for my flat: "You know how much people charge for rental space in Xiamen City's Special Economic Zone? Four dollars local currency

[RMB] per square meter [about U.S.$1.60]. Of course I will not ask that much from you. I think RMB$2.50 per square meter would be reasonable. That means for this approximately one hundred square meter flat that you want to rent from Comrade Lin, you should pay RMB$250 per month."

Two hundred and fifty dollars local currency per month! It would be about U.S.$100 per month for this lousy two bedroom plus living room flat! I was furious about this exorbitant charge and felt a sudden, unbridled urge to throw the plate of preserved food in his face.

Certainly I could afford to pay the price, since my visit to China was financed by two U.S. foundations, who paid me reasonably well. Nor was this charge any more outrageous than the rent I was paying to the local university in Xiamen City for a room that I kept there, about U.S.$200 per month. But I knew how much rent the local people were paying. For a flat like this one, the normal rent would be about RMB$10 or $15 at most, not the RMB$250 Ye wanted to charge. I resented Ye's ripping me off. I would not be surprised to find city people in China, like city people elsewhere in the world, haggling and taking advantage of outsiders. But I was unprepared to see that happening in the village. I also resented his negotiating with me about my rent; he didn't even own this house. I cursed myself for the bad luck I had had in my journey to China, and wondered why I had come to China at all.

Reflections on My Coming

For a short moment I lapsed into deep reflection, not only wondering why I had come to China in the first place but further questioning the wisdom of setting up my residence in this village. In assessing my situation, I quickly examined the reason for my presence in China and the dilemma that I was encountering.

China had been my homeland, but I had not lived there for years. I was born there at the end of World War II to a family of government officials belonging to the ruling Nationalist Party. When the Communists swept through China in 1949, my family fled to Taiwan with the Nationalist government. Since I left the mainland as a toddler, I had virtually no memories of China. My years in Taiwan through the 1950s and 1960s were typical: elementary school, junior high, high school, and then college. Upon my graduation from National Taiwan University, I came to the United States for an advanced degree in anthropology. When I was about to complete my doctorate in anthropology at Michigan State University in 1975, I was hired by Iowa State University.

In 1984, I earned a one-year sabbatical from my teaching post at Iowa State to teach and conduct research abroad. Where to spend that year became a problem for me and also for my wife and two children, for by then I had a family in Iowa. One possibility was to go to China, an attractive choice for several reasons. First, China was gradually opening up. I had had a chance to visit Xiamen City (formerly called Amoy) in southern Fujian Province, along China's southeastern coast for one week in 1981. During that week I had established good rapport with some of the faculty at Xiamen University. The university was re-establishing its anthropology program after a hiatus of thirty years, during which all social science branches had been abolished in China, so there was a shortage of people to teach the subject. A year spent there to teach and to conduct research would make an immediate contribution to the re-establishment of this discipline. I also thought about my children. A year-long experience in China would give them a better understanding of their cultural heritage and the opportunity to learn some Chinese. Another more pragmatic consideration was career growth. Up to that point China had been consistently refusing to allow Western social scientists to conduct research in the countryside. If I went there to conduct research, I would be able to establish a lead over my colleagues in the United States.

I expressed my interest in going to Xiamen University through correspondence with a friend there and received positive responses from him and a formal invitation from the university. I would be invited to teach anthropology, and in return the university would sponsor my research in the countryside by providing the necessary official letters.

In my proposed research in the countryside I would be studying a dramatic policy change, the establishment of the so-called Production Responsibility System, that was taking place in rural China in the early 1980s. This event had been widely reported in the Chinese press but had never been studied by non-Chinese researchers. From what was being reported in Chinese official newspapers, this Responsibility System involved the dissolving of the collective communal organizations in rural areas, first established in the 1950s. An even more daring aspect of this new policy was the virtual restoration of private property and family farming as the centerpiece of China's agriculture.

A study of this changing policy would shed light on several intriguing questions: How did the peasants react to their new rights in farming and property management? How would this newly revised emphasis on family farming affect parent-child relationships? Would this change undermine women's status as they once again became a part of the patriarchal family as they had been before the Communist Revolution? If the collective communal system was ineffective in rural China, what were its main problems? What could we learn about the nature of Chinese society and, at an even more abstract level, about human nature, when China changed its policy from a collective system back to private ownership? All these questions appeared to be sensible, and research along this line would make an important contribution to our understanding of China.

I soon discovered that this journey would not be as smooth as I had anticipated. Shortly before departure, I received a letter from Xiamen University claiming that because of a shortage of living space on campus, I would not be allowed to bring my family. By then, it was too late for me to change my plans. I had worked out all the arrangements with Iowa State University for the year-long absence and a replacement had been hired. Had I known about not being able to take my family along, I would have chosen to spend the year in Hong Kong or Thailand or Japan, where I could have easily developed a research project.

But it was already too late for me to change plans. I did a bit of mental juggling, pointing out the potential benefits of my trip to China, and bade farewell to my family.

I arrived at Xiamen University in late August 1984. Once classes started, I found out that my teaching would not be very productive. The liberal viewpoints and research methods espoused by American academicians were treated with great suspicion in this rigid, doctrinaire education system. The only acceptable truths were quotations from Marx, Lenin, and Chairman Mao. Academic viewpoints and discussions were constantly tailored to fit current policy lines. It was futile for a teacher to encourage creative thinking or to initiate debates on controversial issues.

Worse yet, the few foreign teachers on campus were kept in a special building and carefully shielded from contact with locals. The building was locked from approximately 9:30 or 10 in the evening, depending on the ending time of the local television program that the building attendants watched every night in the lobby of our building. It was unlocked at 6 in the morning to let the residents out for morning exercises. Whenever the building was not locked, one of the eight or nine building attendants would be sitting at the front desk in the lobby, monitoring those who came to visit us, the foreigners. Students who came had to register at the front desk, giving their names, addresses, and departmental majors plus the time of the day and reason for the visit. Given the experiences of local people in past political campaigns, during which Chinese who had any contact with foreigners were harshly attacked as traitors or foreign spies, it became apparent that any sober-minded Chinese would be reluctant to befriend us. Socially, we were completely isolated. I quickly became bored and homesick. Seeing no point in spending my time at the university, I pressed for permission to conduct my research in the countryside. Chinese peasants would be more hospitable and honest, I thought, and my research would be a diversion from the monotony and boredom I was experiencing.

After two months in bureaucratic limbo, I finally received permission to conduct my research in the countryside surrounding Xiamen City (see Map 1.1). Lin Village was recommended by the city government as a possible site. Based on briefings provided by a city official, I learned that Lin Village had about one thousand residents living in two hundred households—the ideal size for anthropological research. Historically a relatively backward agricultural community due to water shortage, I was told, Lin Village had made tremendous progress after the Liberation and the construction of a reservoir. Furthermore, the villagers were embracing wholeheartedly the new policy of the Production Responsibility System and were successfully developing new sideline economic activities. It was a model

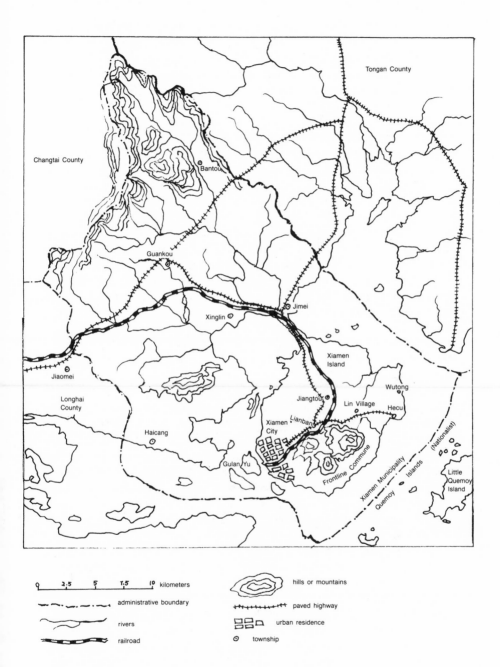

Tongan County

Changtai County

Bantou

Guankou

Jimei

Xinglin

Xiamen
Island

Jiaomei

Longhai
County

Jiangtou

Wutong

Lin Village

Hecu

Xiamen
City

Lianban

Haicang

Gulan Yu

Frontline Commune

Xiamen Municipality

Quemoy   Islands

(Nationalist)

Little
Quemoy
Island

0   2.5   5   7.5   10 kilometers

administrative boundary

rivers

railroad

hills or mountains

paved highway

urban residence

township

MAP 1.1   Xiamen Island and vicinity (scale 1:250,000)

village (it was still called a brigade then, an economic and administrative unit under the commune) in the entire region and had a per capita annual income of over RMB$600, twice the national average that year.

The distance between Lin Village and Xiamen City is about ten kilometers. An asphalt road that connects Xiamen City and Hongshan Village, about one and one-half kilometers south of Lin Village, is served by six scheduled buses daily. From Hongshan Village it would take another twenty minutes of walking on a dirt road to Lin Village. Since I would be commuting between the university and the village, the distance appeared to be manageable.

Lin Village: First Impressions

The moment I arrived in Lin Village in early November 1984, I was attracted by the tranquility and scenery of the area. When viewed from a distance, the village stands imposingly above the glittering, lushly green rice paddy; its many newly built, colorfully painted two-story buildings attest to the newly gained wealth of the villagers. Even though most of these new houses incorporate modern construction material, such as steel beams, glass windows, and cement facades, they still preserve many traditional architectural designs and elements, thus providing a tasteful blend of new and old. The ground level of a typical house contains a walled-in court, with two pairs of smaller rooms at the front: a kitchen, a dining room, a washroom for bathing, and a storage room for farm tools and surplus grains. The rear of the house has three larger rooms: In the middle is a living room or guest room, and on each side are two bedrooms (see Fig. 1.1).

In the middle of the ground level is an open courtyard where many family activities take place. Many farmers also grow dwarf kumquat plants in ceramic pots in the central court for decorative purposes. These round or oblong shaped fruits are certainly not grown just for aesthetic reasons; most Chinese artifacts seem to have both utilitarian and artistic value. My landlady sometimes picked a handful of ripe kumquats and boiled them in sugar and water to make a kind of orange-flavored syrup. It was the standard remedy she made for me whenever I had a hangover from a village banquet. Maybe it was psychological, but this remedy was very effective in curing the problem.

The ground levels of village houses are constructed mainly with granite slabs that are chipped out with hand chisels from nearby quarries and purchased by the villagers to make the floors, room partitions, and sometimes even ceilings. Virtually no wood or steel is needed, obviously reflecting the ingenious ways local people coped with the general shortage of wood and steel in this part of China. But with those smoothly polished granite slabs piled up to build the wall, it is certain that the lower level of the house was able to support the much lighter weight of the second floor.

The second story of village houses is generally built only above the back rooms of the ground floor, with one central living room and two bedrooms. Red

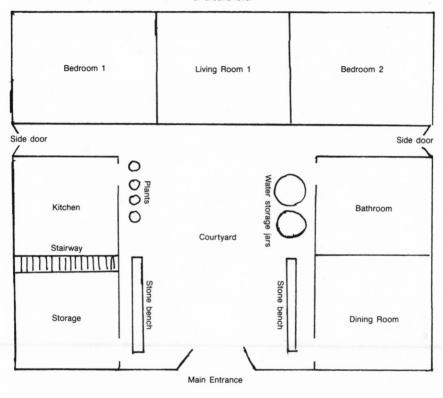

FIGURE 1.1 Traditional house plan in Lin Village

bricks and white plaster are often used for the second floor to provide a sharp contrast to the grain-colored granite slabs of the lower level. One bold villager even pasted a colorful picture on the front wall of the second story of his newly built house. The picture was a mosaic composed of many painted four-inch by four-inch clay squares that were then glazed over and fired into ceramic wall tiles. The picture itself had a dragon and a phoenix, the traditional symbols for good luck. The lavishly used green, red, and yellow drawn over the white porcelain might be considered garish by art critics, but to the villagers it was certainly a strong statement of their recent prosperity.

The village is bordered on three sides by the blue, transparent water of a man-made reservoir. The beach around the reservoir had a greenbelt of tropical pine, a rare scene in southern China. About 1,000 meters to the south of the open side of the village is a chain of small hills with huge, exposed granite boulders. The grayish-purple rock formations rise majestically above the green of the surrounding rice paddies, reminding me of an impressionist painting by a nameless painter that I saw in Taiwan a long time ago.

I could imagine myself living in this village, taking my morning stroll along the lakefront and my afternoon hike in the hills. I saw myself interacting with the villagers as a normal person and studying their changing way of life—the theme of my research. During my first visit to the village in early November 1984, I had spotted a newly built house with a vacant upper floor that I thought would be ideal for my stay in the village. I discussed with my prospective landlord, Mr. Lin Qishan, the possibility of renting his upper level and boarding with his family while I lived here. Mr. Lin, like many farmers in rural Taiwan and Hong Kong that I know of, cheerfully agreed to both my requests. We agreed that I would pay him RMB$60 per month for meals for the approximately fifteen days of each month that I would live in the village. About rent, Mr. Lin said in an offhanded manner: "Don't mention it! We farmers in the countryside build houses to live in, not for profit making. Just move in and live with us. The only costs will be for the electricity that we will split each month." With all these agreements reached, I told Mr. Lin that I would be moving in the following week.

When I carried my personal belongings, stuffed into two suitcases, to Mr. Lin's house, he greeted me with uneasiness and a bit of embarrassment. He told me that the secretary of the village Communist Party, a certain Comrade Ye, had heard about my intended stay in this village, and would like to greet me personally. While Mr. Lin talked my eyes became gradually adjusted to the darkness of the room, and I noticed the silhouette of another person sitting quietly in a corner of the room. Party Secretary Ye stood up at that moment, slowly approached me, and shook my hand. He then cleared his throat by coughing a couple of times and started his speech. Right at that moment I knew that I was not to expect hospitality in this village. My hopes were completely shattered when this diminutive person, P.S. Ye, pressed his "reasonable" demand on me.

For a while I thought about turning him down, calling him a few dirty names, and moving on to another village. Then I realized that it would be futile. First, it would be difficult to find a comparable village in this vicinity that would provide the same living arrangement. Second, I realized that other villages would probably have the same kind of greedy local officials as Ye. If I were to be ripped off in China, I might as well find the best location for this inevitable end. Finally, I desperately wanted to get out of the stifling environment of the university. So I meekly mumbled a few protests as a gesture and then declared that I would accept his "suggestion." Behind the smoke screen I detected a glimpse of a grin. I cursed him many times in my mind and decided to stay away from him as much as possible during my stay.

Getting Acquainted

That was my first impression of Ye. To me, he represented the worst type of Communist Party cadre in the countryside: cunning, unpredictable, nosy, and domineering. During my first month in Lin Village, I tried to maintain a cordial but distant relationship with Ye. At that point I was still busy setting up my apartment and commuting to the university for my teaching. My weekly schedule was split into approximately two equal halves between the village and the university. When I first came to the village I kept myself busy exploring the environment and getting acquainted with my landlord's family and neighbors. I encountered Ye once in a while. When that happened, I would greet him politely, exchange a few pleasantries, and then find an excuse to retreat.

My carefully guarded peaceful co-existence with Ye lasted for about a month. In late December things began to change dramatically. Late one evening when I was doing some leisure reading in my room there was a knock on the door. I opened it and there was my chief adversary. He looked like a battered cock. His head was down. His entire body seemed deflated. He raised his bloodshot eyes and asked in a shaky voice: "Are you retired already? Hope I didn't interrupt anything."

I hesitated for a moment and replied, "No, not at all, come in."

He walked straight to a chair and threw himself in it. I brought out a thermos (a necessity in every Chinese household) to make a cup of tea for him. He sat silently staring at the floor. I didn't know what to say and just found myself a chair to sit in.

After a few moments he looked at me and murmured: "Why did they do that to me? How could they treat me like that after all the good things I have done for them in the village?"

I was completely puzzled and didn't know what to say. I carefully asked a few questions and found out what Ye was talking about. Something unforgivable had happened to his father's tomb at the foot of the hills. Just one year earlier the tomb had been elaborately built in a choice location to commemorate his father. Now the stone slab erected in front of the tomb was smashed into two pieces and the cement surface of the tomb's dome-shaped, above-ground covering was also damaged. Footprints were stamped into the ground at the back of the tomb. According to Ye, this was no ordinary vandalism. Someone in the village had deliberately damaged his father's tomb as an attack on him.

I knew traditional Chinese strongly believed in geomancy, that the composition of the five elementary forces of the universe—the *wuxing* of fire, wood, water, metal, and earth—powerfully determine people's lives and fate. Within a certain geographic area, the strengths of these five elementary forces would be carefully measured. In order to maintain a perfect or nearly perfect harmony among these five forces in a given area, people selected specific locations to build houses for the living and tombs for the deceased. This geomantic concern not only influences the selection of the location of houses and tombs, it also dictates the cardinal directions to which the houses and tombs are oriented and their architectural styles. Damage to an ancestor's tomb is the equivalent of a curse applied to the spirit of the deceased ancestor, and would ultimately bring bad luck to the offspring.[1]

My curiosity was aroused. Several questions immediately popped into my mind: Did they still consult geomancers in building houses and tombs? I thought that all these "feudalistic" superstitions—anything that originated before 1949 and that the government didn't like—had been suppressed and completely wiped out in China. Ordinary citizens might still carry on some of those practices clandestinely, but here was Mr. Ye, a party cadre, apparently subscribing to these supposedly "reactionary" beliefs! The next question was, Who could have done this in direct challenge to the village ruler? Was this an indication of internal strife within the village? Or factional conflict? I began with an obvious question: "Why do you think it is a villager who did this to your father's tomb?"

P.S. Ye raised his voice impatiently: "It must be the villagers. Who else would come here to do this to me? Peasants never appreciate anything! Despite all the things I have done for them, to raise their income levels and to maintain law and order in the village, they are never appreciative. It must be someone I punished for breaking a village ordinance. Now he seeks revenge by disgracing my father's tomb!"

Seeing my puzzled expression, he began to explain the problems that he, the village Party secretary, faced recently. With the dismantling of rural communal organizations in this part of China in early 1984, most local officials and Party cadres had abandoned their previous duties. But as the top Party cadre in the community, Ye had to set an example for the others. He had been quietly taking on the responsibilities discarded by other officials. For instance, he explained, the punishment against offenders of village ordinances, the *xianggui minyue* (country rules and civilian regulations, a kind of quasi-law developed in China in the late 1970s), should be the responsibility of the village's public security head. But since this person had been busy with his new sideline, operating his truck hauling business, he was simply not around to assume his duty. As a result, Ye had been in charge of public security, a job he had had before he was promoted to Party secretary.

But I was unconvinced: "What makes you think the villagers resent you more now for punishing public offenders than they did when you were head of public security?"

"Well," he said, "the government has recently been relaxing its control in the countryside. Many peasants have taken this to mean that they can do whatever they want to do, such as gambling, stealing, and fistfighting. They interpret my intervention as a violation of their rights, but I don't think that this is a correct interpretation of the new government policy. Another reason they are more resentful of my work now than before is that they think it is not my job to take charge of this public order business. Nobody grumbled when I punished someone for a minor crime when I was head of public security. But now they grumble that even the formal public security head is not bothering other villagers, so why should I intervene in petty matters?"

Then I asked him who the most recent offenders of the village ordinances were and what kinds of misdemeanors they had committed. He gave me several cases, one by one, explaining the nature of the crimes and the punishments he had assigned to them.

P.S. Ye must have found in me a good and sympathetic listener, for we chatted for about two or three hours that night. And after that, he seemed to take me as his confidant. He came to chat with me regularly when I was in the village, about once every day for an hour or two. When he was invited to banquets offered by other villagers, he would take me along. If I stayed at the university for two or three days, when I returned to the village he would immediately seek me out to tell me the latest village news and the new problems he faced. Occasionally he would ask my advice in handling more difficult issues. For instance, when he and several other villagers pooled money together to form a new trading company in the village, I spent over two days working with them to draft the bylaws and organizational plans for the company. As our friendship improved, he also began to take a keen interest in my research. When I wanted to interview a certain informant in the village, he would go along, introduce me to the person, and make sure that I received full cooperation from that person. When I designed a questionnaire for my research project, I asked him to read it and to make suggestions for modifications.

As we began to talk more, I came to understand better the problems he faced in the village. As one of only two high school graduates in this village over forty years of age, he obviously had better knowledge and a broader perspective about current events in China than most other villagers. Also, as the head of the local Party branch, he had to consider things not just from his personal viewpoint but also from a villagewide perspective. His charging me an exorbitant rent for my flat on behalf of my landlord was not because he received a cut of the rent, as

P.S. Ye in a lighthearted mood, wearing a borrowed police hat

I initially suspected, but because he felt that it was his responsibility to look after the interests of the villagers. The gain of each of the villagers would ultimately be the gain of the collective whole, the village. A dedicated Communist, Ye still maintained strong beliefs in collectivism. To the other villagers, however, he represented the menace of the failed policies and promises of the past.

But then I found Ye was not a blind follower of Maoism, either. He often asked me thought-provoking questions, such as about presumed human nature as I understood it in the capitalist United States. Based on my descriptions, he would compare them with what he had learned from his Communist education. He would then evaluate these two sets of premises by examining the situation in China in the past thirty-five years under Communist rule. He often drew actual examples from the village or from the villagers and then asked whether these incidents were intended results of orthodox communism. He also engaged in lengthy discussions with me about the philosophical basis, or lack of it, in Chinese Communism. He was sometimes so sharp and critical about many fundamental premises and principles of communism that I was reluctant to write them down for fear of their being used to implicate him in future political turmoil.

I also found Ye to be a humorous, colorful person. In dealing with other villagers and sometimes high-level government officials, he could alternately cajole, threaten, complain, or invoke public pressure to achieve his intended goals. An eloquent orator, in spite of his high-pitched, staccato voice, Ye's use of slang was the best I encountered. In a heated argument he could burst out a chain of obscenities that would embarrass most villagers.

But despite his public image as a tough, feisty, and arrogant local tyrant, Ye also had his soft, tender side that he carefully concealed from the public. He was the only adult I knew in Lin Village who played games with children. He would spend hours playing poker with three or four children in his backyard. Also a dedicated family man, he had tremendous affection and respect for his wife, Baozhu. This was so great a departure from the established tradition of patriarchal domination in this part of China that many villagers considered him henpecked.

After my first conversation with P.S. Ye that night, I began to take notes on the content of our conversations, as normal anthropological fieldwork procedure requires. Through him I not only gained access to village events but also accumulated a large amount of information about his life, aspirations, and beliefs and opinions on many issues. I was sure that he knew I was taking notes after each conversation. One day when I mentioned something another villager had told me and that it disagreed with Ye's observation, he jokingly said: "You remembered it wrong. Why don't you go back and check in your notebooks!"

The idea of writing his biography came to me about six months after I arrived in the village. I told him tactfully that since I had learned so much about him, I would like his permission to write his biography and publish it in the United States. He was stunned by my suggestion.

"What a ridiculous idea!" laughed Ye. "Let me ask one question: Who are the contemporary Chinese who have their biographies published in the United States?"

"Well, I guess people like Chairman Mao, Premier Zhou Enlai, and perhaps Marshall Zhu De," I replied meekly, for I could see what he was leading to.

"So, you think I am of the same rank as those important people, ha!" he said triumphantly. "The villagers have been criticizing me for being obnoxious. Wait until they find out that there is a book published about me in the United States!"

"Well, you see . . ." I tried to figure out the best way to express my views in the most logical manner: "My point is that what Western people have learned about China is mainly from the perspective of those important people like Chairman Mao and Marshall Zhu De. What about the ordinary cadres, the people who work at the village level to make China move? You grew up with new China. What happened to you during the past thirty years must have been shared by many people in the countryside. This type of experience must be very different from Chairman Mao's or Marshall Zhu's experiences."

My argument must have struck P.S. Ye as something novel, for he fell silent. Then, a few days before I was to leave the village, he came to see me and said quietly: "I have been thinking over what you told me about the significance of seeing things through the eyes of ordinary folk. Now I realize that you do have a point there. If you think that there is anything worth writing about in my life, feel free to do it when you return to the United States. I will someday write up something about myself and send it to you by mail, too."

I seized that opportunity and asked him to let me tape-record an interview with him to clear up a few dates and locality names that he had mentioned before. The next day he spent about eight hours answering my systematic questions about his life. This taped interview provides the basic frame for this book.

After I returned to the states and looked through my notes and listened to the tapes I had compiled about Ye, I saw a rich, broad view of China over the past three-and-a-half decades through the eyes of a country cadre, with corroborations based on months of observation and interviews with other villagers. The zeal in political movements and mass campaigns, the remarkable achievements in eradicating poverty, illiteracy, and unhygienic conditions in rural China within a relatively short span of time, the violence and brutality of persecuting certain people in order to pursue specific political goals, and the treachery and betrayal at the national level in China during the past thirty-five years also had their miniature reflections at the village level. Through the life and work of Ye, we can witness the turbulent process of the birth of a nation. The mixture of joy and pain, the wobbly attempts to stand up with feeble feet, and the achievements and failures based on trial and error that P.S. Ye saw in Lin Village can be magnified hundreds and thousands of times to form the conglomerate called "China."

I thought for a while about how to record the history of P.S. Ye and his village, and decided to use as many of his words as possible to preserve their authenticity. I did, however, reorganize my records according to chronological order, so readers will be able to follow his life more easily. Furthermore, to make certain phenomena and issues explicit to non-China experts, I added a little background information or illustrative phrases in the text to make them understandable. For more complicated issues, I used notes for clarity. Relevant articles or books that I think may be useful to readers who might be interested in a specific subject are also cited in Notes and in the Bibliography. A few local terms are used in the text as they originally appeared in my notes. I did translate these terms from the local Minnan dialect to the official Mandarin language according to the current pinyin system used in China. Chinese characters for these terms can be found in the glossary of Chinese characters at the end of the book.

To protect the anonymity of the village and its residents, I invented the name Lin Village and used pseudonyms for all people except P.S. Ye. I used Ye's real name because, when he agreed to let me write his biography, he indicated that he would rather see his real name appear "in the fine print." Real names are also used for public figures at the city, provincial, and national levels. I hope the publication of this book will not in any way jeopardize the well-being of P.S. Ye or the villagers.

Family History

2 My first in-depth interview with Ye, as it turned out, was the day after his late-night visit following the vandalism at his father's tomb. As he was leaving that night he asked if I would go with him to his father's tomb the next day to take pictures. He wanted to collect evidence about this crime for future investigations. He had reported this incident at the township police station, but the police were slow to handle this unimportant type of crime. He felt that by the time the police came a week or two later much of the evidence, such as the rocks used to damage the tombstone and the footprints, would be gone or obliterated by rain or cows grazing in the hills. I was the only person he knew who owned a camera. He would reimburse me for the expense of the film and developing. I was more than eager to take a firsthand look at this scene that revealed so much to me about village "superstition" and agreed to meet him early the next morning to go to the hills.

A Walk to the Tomb

It was a sunny but cool December morning when Ye and I took our stroll to the hills. The air was still humid, but the breezy northeast wind and low temperature of about 15°C had made the walk a pleasant outing. To Ye, as well as most other villagers who were used to the subtropical heat, this was already the beginning of winter. He wore a heavy gray army jacket with cotton padding between the linen. Seeing my short-sleeved shirt, he mumbled: "Don't you people have any sense? This is already winter!"

The path from Lin Village to the hills was a straight dirt road, ostensibly used for farm machines or trucks. Many diligent village women were already working in their still-green gardens on both sides of the road. Lin Village's collectively owned land was partitioned in mid-1984. Each village family had received its portion of contract land. Also, private ownership of productive instruments or enterprises was now accepted by the authorities. Seizing upon this newly gained liberty, most village men had purchased walking tractors ("iron bulls" in local dialect) and turned them into transportation vehicles that provided them with lucrative income. Some other village men invested in small-scale machine shops or cottage industries and spent their workdays indoors. It was countrywomen, like their ancestors, deemed not important or sophisticated enough for these new trades, who were reserved for low-prestige and low-income farm jobs. Looking at these women working feverishly in their family plots made me realize how industrious the Chinese can be, and I could see why the new policy of the Production Responsibility System had been successful.

From a distance, the green foliage of a common tropical plant, the red bean trees (*Abrus precatorius*, also called "lovesick tree" in Chinese literature), dotted the lower slopes of the granite hills. Our destination, the village cemetery, was about three kilometers' walking distance.

Ye and I walked slowly. He often lapsed into silent reflection. Occasionally he nodded to a village woman who greeted him as he passed by. But mostly he was silent. Suddenly he turned to me and said: "It is unfair! My father lived a miserable life! He worked so hard his entire life that he was no better than a blind water buffalo. I regret that I didn't give him the best things that I could afford then. He died when I started building my new house, which means I didn't have any spare money then, and before I was able to make a lot of money from investing in village enterprises. By the time all his sons had become independent and well-to-do and able to give him good things to eat and use, he passed away." He seemed to have blurted out all his thoughts at once, and struggled to recatch his breath.

"Does your father have any brothers or sisters in this village? Was your father the first person in your family to live here?" I asked cautiously. My anthropological readings about this part of China told me that during the "feudalistic era"[1] people lived with their paternal kin only. People who lived in the same village were often descendants of the same male ancestor and thus shared the same surname. Often a village was named after the major kin group, such as the name Lin Village, whose residents were presumably once all Lins. In this kind of "single-surname village" all residents shared certain ancestral estates and formed a tightly knit kinship organization called the "lineage." People in one lineage often fought against other lineages living in other villages.[2] My speculation was that Ye's family had not been living in this village for long.

"No, my family has been living in this village since my grandfather's time," Ye replied.

"But how could your grandfather come to live in a village that is supposed to be dominated by the Lins?" I asked.

"Well, this is a long story," Ye replied thoughtfully, "and I will have to explain it to you slowly. From my family history you will be able to gain insights about some basic characteristics of this village. Only with this understanding can you possibly comprehend the historical roots of internal fighting in this village, and the delicate nature of my position as the brigade Party secretary today.

"The area where Lin Village is now located was not a highly desirable area for farming. The soil here is sandy." Ye pointed to the fields along our path.

"The small hills to the south blocked easy passage to Xiamen harbor. With barren soil and insufficient water during the dry season from May through October, except for typhoons, this area was unsuitable for rice terracing. Early residents here depended mainly on sweet potatoes for a living. Most of the able-bodied from this area moved out, either to Xiamen City or to the South Seas (*Nanyang*, Chinese for Southeast Asia) to pursue a better lifestyle.

"The original inhabitants of this village were the Lins, that was how the village came to be known as Lin Village. The Lin people must have migrated to this place from Anhai Township in Quanzhou Prefecture about one hundred kilometers to the north. Nobody knows exactly when the Lins moved down here, but perhaps it was 200 years ago. I heard from my grandmother, who was herself a Lin, that during their heydays approximately 120 years ago, the Lins occupied a dominant position in this area, not only in this village, but also in several adjacent villages. This village alone had more than 1,000 hearths, implying an equal number of Lin families. The Lins owned a lot of land in the vicinity and engaged in intermittent warfare with other surnames or lineages in neighboring villages. One of the Lins' archenemies was the Chen family of neighboring Mudhole Village." Ye pointed to a cluster of houses about two kilometers from us and said, "That is Mudhole Village, where my wife Baozhu was born and raised."

"Why did people fight then?" I pretended to know little about local history.

"Most of the fighting involved negligible issues, such as conflict over irrigation water in ponds, graveyards, or petty theft. Because the Lins were numerous and strong, they abused others. For instance, they refused to let non-Lins live in this village, including their own tenants who worked for them. The Lins also charged people fees for right of passage when they passed through here to Xiamen City.

"According to feudalistic superstitions in the past, which I don't believe in myself, the Lins ran out of luck about a hundred years ago. This happened when the geomantic composition of the Lin lineage ancestral shrine was accidentally damaged. This incident subsequently caused the collapse of the entire lineage."

The term "geomancy" aroused my interest immediately. I interrupted eagerly: "How did this happen?"

Ye replied, "The Lin lineage used to have an imposing ancestral shrine, which was situated in the slope north of our village, but it is currently inundated by the reservoir. The ancestral shrine was owned by all Lins, who came here twice a year, on the fifteenth of the second month and the winter solstice,[3] to offer sacrifice to their ancestors. The ancestral shrine had its own trust land, approximately five or six *mou*[4] of rice paddies, the best land in this village. The rents collected from the trust land, about 300 or 400 catties [one catty equals about half kilo] of unhusked rice every half year, were used to pay for the ancestral rites. The remaining funds were used to provide a feast for all the Lin descendants, called *chizu*, "eating the ancestors," in the local dialect. If there was still money left after the feast, it was used to purchase pork to be divided among all the male descendants of the Lins. I know about this custom because the Lins continued this practice all the way down to the post-Liberation period. It was only in 1952, after the Land Reform confiscated all the ancestral land, that the Lins stopped this practice."

"But you still haven't explained how the Lin ancestral shrine was damaged," I reminded him.

"Oh, yes," Ye replied. "The shrine was built along the slope, with the front door facing the low land and the back wall leaning against the high ground. During the rainy season the running water gushing down the slope splashed against the back wall of the shrine and caused minor but visible damage. According to local legends, it was Lin Chenghu's grandfather, a scholar among the Lins, who suggested that a ditch be dug at the back of the shrine so the running water would be channeled away from it. The suggestion was accepted by the Lin elders, who sent several laborers to dig the ditch. When the workers dug the ground at the back of the shrine, they shoveled into a small spring that spouted out red, bloodlike water that soaked the surrounding soil. The workers were frightened by this and all fled. Something horrible had happened. The legend has it that the digging had accidentally cut into the neck arteries of a reclining dragon that constituted the local topographic contour and had provided protection and prosperity to the Lins. Once the dragon was injured, the Lins were no longer protected by this favorable geomantic force.

"Once the damage was done, major disasters began to befall the Lins. The first calamity came in the 1880s, an outbreak of the black death in this village. Nobody knows exactly how many people died, but a rough estimate was that about half the original village inhabitants died within one single year. Many surviving Lins were so frightened that they fled to other villages or to the South Seas.

"Tragedy struck again about seventy-five years ago, around the end of the first decade of this century. It was a black death epidemic again. When one person contracted the disease, all other family members would soon be infected and die. My grandmother remembered this second black death epidemic vividly because she witnessed it as a child. She told me that when the epidemic came it was already late fall that year. The Lins had already harvested their sweet potato and rice crops. They were preparing for the birthday celebration for the local patron god, Lord Liu (*liufu yuanshuai*), on the fourteenth of the tenth month. An opera troupe was hired from Fuzhou City for three days' performance. As the performing troupe was carrying wooden boxes and crates containing their paraphernalia to the village, the villagers were busy carrying wooden coffins out for burial. Again, large numbers of Lins died during this period, and many more fled the village, considering it a cursed place.

"In between these two epidemics the Lins discovered an even more threatening problem: Many Lin wives had become barren. In this part of Fujian Province people observed strict marriage rules that prohibited a man from marrying a woman of the same surname or from the same village. Men from Lin lineage had always acquired spouses from villages with which they did not engage in warfare, about sixty kilometers due north in the hills in Anxi County. These women, due to their harsh living environment and industrious work, were strongly built and bore large numbers of sons for the Lins. After the first epidemic, however, many Lin wives stopped bearing children. Even those who were still able to conceive produced only daughters. The immediate threat was that without a son in the family the parents would have no one to depend upon for their old age. Even more threatening was that, without a son to carry on the family line, the parents would die without anyone to offer ritual sacrifice for them. Those uncared-for ancestral spirits would become wandering ghosts. Without a male issue in the family the lineage branch would be ended (*daofang*, 'house collapse')."

At this point Ye stopped for a rest under a red bean tree. We were at the foot of the hills and close to the cemetery. He unbuttoned his heavy army jacket, for it was becoming warm as the sun rose higher.

"What happened then? And how is it related to your grandfather's coming to live in Lin Village?" I persisted, not wanting him to end the story then.

"Well, to remedy the problem of no male issue," he continued, "a family had one of several alternatives. The first was for the family head to adopt a son from his paternal cousin, if the latter had more than one son and was willing to give one away. If the man of the house didn't have any paternal cousin, or the latter didn't have more than one son himself, the family could purchase a boy and adopt him as their own son. The third option was that if this family had one or more daughters, the parents could keep a daughter home and bring in a husband for her. And that was how my grandfather came to live in Lin Village. My grandmother was the only child of her family. Her parents, that is my great-grandfather, decided to keep her at home. My grandfather was brought in to marry my grandmother."

I knew that this practice, called *zhaozhui*, "adopt a son-in-law," contradicts the ideal traditional Chinese custom of patrilocal residence, where a woman moved to her husband's house upon marriage. Instead, in the *zhaozhui* situation, the son-in-law comes to live with the wife's family and becomes a part of her group. Under this adopt-a-son-in-law practice, when the daughter has sons, at least one of the sons would be given the wife's surname to carry on the maternal family interests. Which one of the sons would be given the maternal surname was an issue to be discussed and decided before the marriage. Generally, this was determined by birth order.

This kind of arrangement carried a certain social stigma in traditional China. To give away a man's own flesh, especially a son, was considered a disgrace. Only men without self-esteem or without proper means of self-support would be willing to accept this kind of arrangement. The son that a man gave to the wife's family was considered a rent or fee paid to her family for the man's inability to support his wife and children. The slang term in southeast China and Taiwan for this practice is "charging the sow's rental fee" (*chou zhumushui*). Surely Ye was aware of the derogatory connotation of this arrangement too, for he never used the term *zhaozhui* when discussing his grandfather's marriage to his grandmother.

"That was how my grandfather came to live in Lin Village," Ye continued. "My grandfather was a poor drifter from another locality that I don't even know about, and was adopted into this Lin family to marry my grandmother. After the marriage my grandmother bore two sons. The first one took the Lin surname and stayed with her. My father was the second one and took my grandfather's surname, Ye.

"My father went to the South Seas, probably Singapore, in his teens and stayed there for three or four years," Ye said calmly.

"So you have overseas connections too!" I exclaimed. I knew that during the turbulent years of the Cultural Revolution, all Chinese who had been abroad or who had friends or relatives overseas were attacked as traitors or foreign spies. I wondered whether Ye had told other people about his father's overseas journey, or whether he had been attacked during the Cultural Revolution because of it.

He seemed to know what I had in mind and said loftily: "Overseas connections mean nothing here. In this part of China, almost every household has kin in the Philippines or Malaya. Besides, most of China's past political campaigns were aimed at high-level party cadres and city residents. The peasants have been mostly immune from abuses like the Cultural Revolution.

"My father went to the South Seas because my grandmother had a cousin from her father's side, a woman, who migrated to Singapore with her husband. They took my father along for the better opportunities there. During my father's absence my grandfather died, followed by my father's elder brother—the one who took my grandmother's family name. That meant my grandmother was left alone. So she went to the South Seas to bring back my father. My father returned because the Lin family still had about ten *mou* of farmland and a house for inheritance. That must have happened in the late 1930s, for soon after my father's return the Sino-Japanese War of 1937 broke out and the connection between China and the South Seas was cut off."

At this point we arrived at Ye's father's grave. It was built on slightly elevated ground at the base of the foothill, facing east. The dome-shaped tomb had a stone facade in the front with a marble stone slab erected in the middle. The stone slab had his father's name, his birth and death dates, and his birthplace inscribed on it. Also inscribed were the names of his sons and grandsons as his living descendants. All these inscriptions were painted in red, in contrast to the grayish marble color.

The dome-shaped tomb was covered with cement mixed with ochre. It looked reddish, even though the rain and dust since its construction had reduced the original red color into grayish-pink. Ye must have learned his lesson well from the village legends, for there was a cement ditch behind his father's tomb to prevent the water running down from the hills from damaging the tomb. Natural damage had been prevented, but the tomb was visibly ravaged by an unknown enemy. The marble stone slab was broken into halves, and there were also rocks and footprints all over the tomb.

There was no question that this tomb was the most extravagant one built recently in this village. Obviously Ye was proud of this tomb too. He turned to me and asked affably: "How do you like it?"

"Well, it was certainly built in an good location." I was cautious in selecting my words. I knew very little about geomancy and wouldn't want to say something wrong to offend him. "From here your father has a good view of the surrounding plains. The construction of this tomb must have cost you a fortune. This certainly demonstrates to the villagers what filial piety you have."

"Well, I didn't pay all the expenses," Ye said with a bit of embarrassment. "My brothers and I were divided when my father died. So we split all funeral expenses. But I was the one who designed the tomb and hired workers to build it."

"It was such a nice burial construction, except for the damage done to it!"

"Yes," the mention of the damage had Ye all agitated. "Now you can see why I was so angry with the people who did this to my father. Can you please take a few pictures for me now?"

As I took my two cameras out from my shoulder bag and started taking pictures, I asked him: "Now, what happened to your father when he returned from the South Seas?"

"During the Sino-Japanese War and subsequently World War II, southern Fujian Province was occupied by Japanese invaders. At that point my grandmother arranged to have my father married. My mother was from Lianban Village, about five kilometers to the west of Lin Village, just outside Xiamen City. She was from a very poor farm family. Few families with adequate means of support in Xiamen City or its vicinity would marry their daughters to Lin Village."

"Why was that so?" I was curious.

"It was not because the Lins didn't have land. Actually, at that point, the Lins here had a lot of vacant land. Around the 1920s and '30s the Lin lineage had been very depopulated by the two black death epidemics and the lack of male issue. When a Lin lineage branch was terminated due to the sudden death of its members or due to the lack of male offspring, the land was appropriated by kin in the next closest branch. Most of the Lin sons at that point carried more than one family line simultaneously and inherited the property."

At that point I had finished taking the few pictures I thought would be important to show the degree of damage. I also asked Ye to pose in front of his father's grave for a few shots. When I finished we headed home, still walking at the leisurely pace we had set earlier.

Ye posing in front of his father's tomb

Apparently Ye hadn't forgotten his unfinished story and took up his narration: "I said that families with proper means of support in the neighboring areas wouldn't marry their daughters to the Lins because life here was harsh. Water had to be hauled from deep wells not only for household uses but also for irrigation. Women spent hour after hour each day fetching water from the deep wells with pails attached to a bamboo-pole lever, called a well-sweep, and then carrying the water to their houses or to the fields using shoulder poles and wooden buckets. The tasks were laborious, and most women developed arthritis at an early age because of it. And for all their hard labor they had only sweet potatoes to eat as their staple. Most young women dreaded marrying into Lin Village because of the hard work. This situation improved after 1962 when the reservoir looping around our village was completed and the water supply problem solved."

"But if women in the vicinity dreaded marrying into Lin Village, then why did your mother marry your father?"

"Well, the situation was quite different during the Sino-Japanese War and World War II." Ye was apparently not offended by my insistence. "During the war the area became attractive not only to the poor from the interior of Fujian Province but also to people from Xiamen City. Due to the disruption of the war and the blockade by the Allies, the Japanese occupation forces imposed food rationing in this area. Food shortages became severe in Xiamen City, so even sweet potatoes became a luxury. It was these circumstances that caused many Lins here to marry women from Xiamen City and from other lowland villages.

"I was born in 1943, the first child of the family. My next younger brother came two years later, in 1945. In all I had six brothers and one sister. Even though my family owned some land and didn't have to pay rent like other tenants in the village, life was still harsh for us. With so many mouths to feed, both my father and mother worked like buffaloes from dawn to dusk. My father was a quiet and unpretentious man. He worked hard and never argued with other people. He tried his best to feed us and to provide us the opportunity for some education. But the burden was just too heavy for him to carry. I was the first one among my brothers able to finish high school. It was regrettable that my next two brothers never had the same opportunity."

"Was your father ever a tenant to the Lins?" I interjected.

"No. My grandmother inherited more than 10 *mou* of land from her parents and passed on the land to my father. But at that point there were many tenants who lived in Lin Village. The disruption of geomantic forces in the Lin lineage, the two epidemics, and the infertility of women very dramatically depleted the number of Lin families. By the 1930s, there were probably no more than two dozen Lin families left in this village. A lot of the marginal land in the vicinity lay fallow. The Lins began to lease out fallow farmland to land-hungry farmers from Anxi, Huian, and Tongan counties to the north. The Lins also allowed these newly arrived tenants to pay rent to live in the Lins' vacant houses. The terms of the land tenancy were comparable to those in other areas in southern Fujian, in that the tenants paid between one-quarter and one-third of their annual crop yields to the landlord. Today, except for my family, all other village families whose surnames are not Lin moved here during the '30s and '40s.

"The influx of immigrants to this village, especially those not related to the Lins, fundamentally changed social life here. The first development was the appearance of internal strife. These newly arrived tenants, who constituted the majority of the village population, didn't like the Lin landlords and accused them of dishonesty. Initially, a Lin landlord would lease out an abandoned field to a tenant and charge only one-quarter of the annual yield as rent. After the tenant built up the terrace and improved the soil quality, the Lin landlord would raise the rent to one-third of the annual yield. If the tenant refused, the landlord would revoke the lease and rent it out to other tenants who were willing to pay higher rent for this well-developed field. Because the Lins were rich and powerful, they bullied the non-Lins and created animosity within the village."

"Did the tenants do something to stop the Lins' abuses then?" I asked.

"Well, they did," Ye said plainly, without showing signs of approval or sympathy. I found his attitude to be peculiar. All Chinese literature and propaganda material present a stereotypic image of landlords in pre-1949 China as greedy, treacherous villains, who lived off the blood and sweat of those poor, defenseless tenants.

"Landlords be damned and peasants be glorified" is the official line to be followed by everyone in China. Apparently Ye paid no heed to this Party instruction.

Ye continued his nonchalant narration, as if this had happened in another place or to different people: "The most vocal opponents of the Lins were two brothers, Wu Ming and Wu Liang, whose family migrated to Lin Village in the late 1920s. This Wu family, like other Wu families in the village, had all come from the same village in Anxi County and belonged to the same lineage group. This kinship relationship contributed to their unusual solidarity. The Wu families, in conjunction with other tenant families and farmhands, resisted the abuses of the Lins. Whenever a tenant was unjustly dismissed by a Lin landlord, the other non-Lins would retaliate against the landlord.

"Wu Ming and Wu Liang were in their twenties during World War II. They were strong and quick to learn new things. They knew how to manipulate external authority to strengthen their own power in the village. Since the Wu brothers didn't have land here and refused to work for the Lins, they drifted in and out of the village and worked for whoever could pay them. For instance, Wu Liang, the younger one, worked as a village constable when the Nationalists controlled this area before World War II. Later on, with the advance of the Japanese occupation forces during the war, Wu Liang shifted his loyalty to the Japanese and was reappointed the village constable. He even picked up some conversational Japanese during those few short years. When the war was over and the Nationalists returned to this area, Wu Liang turned around and became a Nationalist local constable again. It was this kind of external connection that helped poor families in Lin Village to resist the Lins. Most of the Lins, however, regarded the Wu brothers as rascals and despised them. The conflict continued throughout the 1940s, and was escalated when the Communists came to power in 1949.

"In addition to these internal conflicts resulting from the influx of immigrants to the village, another change has been the development of a new marriage pattern. In the past the Lins strictly followed the rule of marrying outside of the village. They had no choice; all residents in the village were Lins and were related. They had to find spouses outside the village and with other surnames. But the presence of tenant families, whose surnames were not Lin and who were not related, altered this pattern. As a multisurname village now, youngsters were able to seek spouses from within the village. Marrying within the village became the rule rather than the exception in the late 1940s.

"Now, can you see why my family occupies a delicate position in this village?" Ye turned to me and asked pointedly. "On the one hand, through my grandmother, we owned our house and land here like the Lin lineage members. Compared with other tenants who came to live here, we enjoyed more security from our maternal linkages with the Lins.[5] On the other hand, we were not Lin lineage members and were excluded from the ancestral cult and the dominant position of the Lins. In that sense we were a part of the non-Lins. Because of this precarious position, my family has been able to remain neutral in the intra-village conflicts that plagued Lin Village from the early days when it opened to non-Lins."

At that point we had arrived at my apartment. I was elated by the rich insights that Ye had given me and was eager to record all the details before they escaped me.

The Importance of Geomancy

What about the destructive geomantic composition that almost wiped out the entire Lin lineage? I asked several elderly residents and found out that they generally concurred with Ye's narration about the causes and results of this incident. The only additional information I gathered was that, according to local legend, this negative geomantic force was mitigated after the completion of the reservoir around Lin Village in 1962. The building of a high dam in the low-lying area to trap water for this reservoir had changed the topographic complexion of the local landscape. The presence of a large body of water had given the hidden dragon a new breathing space for healing and growth. Local elderly people also believed that the two embankments of the reservoir, one to the north and another to the east of the village, helped to conserve the good fortune allotted to this village that had been drained away to the low land in the past. One clear sign of this improved fortune to the Lin lineage, most of the village's older residents pointed out, could be seen in the number of sons the Lin families had produced since the construction of the reservoir.

In later conversations with Ye I found him to be very evasive about anything spiritual. For instance, when I asked him whether Lin Village had a village temple built after the government stopped its attack on folk religious practices in 1982, he flatly denied it. Needless to say, he also denied the existence of spiritual mediums, or shamans, people who could be induced into trances and communicate with spirits. But then, in January 1985, after I had been in Lin Village for about three months, I discovered the newly built temple in a remote corner of the village. Through my interviews with villagers, I also found out that there were several spiritual intermediaries who practiced extensively. I collected the names of two villagers who practiced spiritual healings. I confronted Ye with these findings, and he was clearly embarrassed.

"I shouldn't have discussed superstition with you when I first befriended you. It is an idealist nonsense that we, the materialists, strongly object to. I am against feudalistic superstitions. As a Communist Party member, I do not participate in our village temple activities. For instance, I have not yet set foot in the village temple since its rebuilding in early 1983. Of the two spiritual intermediaries you mentioned, I consider both of them charlatans who profit from the peasants' ignorance and misery. I despise them. When they collect money for temple ceremonies, I contribute my share under my first son's name. This is an indication to them that as a member of this village, I am willing to be a part of community activities, even superstitious ones. But as a Party member, I disapprove of their activities. I would not have my name listed in their donors' list."

"But this stance didn't stop you from believing in geomancy!" I responded, not without sarcasm.

"The issue of geomancy is quite different from idol worship in the temple," Ye insisted. "Geomancy doesn't involve spiritual intermediaries or deities. It is directly related to our day-to-day life in that geomantic concerns are related to the cardinal directions of our houses and ancestral graves, which in turn affect our well-being. You don't have to rely upon those temple quacks to understand the significance of geomancy. Let me explain to you how these principles operate."

He took me to the new house he was building. It was without a doubt the most imposing two-story house in the village. It not only had the traditional enclosed courtyard, but there was another wall with an iron gate enclosing the entire housing compound. A couple of carpenters were adding finishing touches to window sills and door paintings. Apparently the entire construction could be completed in a matter of days. We went up to the balcony of the second floor where we had a good view of the south side of the village. In the distance were the granite hills of the village cemetery. Ye cleared his throat, spit out the phlegm on the ground as most villagers do, and started to give me a lecture on his view of geomancy.

"Look at the houses out there," he pointed at rows of houses on the southern fringe of the village. "You can easily detect a certain pattern. In building their houses villagers generally favor southern exposures, for south symbolizes warmth, growth, and prosperity. The second choice would be east, in that the rising sun from the east implies the beginning of life. West is less favored than the other two, for it indicates the end of a day's activities, and hence the analogy of termination of life. The worst choice would be north: dark, cold, and lifeless. From a pragmatic viewpoint, a house facing north would be exposing itself to the cold north wind in the winter, definitely not a good direction. So you can say that cardinal directions constitute the first principle in geomantic considerations."

I listened attentively but was not impressed by Ye's discourse, for the realtors in Iowa could have given me the same advice if I purchased a house in the country. I interrupted impatiently: "What will be your second principle, then?"

Ye showed no sign of displeasure with my rude manner and continued: "Another general principle in selecting a direction for a house is to have the back of the house leaning on high ground, while the front faces the low land. This position is stable and secure, like a man squatting on the ground: You rest your back toward the high ground while facing potential enemies from the low land. This provides a panorama of the surrounding area. When you apply these two principles to house building in Lin Village, you will immediately see the problems we face. Our village is situated on a slope tilting high to the south while descending to the north. In such a position we simply can't build our houses facing south, for the hills and high ground to the south will block air flow to the houses while the backs of our houses open to the low land. The local slang calls this kind of inverse geomantic orientation 'tumbled upside down' (*daotouzai*). Houses built in this fashion will bring bad luck to the residents. If we can't build our houses facing south, the most favored direction, this gives us only three other choices: north, west, and east. But, as I mentioned before, nobody wants to build a house facing north or west, so the only direction left is east. If you look at houses in our village today, you will see almost all of them are facing east."

After Ye's explanation, I looked again and realized that, indeed, most of the village houses were facing east. But there were three or four houses that instead of facing east, tilted slightly toward the south. I pointed to those irregular houses and asked him, "How come those houses don't follow the general pattern?"

A small grin appeared at the corners of his mouth, as if to say: "I knew that you were going to ask that question."

He cleared his throat again and replied, "See, that's what I mean when I said geomantic concerns affect people's day-to-day lives. These were villagers who in the past tried to manipulate geomantic principles when building houses. Even though they knew they couldn't build their houses toward the south, they thought that if they could slightly twist their houses in a southeasterly direction, they would still be able to enjoy the benefit of southern exposure. When they did that, however, disasters befell their families."

"Disasters?" I raised my voice.

He glanced at me and replied: "Let me give you an example I witnessed personally. One of the owners of those irregular houses was a man named Li Ai, whose nickname was Shorty because of his diminutive body size. When Shorty built his house in 1968, he faced the house slightly toward the south. He probably thought that even though he couldn't build a south-facing house, this southeast orientation would still bring good fortune to his family. When he hired a contractor to build the house, the latter advised against this plan and warned that there would be bad fortune descending on his family. But Shorty was a stubborn man. He said that since he was a Communist Party member, he didn't believe in that nonsense. He repeatedly ignored the plea by the contractor to change the house plan to straight east.

"There were continuous problems during the construction process. The wall at the back of the house just didn't hold up and collapsed repeatedly. It had to be built several times before it became stable. By 1969 the house was completed and Shorty's entire family moved in immediately. By the end of 1969, Shorty's thirty-nine-year-old wife died from a mysterious illness. Three months later, in January 1970, Shorty himself died from cancer, at forty-two. Another four months later, Shorty's mother, who had been living with them, also died from an unidentified illness. Thus, within one short year, all three adults died, leaving behind four children. The children and the neighbors were extremely sorrowful and fearful. People believed that the house was built against proper geomantic dictation. It was cursed. It was dangerous to live there.

"Since Shorty's oldest child, a daughter, was only nineteen then, too young to take care of the entire family, his wife's brother came to live with the children as their guardian. Their maternal uncle reported experiencing many horrible things in this house. For instance, in the dark of night, he often heard howling and screaming on the roof. One day he went up to the attic to search and found several pieces of spiritual money, the kind of yellowish, straw-paper money people use on ceremonial occasions, stuffed under the house beam. Apparently it was the contractor who had done this when building the house."

"Why would the contractor do that?" I asked.

This time Ye showed displeasure with my interruption. He said, "Let me finish the story; then you will find out why."

"A few years later, more evidence showed up to indicate that this house was indeed cursed. It was in 1975, when I was appointed the village public security head. I was called up one day to take a look at something mysterious that had been found in Shorty's house. The back wall of the house had collapsed again. When people looked through the rubble, they found a piece of human kneecap nailed to a miniature wooden shoe with piece of red string tied around it. People were scared. Nobody dared to touch it. When I came over and took charge of the situation, I was scared too. Apparently that was another magical item hidden during construction by the contractor to harm Shorty's family.

"The local legend has it that when a house is built against geomantic principles, either the builder or the occupants of the house will suffer from ill fortune. If the contractor wants to make sure that he will not be the one to suffer the consequences, the best strategy is for him to put a few omens in the house. The owner would have bad luck, but the contractor would be spared. Now, when the kneecap and wooden shoe were discovered in Shorty's house, the last charms were removed from Shorty's remaining children. The movement of the bad force was, at that point, redirected toward the contractor, who by then was living in another village. We heard that this man went out one night and got drunk. On his way home he fell into a roadside pit peasants used to store manure and was drowned. When this contractor built Shorty's house, he was living with a young female worker, who bore him a son. When he left our village he gave this son to a village family. Shortly after the contractor's death, his son also died.

"Another village family who suffered a very similar fate because of negative geomantic forces was the family of Lin Leshan, who used to be the head of this brigade and who was a very stubborn man. Lin, whose nickname is Thunderbolt because of his loud voice, built his house in 1968. Before Thunderbolt built his house, a villager with some knowledge of geomancy warned him that the house site was not balanced with all five essential ingredients: the minerals, wood, water, fire, and earth. To correct the problem, Thunderbolt was advised to dig a ditch behind the house. Thunderbolt Lin, again a Party member, dismissed this advice completely. A few months after the completion of his house, Thunderbolt Lin lost his position as brigade head. Soon after, he died of cancer. But that was not the end of the family tragedy. In September 1983, Thunderbolt Lin's oldest son, driving a hand tractor and hauling earth from a mountain slope to make sand bricks, was buried alive in an avalanche. Villagers believed that Thunderbolt's house was also cursed."

I was fascinated by Ye's discourse. Later, when I was able to copy the village household registration records, I looked for Li Ai's and Lin Leshan's household history. Under the names of Li Ai, his wife, and grandmother, plus Lin Leshan and his son, the record of their death dates and causes of death all coincided with Ye's description. Apparently, geomantic concern had been a persistent factor throughout Lin Village history. It could not be erased by government policies or practices.

The Liberation

3 I was well settled in Lin Village when winter suddenly descended on this part of China. I use the term "suddenly" without exaggeration. It was either the last few days of 1984 or the first part of 1985 when the clear sky that had brought plenty of sunshine to this area was replaced overnight by thick, dark clouds and occasional sprinkles. Winter monsoons, which are supposed to bring dry and cold air masses from inner Siberia across the continent to cover much of China, twist when they collide with the warm air off the Pacific Ocean. The original southeast airflow picks up moisture from the warm body of water, turns southwest, and dumps its humidity on China's southeast coast. "The plum rain season," as the local people call it, lasts for about three months, from late December to late March.

One may wonder whether winter really exists in subtropical areas such as southern Fujian. The absolute temperature was not that low, around 5 to 10°C. Neither was the rain the kind of downpour that is common in July or August during the typhoon season. But winter exists. Most houses in this area are poorly insulated and unheated. There are cracks and leaks in windows, doors, and the roof that invite the cold air to penetrate. It would be futile, as I did initially, to try to heat the room with a charcoal burner or an electric heater. The blowing and howling northeast wind that sweeps across every room simply sucks up the heat and carries it away.

Villagers bundled up with cotton padded coats to ward off this bonechilling cold. Older men and women sometimes carried small bamboo baskets with small earth stoves and a few pieces of burning charcoal in them to warm their hands. Most people cut short their daily work in the field. There was not much to do in their gardens anyway, for plants were not growing as rapidly as they did during the summer. When the drizzle intensified, the village brick factories and kilns stopped production. Young men, furloughed from work, took this opportunity to gamble in groups of three or four in an inconspicuous room in one of their houses.[1] Middle-aged men, generally less interested in gambling, gathered in early afternoon to drink. In the village social context, drinking definitely carries a strong masculine image. A drinker who can outdo the others in volume consumed, especially of the locally distilled rice wine, is admired by other villagers. I was sometimes invited by villagers to join them in these drinking gatherings, so I used these opportunities to conduct my interviews. But, as the party progressed and some of them became intoxicated and incoherent, it became difficult to carry on meaningful conversations.

Never a good drinker, or perhaps too self-righteous to be involved with villagers' less-than-desirable drinking habit, Ye seldom participated in these gatherings. Most often he came to visit me either in the afternoon or early morning. We chatted over a pot of hot tea and some preserved fruit—never my favorite food item, but commonly served by villagers when entertaining guests. Sometimes Ye invited me to his house and had his wife prepare a light snack to accompany two or three bottles of Snowflakes brand beer, brewed in Shanghai. It was on those occasions that I was able to record systematically rather detailed information about Ye's early childhood and his perceptions of village life in the immediate post-1949 era.

The Land Reform

"I was six years old when the Liberation came in 1949." Ye spoke more slowly when discussing his early life than when engaging in his usual high-pitched, fast-paced conversation. "The establishment of the new government didn't have much impact on my family. At that point my family had about 10 *mou* of farm land. But there were six people in the family who relied on this small amount of land for a living: my grandmother, father, mother, two younger brothers and me. Crop yields from the land were barely enough to make ends meet. Because my family owned some land, we were classified as middle peasants during Land Reform."[2]

"So there wasn't much change in your family?" I asked.

"That is correct," Ye agreed. "But to most other families in Lin Village the Liberation was a complete reversal of their previous social positions. The landlords and rich peasants lost their land holdings and their status, and former tenants and farmhands were proclaimed newly honored citizens of China.

"The most dramatic event in our village," Ye spoke with a trace of cynicism, "was that the triumph of the People's Liberation Army brought back the Wu brothers, Wu Ming and Wu Liang, to this village. Again, Wu Liang's rise to power was most spectacular. When I look at his life, I sometimes wonder if there is an invisible hand in heaven directing our lives according to certain written scripts."

At that point I had some familiarity with many villagers, and Wu Liang was one of them. He was introduced to me as the retired serviceman who now served as the receptionist who watched over the brigade telephone—the vital link between Lin Village and the outside world, especially for business transactions. He was sixtyish, with slightly graying hair. One crippled leg made his walking posture awkward. His bloodshot eyes and bloated, reddish face clearly indicated that he was an alcoholic. He was generally quiet, courteous, and unassuming when I went to the brigade office to use the phone. Other than those images, I was not particularly impressed by Wu Liang, especially after my earlier talks with Ye, who seemed to indicate that Wu was an important person in this village.

"Tell me more about Wu Liang then," I urged. "How did he gain his power?"

"In 1948 and early 1949, when the war between the Nationalists and the Communists in north and then central China intensified, the Nationalists began to draft young men en masse to fill their ranks. Since the Nationalists were losing forces very quickly, either through defeat or defection, the draft was extended to the countryside in southern Fujian. Rich families that tried to keep their sons away from military service, as rich Chinese always have, simply purchased another man as a substitute for the draft call. To no one's surprise, Wu Liang discovered a new way to make a quick profit. He sold himself to a rich family as a substitute draftee to the Nationalist army for an exorbitant amount of money. He went along with other new recruits through basic training and then to the front. When he had the opportunity, he deserted the army and returned to the village. He then sold himself again to another rich family for the next round of the draft and completed another cycle of service and desertion.

"Wu Liang played this game a few times and, according to the village legend, ran out of luck. On his last try, the Nationalist officers had tightened up their monitoring of new recruits. Wu Liang couldn't find a chance to sneak away and was forced to go into real battle. He was soon captured by the People's Liberation Army and so he defected to the Communists. To him, the defection probably did not mean anything. He has no interest in politics relating to either the Nationalists or the Communists. He would do anything or go any place where he could gain financially. That was how Wu Liang became a foot soldier in the Liberation Army and marched south with the Communist forces. Nobody knows what happened next, but what we now know is that Wu Liang was wounded in the right leg by Nationalist shrapnel during a battle. He became a cripple and was discharged with honor from the Liberation Army."

Now I could see why Ye felt Wu Liang's rise to power was ironic. Being a discharged Chinese Liberation Army soldier is like holding a gold plate for life. For an opportunist like Wu, that was indeed a twist of fate.

"By late 1949, the last Nationalists were completely driven out of mainland China and the new people's government established. Wu Liang and his older brother Wu Ming returned home with the triumphant Liberation Army. They possessed all the right ingredients to become the new rulers of the village: They were landless and, by definition, belonged to the oppressed class in the old feudal society; Wu Liang served in the Liberation war, was wounded in battle, and hence was a war hero.

"Even though Wu Liang and Wu Ming were completely illiterate, they were made the village mayor and deputy mayor. Cynics in Lin Village called Wu Liang 'three dynasties red' (sanchaohong). He is always red, the positive social emblem in contemporary China, in all three dynasties: the Japanese, Nationalist, and now the Communist dynasty. The injury to his right leg forced him to rely chiefly on the left leg for body support. When he walks, as you can still see today, he only temporarily entrusts his body weight to the right leg and then quickly shifts back to the left leg in an almost hopping gesture. For that he gained the nickname 'Hopping Toad Wu,' which villagers only dared to use behind his back when he was in power. But now, since his public humiliation in subsequent political campaigns, everyone calls him this to his face. It is one indication of how little the villagers think of him. When such a social outcast comes to power, you can predict what kinds of abuses and excesses he will commit.

"I sometimes wonder how many mistakes and abuses early cadres made to have created so much internal conflict and hatred in rural China. Most of the early cadres were from very poor families and hence were generally illiterate, just like the Wu brothers. They knew nothing about Communism or the purposes of this revolution. In fact, many of them were pure opportunists. When they were elevated to power by our government, they took that as an opportunity to carry out their personal vendettas against those who had been rich and powerful. Since they were 'oppressed' during the feudalistic era by the rich and landowners, these cadres figured that they could take back whatever they wanted. They attacked the rich families in 'class struggle' sessions and confiscated their family belongings for personal uses.

"Let's take Hopping Toad Wu as an example. If a Chinese written character is as big as a watermelon, Wu can read no more than two basketsful of words! How could you expect him to understand the meaning of policy directives when he couldn't even read them? The establishment of the people's government in the countryside in 1949 and Land Reform in 1951 were merely seen by the Wu brothers as opportunities to legitimize their revenge against those who had looked down on them before. This produced a reign of terror in the countryside, and also sowed the seeds of internal hatred."

"I assume that the former rich and the landlords were the ones who suffered most in those years?" I wanted to have more specific information about how the Wu brothers abused their power, as Ye had hinted earlier.

"Yes," Ye seemed to be taking my lead. "The most dramatic downfalls in Lin Village during the immediate post-Liberation years were among the large landowners, who were mostly Lins but there were also a couple of non-Lins. Among the Lins, the one who once had the most land was Lin Boting's father. In its heyday of the 1930s this family owned over 100 *mou* of land (about 6.6 hectares) in the area. Most of this land was inherited from other Lin families who had had no male issue to carry on family lines and thus had been terminated. Before 1949, however, Lin Boting's father had already sold a substantial amount of his land to support his opium addiction and had only about 30 *mou* (about 2 hectares) left. It was lucky that Lin Boting's father had dissipated most of the family estate. His opium addiction reduced some of the trouble that Lin Boting was to face in the post-Liberation period.

"After Liberation Lin Boting was classified a rich peasant, not a landlord. The first thing our government did after 1949 was to divide peasants into a classification determined by a complex formula called 'levels of exploitation.' Every rich family was measured for its exploitation level, considering the amount of farmland, the number of dependents, the number of family laborers who participated in farming family land, the number of long-term or short-term laborers hired to work the land, and how long they had hired workers or leased out land to tenants. After some careful calculation, Lin Boting's exploitation level was determined at 27.3 percent, slightly below the 30 percent required to be classified as a landlord. He escaped this 'landlord' stigma and avoided some harsh treatment given to former landlords. But his miseries were far from over, even without the landlord label, until the tragic end of his life."

"But wasn't this classification of people a national policy, not something that the Wu brothers could have done independently?" I insisted.

"Yes, it is true that this was a national policy," Ye conceded. "But in implementing this policy the early cadres carried the directives to extremes. A rich peasant should not be treated like a landlord. But Lin Boting, a mere rich peasant, was cruelly abused by the Wu brothers as if he were a landlord. That was something I consider intolerable.

"Lin Boting's miserable life has made a lasting impression on me. He was about seventeen or eighteen years older than I. I was still a small child during the Liberation, but Lin was already in his mid-twenties. Because of his family's wealth, which meant that he didn't have to go out to work like other peasants under the scorching sun, and that he enjoyed the proper food, Lin grew up with a light complexion and he was a bit overweight. That was how he earned the nickname 'Chubby Lin' from other villagers. Chubby Lin seemed to understand the plight that he and his family would have to endure under the new government, and tried to make the best of it. He always wore a ready—but clearly frightened—smile, even when confronted with the most difficult adversaries, and meekly accepted the abuses directed against him.

"Chubby Lin's timid, sullen, and helpless image occupied a lot of space in my childhood memory. Whenever he walked around the village streets children would follow him and quickly form a small crowd. The kids, probably imitating adults, would throw stones at Chubby Lin or call him dirty names. Chubby Lin wearily accepted all these insults and ridicule, bowed his head down even more, and darted to the closest house for refuge. He did all this without the slightest expression of anger or resentment.

"In my early childhood, my father had made it explicitly clear to me that I would not be a part of this unruly group who publicly humiliated Chubby Lin. My father said that even though Chubby Lin's family had owned land before, neither Chubby Lin nor his father had mistreated any tenants or villagers. Even though this family had fallen into political disfavor, my father insisted this didn't give us the license to abuse him. I heeded my father's instructions, and watched these unfortunate events from a distance. In doing so, I even developed some sympathy toward Chubby Lin and people like him, even though Communism taught us to hate these class enemies.

"Chubby Lin was probably the most tragic person among the rich Lins in this village. At the time of Liberation, there were four or five of the Lin families who had some land but they did not own enough land to be classified as landlords. They were labeled rich peasants like Lin Boting. The rest of the Lin families were classified as middle peasants, except for a few drifters who, by Liberation time, had used up all their family fortunes through gambling, whoring, or opium addiction."

"How important were these class labels to a person's life?" I asked.

"Very, especially the distinction between rich and middle peasant. It was the demarcation line between two different worlds. Rich peasants, by virtue of leasing out part of their farmland to tenants or hiring a few farmhands before the Liberation, were regarded as practicing exploitation against the poor, although their sin was considered not as grave as the landlords'. During major political campaigns, and especially when public rallies were organized by higher-level authorities to 'struggle against' class enemies, the rich peasants—along with former landlords, officials of the previous regime, criminals, and counter-revolutionaries, all those 'bad elements' (*huai fenzi*)—would be dragged up to the podium and attacked, either verbally or physically, by the masses. But during minor political campaigns the rich peasant families could sometimes be spared. Only the real landlords and anti-revolutionaries would be attacked. The real punishment for the rich peasants was that, because of their class label, their children would have few chances to receive advanced education or to join the People's Liberation Army. By contrast, the middle peasants could avoid all these limitations because of their non-exploitative nature."

"Were there any landlords in Lin Village then?" I asked.

"Yes and no," Ye replied. "Besides the few Lin families classified as rich peasants, there were two families whose large landownership would have put them in the landlord category. They were not related to the Lins, and came to possess land here rather late. The first one was a former sharecropper named Wan Li. Because his living conditions were limited in this village, Wan Li went to the South Seas in the 1930s as a laborer and left his wife and children here. He made a lot of money and sent a major portion of it back to his wife to purchase land from the Lins. By 1948 Wan Li returned to the village to enjoy the fruit of his labor, by then over 40 *mou* (about 2.7 hectares) of prime farmland. His dream perished the next year with the establishment of the new government. Even though the amount of land and the number of tenants he had would have put him in the landlord category, he was not labeled as such because he had been back for only one year. The length of time required for someone to be classified as a landlord with land tenancy was at least three years. He was thus spared.

"But Wan Li's former farm manager was not so lucky. Before 1949 it was quite common for absentee landlords to hire managers for their farms. These managers leased out land to tenants, arranged tenancy contracts, and collected rents. When Wan Li accumulated land by sending his earnings back from the South Seas to his wife, he also hired a Zhang person to manage the land. This Zhang manager was widely hated by the tenants because of the ruthless way he collected rent. Even though Zhang didn't own any land himself but merely acted as the manager for Wan Li, he was labeled a landlord and was executed during the Land Reform of 1951.

"The second landlord in Lin Village was Hong Ahui, one who had an experience similar to Wan Li's. In his youth he went to the South Seas to make money, and returned home to purchase land before the Liberation. Hong had about 30 *mou* (about 2 hectares) of rice terrace in 1949, but was not classified as a landlord because he had returned to Lin Village less than three years before 1949. So, you see, we had landlords who owned some land here before the Liberation, but technically they were not classified as such. Without a distinct landlord class in our village to serve as the 'class enemy,' the Wu brothers made rich peasants like Lin Boting targets of abuse during struggle sessions. It didn't have to happen that way.

"As I look back on what happened in Lin Village during the early years after the Liberation, I felt lucky that my family was in the middle peasant category.[3] Had my family been in the rich or landlord categories, we would be suffering all sorts of humiliation and punishment. Being a 'class enemy' of the masses, I would never have been allowed to go to high school or to join the Party. On the other hand, had my family been classified as 'poor peasant' or even lower, we would have been tempted to grasp power and abuse other village families, and thus be part of the never-ending cycle of hatred and violence."

"What you are suggesting is that in the early years of Liberation, the incompetent rural cadres like Wu Liang made a lot of mistakes. And that was the source of many problems that developed later," I commented.

"No," he corrected me, "the situation is far more complicated than abuses of political power by rural cadres. Abuses of power by cadres could have been easily corrected. In fact, when the national government noticed these problems in the early 1960s, they tried to correct the situation by launching political campaigns to purge the original cadres. They elevated another group of poor peasants to power and denounced the original cadres. These new 'pure proletarians' were essentially the same type of illiterate opportunists, but they happened to have been excluded from the original power share. They seized the opportunity for self-aggrandizement the same way their predecessors had done. They attacked not only the landlords but also the former cadres. A new cycle of violence developed, further increasing internal hatred in the village. As for Wu Liang and his brother Wu Ming, even though they wielded tremendous power in the post-Liberation period, they were repudiated, disgraced, and dethroned a few years later."

"Are you saying that the government's policy was wrong in the post-Liberation years when it elevated poor peasants to power?" I was a bit stunned by Ye's frankness and wanted to make sure I understood him correctly.

"No." He was rather emphatic in his response. "The problem was more than just policy. Sometimes I wonder whether the notion of class struggle and the attempt to classify peasants into various classes is a fundamental error of our government. Humans are not created equal: There are those who are smarter than others. There are also those who work harder than others. If we punish those who work hard and accumulate land, and reward those who are either inept or lazy, we are passing an incorrect message to citizens and to the next generation. How can you expect people to work hard and be innovative when they see what happened to their parents or neighbors who were hard-working before the Liberation?

"So, you see," Ye turned to me, "the problem we have had is not just the problem of policy: It goes much deeper. It involves how an individual perceives society and the people living in it. We cannot build a society on the basis of mutual hatred. Class differentiation encourages mutual hatred. The government made a good decision in 1978 when it abolished all citizen classification in China. If you look at the household registration records in the village today, you will find that the column for 'class standing' has been eliminated. We no longer consider a person's class before the Liberation as a factor in passing judgment. In doing so, we are undoing some of the injustices done in the name of class struggle."

"Was there any significant impact on your family in the post-Liberation years?" I asked.

"Not much," Ye replied. "All this turmoil in the post-Liberation period had very little effect on my family. My father worked hard on his land to make ends meet, and never got himself involved in village politics. He reminded us all the time that we should work hard and should not betray our morality by hurting innocent people. We were poor then. I still remember having barely enough food, chiefly sweet potatoes, to eat as our staple day after day. As the oldest son of the family I began to work with my parents in our field before I even attended school. I hated those early morning chores when I had to get up before dawn on cold winter days with my parents, wearing patched clothes and no shoes. I remember that I began to handle a plow when I was barely tall enough to reach the plow handle. As I plowed the sweet potato field I always carried a small basket with me. Whenever I turned up a small fragment of sweet potato, sometimes the connecting joint between the stem and the root, I picked it up and brought it home in that basket.

"The Land Reform of 1951 did not provide any practical benefit to my family either. At that point there were about 400 people in this village. The total amount of farmland was slightly over 800 *mou*, which came out to about 2.1 *mou* per person according to the land redistribution process. At that point my family had 10 *mou* of land and 6 people. We could have received an additional 2 *mou* of land according to the Land Reform formula. But my grandmother died in early 1951, before the land was formally allocated. With 5 people and 10 *mou* land, my family was denied any additional land."

School Years

Another long conversation with Ye that reveals a great deal about his childhood years occurred one afternoon when we were sitting in the upstairs living room of his newly finished two-story house and looking out the window that faces a small alley. It was almost 5:00 in the afternoon on a cloudy, humid wintry day in February. Several children, apparently just finishing school, ran through the alley yelling and chasing one another. Ye watched the youngsters and remarked in an envious tone: "Children today don't know how lucky they are. They never have to worry about enough food to eat, or money to pay for school supplies, or even be concerned with whether they can attend school."

"But you attended school youself!" I remarked. "Not only primary school, but also junior high and high school. What is so unique about children going to school today?"

"It was different," Ye insisted. "Not only was I a special case among the village children, but I also encountered difficulties throughout my school years. What type of education we had then! Today's kids could never imagine.

"I began to attend school in 1950, not a formal school, but a traditional private tutoring class. There was no formal school in this village then, one year after the Liberation, but the countryside had regained its tranquility. In Lin Village, a middle peasant of the Lin lineage was concerned about providing education for his children. He called upon other families with school-age children to establish a tutoring class. These families met and decided that a fixed fee, tuition, would be collected from each student and would be used to hire a traditional tutor. Class instruction was held in the Lin ancestral shrine located on the northern fringe of the village. Even though my family was poor, my father managed to raise the required sum to pay my tuition. I guess my father sent me to school because he felt that I had the most potential among my brothers to succeed. As a child I was not especially bright, but I learned things quickly. From my father's viewpoint, the investment in my education represented the best chance for my family to move ahead.

"I studied for one year in this private tutoring class. I didn't like the school much. The teacher was a traditional Confucian scholar who often mumbled classical prose we didn't understand. The instructional material was also traditional, such as the 'Three Characters Classic,' which we had to recite from morning till night without knowing its meaning.

"In 1951, the government established a primary school in Hilltop Village, about one kilometer to the northeast of Lin Village (see Map 3.1). The reservoir that now separates these two villages wasn't built yet, so we could walk straight to Hilltop Village in about 30 minutes by crossing the shallow ravine. When this new school was established, all the children in our class immediately switched over to the public school, which was free and provided better instruction. I was already eight years old when I attended first grade, the oldest one in my class. When the school started I also came to know a girl in my class from Mudhole Village, the archenemy of our village two kilometers to the south. Her name was Chen Baozhu, and she was to become my wife. Every schoolday morning she walked from her village to Lin Village, then further on to Hilltop Village. I often walked with her when she came past our village. Maybe it was fate. She was my classmate not only for all six years in primary school, but also during the next six years in junior and senior high. Not only did we go to school together, we were also assigned to the same work team in political campaigns after high school. It was through this long association and mutual understanding that Baozhu and I were able to stand firm together and to overcome the prohibition against marriage between our two villages."

"Who prohibited residents of the two villages from marrying each other?" I was interested in local customs as part of my anthropological inquiries.

"Well, this is a long story. The animosity between Lin Village and Mudhole Village had a long history. It is also a good way to illustrate the feudalistic nature of traditional China. The dominant surname group in Mudhole Village was the Chen lineage, who had been fighting with the Lins in this village indefinitely. The causes of the fighting were often petty conflicts. A cow owned by the Lins strayed away from the pasture and trampled over the Chen garden. Or a Chen man stole a few tree branches from the Lin gravesite for firewood. The situation didn't improve in the early twentieth century when other families gradually moved into these two villages. The diluting of direct lineage dominance of Lins in Lin Village and of Chens in Mudhole Village didn't lessen the tension between these two communities. New residents who moved into these two villages were automatically absorbed into these ongoing conflicts. During periods of high tension, a villagewide militia was organized by each village to patrol its territory and to prevent theft by the opposing side. When conflicts flared up into full-scale warfare all village adults would take up arms and plunge into the battle.

"My marriage to Baozhu in 1968 was of particular significance in breaking down this inter-village animosity. Baozhu's father was a direct victim of such conflict. Legend said that Baozhu's father, old man Chen, was a master of traditional Chinese martial arts. He could jump onto a rooftop with ease, and run over rugged terrain like he was skipping over smooth water. He could defeat several armed men single-handedly. It was late in the 1940s, before Liberation,

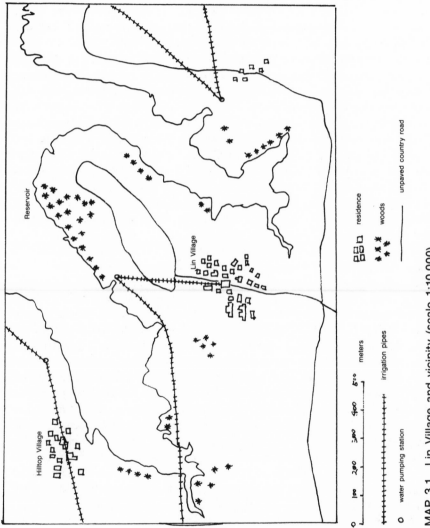

MAP 3.1 Lin Village and vicinity (scale 1:10,000)

Reservoir

Lin Village

Hilltop Village

0   100   200   300   400   500   meters

+++++ water pumping station

o irrigation pipes

residence

woods

unpaved country road

that old man Chen was ambushed and killed by Lin villagers. It was an unfortunate event and, in retrospect, neither side was solely responsible for the mistake. There had been a lot of thefts in this village and the residents had set up sentries and armed militia to guard the area at night. Unaware of the preparedness in Lin Village, old man Chen sneaked over one night, apparently to steal a chicken. He was so confident of himself that he was not even armed. Chen was noticed when he entered the heavily guarded village and was surrounded immediately by our armed men. He was overcome and mercilessly slaughtered."

"I assume that Baozhu knew the cause of her father's death?" I asked.

"Of course Baozhu knew that her father was killed by Lin villagers. I also understood why there had been resistance in both villages to our marriage. But Baozhu and I reasoned that what happened between these two villages before the Liberation was a part of the feudalistic legacy that we should forget as quickly as possible. Both Baozhu and I belong to the new generation that has grown up with new China. As such we should have the courage to leave behind all the historical baggage of the past. Marriage was the best testimony of our determination. Time was on our side, too. After the Liberation all inter-village or inter-lineage warfare, so common here in the past, was banned by the new government. Our marriage provided new opportunities to develop relationships between our villages. After our marriage there were several other marriages between these two communities. So far, two girls in our village have married men from families in Mudhole, and, besides Baozhu, two other women from Mudhole have married into our village."

"So you have known Baozhu since your first year in school." I tried to steer the conversation back to Ye's education.

"Ha! You see," Ye noticed the diversion from the original topic and mockingly extended his apology to me, "how I could easily be distracted by unrelated issues that nobody is interested in!

"Well, let's talk about my education. Even with the establishment of this new public school in Hilltop Village, my schooling didn't continue without further problems. In 1953, the shelling between us and the Nationalist bandits began. Xiamen Island is only about 3 or 4 kilometers away from Quemoy Island, controlled by the Nationalists. Since our village is on the eastern side of Xiamen Island, facing Quemoy Island directly, this entire area was under heavy gunfire. Many fortresses and underground shelters were built here. Even today, if you go to the rocky hills south of the village, you will find an entire area carved into underground tunnels and fortified bunkers. During periods of high tension, bombshells occasionally dropped on our village.

"No one in our village was killed by bombs. The real problem I remember during this period was that the tension continually disrupted classes. Sometimes in the middle of a class the shelling began. Everything had to be dropped and students were rushed to the nearest shelter for protection. During periods of heavy shelling in early 1954 our entire village was evacuated to Longhai County on the mainland. We were so glad when the tension lessened a few months later. The shelling first turned from a daily event to alternate days. Then it changed from real bombs to propaganda shells, which, upon explosion, distributed propaganda flyers.

"Despite the problems at the village and national levels, the years immediately after the Liberation I remember as relatively good years. Living conditions were still harsh, of course. I remember that I had to work in the field with my parents whenever I was not in school. I took care of the family cow, hauled water from a well for irrigation, and weeded the rice paddy. Sometimes I went after school with other children to collect straw and grass in the hills for my mother to use as cooking fuel. There were constant shortages of certain consumer goods, such as matches, kerosene oil, and clothes. But people could see the tangible progress being made within a relatively short time. Landlord abuses were eliminated. Former landlords and rich peasants suffered from their downfall, but they were only a small fraction of the village population. A new social order was established. The production level in our village first returned to and then surpassed its pre-Liberation level. Everyone was optimistic that the next day, next month, and next year would be even better. Those few years were probably the high point of the Chinese Communist Party. It proved that it could deliver prosperity to the peasants. Chairman Mao became a demi-god, beyond any living human's challenge.

"Riding high on this positive national mood, the Communist Party easily implemented its mutual aid team campaign in 1953. The concept of the mutual aid team was that the small peasants, about ten families in a group, would pool their land and farm equipment for cooperative management. But the peasants still owned title to their land. Return from their joint farm would be divided according to the amount of land, equipment, and labor each family contributed during the growing season. In a sense they joined the team as shareholding partners in a firm. This scheme seemed to work well and rural people achieved a prosperity they had not anticipated. In this campaign, Hopping Toad Wu and his brother Wu Ming initiated the first mutual aid team in our village. At that point Hopping Toad was elevated to the post of deputy director of the *xiang* (rural township) and his brother Wu Ming became the mayor of Lin Village.

"A year later, in 1954, a new campaign was launched to organize peasants into Elementary Agricultural Producers' Cooperatives. This was different from the mutual aid team in that it was much larger, about the size of two or three mutual aid teams pooled together to form an elementary cooperative. This new cooperative was to elect a committee, mostly poor peasants, to manage the farm work. This type of farm cooperative allowed the small peasants to pool their resources together for better management. They committed their land into the cooperative and received payment from the cooperative on the basis of their contribution in land and labor. During this campaign, the Wu brothers again took the lead in forming the first elementary cooperative in our village.

"Two years later, in 1956, before the peasants realized what they had gotten into, these Elementary Cooperatives were combined into Advanced Agricultural Producers' Cooperatives, as the national government instructed. The advanced cooperative was quite different from the elementary cooperative in many important ways. First, it was much larger, with as many as three hundred families in each advanced cooperative. In this area all the neighboring villages, including Lin Village, Hilltop Village, and Mudhole Village, were lumped into one single advanced cooperative. Wu Liang was appointed the director of the cooperative, and his brother became the deputy director. The second major difference between the elementary and the advanced cooperative was that in the latter the peasants forfeited all claims to their land. They were ordered to join the advanced cooperative and contribute their land into the collective. All return from the cooperative was to be divided according to the members' labor, without regard for how much land they owned after Land Reform. Peasants were turned into merely farmhands. In a single stroke the government took away all land owned privately by peasants."

"Was there any opposition to this new move?" I asked.

"Very little," Ye replied. "Some villagers were reluctant to part with their family land. They grumbled privately about the coercive manner in which the peasants were herded into collectives. But they were a small minority, who did not dare oppose the government. Most villagers still had fresh memories about the execution of manager Zhang and struggle sessions against rich peasants in our village during the Land Reform era. Another more important reason why opposition to this land confiscation was muted, I believe, was that the peasants were overwhelmed by the Party. Wasn't it true that the Party had brought an end to their previous miseries? Wasn't it also true that their living conditions improved significantly in the years immediately following the revolution? They had had so much trust in Chairman Mao and the Communist Party that most peasants probably believed that all these changes were necessary for the arrival of the ultimate paradise promised in government propaganda.

"Amidst this optimistic national mood," Ye brought this conversation to an end, "I finished primary school with honors in 1957. I took the entrance exam to junior high school and passed it. The school was in the market town called Jiangtou, about four kilometers from here, the only junior high in this entire area. It took me at least one hour to walk from Lin Village to my school in the morning, and another hour to return home in the afternoon. Even though the trip was long and sometimes frightening, especially in the winter when the sun sets early and the country road is dark, I was in high spirits and full of appreciation. I was the only person attending junior high in my village. Baozhu, the girl from Mudhole Village, also passed the entrance exam with good grades. Had it not been for the Communist Revolution, which brought total liberation from the yoke of feudalism, I would never have had this opportunity to attend junior high school."

Hunger, Hunger

4 One important ceremony people in rural China observe is Qing Ming, which literally means clarity and transparency. This is the occasion for people to pay respect to their ancestors by going to the graveyards and sweeping and repairing their ancestors' tombs. This ceremony occurs in early April, when the spring air is fresh and cool, as the term *qing ming* implies.

A few days before this ceremony I began to detect unusual activity in Lin Village. Families began to send their children to village stores to buy incense, spirit money, and firecrackers. Two or three days before the festival village women were busy preparing special sacrificial food. They scooped out polished rice from family storage bins and took it to the brigade rice mill, where for a fee of RMB$.50 the rice was processed into rice powder. They then mixed the rice powder with water and sugar and pressed the dough into wood-carved molds to make small cakes. The cakes were then placed in large bamboo steamers and stacked up three or four at a time over a pot of boiling water. In the meantime, children gathered around the kitchen anticipating the freshly cooked rice cakes.

Ye's wife, Baozhu, sent her second son with a plateful of these steamed cakes to me two days before the Qing Ming festival. I tried a piece but didn't particularly enjoy its doughy taste. I put the rest of the cake in a glass cabinet in my living room and soon forgot about it completely.

Qing Ming festival day was bright and sunny. Early that morning I went with Ye, his family, and his three brothers' families to the rocky hills south of the village where their grandmother and father were buried. Once outside of the village and in the open fields I was surprised by the crowds of people from all directions marching toward the foothills. It seemed that the entire village was congregating there, along with a few families from neighboring villages whose ancestors were also buried there. They carried baskets with three or four dishes of food, spirit money, firecrackers, liquor, cigarettes, and special long rectangular white paper strips to be laid atop the tombs after the ceremony. Young adults also carried sickles and hoes to clear weeds and saplings that grew on the tombs. A few families who arrived early had already cleared away the weeds around their ancestors' tombs. They offered the food to their ancestors by laying the dishes out neatly in front of the tombs. Children helped with burning incense and spirit money as sacrifices. Echoes of firecrackers occasionally broke the tranquility of the countryside, signaling the completion of a family's ceremonial obligations to its ancestors. One villager, nicknamed Tiger, even lit three Marlboro cigarettes and placed them on the small stone altar in front of his father's tomb. When he saw my perplexed expression, he grinned and said: "My father used to be a heavy smoker. He would definitely enjoy these good quality American cigarettes."

I chatted with many villagers about their ancestors and took photos for them at their request. While I was impressed by the persistence of tradition in the countryside, in spite of the government's negative campaign in the past thirty years to eradicate "feudalistic superstitions," this episode didn't concern me much because I was busy designing questionnaires for my research project. Three days after the Qing Ming festival Ye came to visit me and I didn't even remember this event.

He noticed the plateful of rice cakes in my cabinet that I had neglected for several days now. He groaned and took the plate out of the cabinet. It was already spoiled, with bluish mildew on it. He carefully scraped away some mildew from a piece, put a nibble in his mouth, and commented, "It was not completely spoiled yet. If you don't like it, I can take it home."

"Are you sure you want to eat this spoiled food?" I asked worriedly, for I was concerned about the possibility of food poisoning if he ate the cake.

"Well, I will let my wife, Baozhu, decide," Ye replied, "since she is the village doctor. But even if this is unsuitable for humans to eat, I can still give it to the hogs."

He then looked me directly in the eyes: "You are like the children in the village because you are so wasteful. I just can't understand how people like you can develop this type of bad habit."

The moment Ye mentioned village children, I knew how serious he was. He sometimes remarked to me about how unruly and unappreciative the village youth had become. Whenever he encountered something he disliked, he equated that to "kids' behavior." Trying to ease his irritation, I half-jokingly said, "Well, don't worry too much about it; it is only a plate of cake."

My attempts to appease him apparently didn't work, for Ye became angrier and blurted out a series of questions in his high-pitched, staccato voice: "Only a plateful of food? Do you know how many lives this plateful of food can save? Do you know how much hunger people in our generation have suffered? I wish heaven would condemn all those who waste food to live through the Great Leap Forward!"

The Great Leap Forward was one of the frenetic periods in Chinese Communist history. Due to policy errors at the national level, production plans in the late 1950s failed. It was never too clear to the outside world just what happened during this period or how much damage was done. Even though it was acknowledged that famine occurred in many parts of China, estimates varied as to how many people actually starved to death. Apparently, in the minds of people like Ye, the Great Leap Forward was synonymous with hunger. It must have been a very painful experience for the memory to have persisted after almost thirty years. It was through Ye's description of this episode in his life and in this village that I was able to gain personal insight into and hence better understand the miseries the Chinese people endured. Several later interviews I had with Ye about the Great Leap Forward form the basis for this summary of the period.

The Great Leap Forward

"The Great Leap Forward was initiated in the countryside with the establishment of the People's Communes. It seemed that very few people had any clear idea of what was to happen when the government proclaimed the establishment of People's Communes throughout China in late 1958. There was a kind of agitation, or perhaps excitement, in the air. The bumper crop in the previous two years had impressed the peasants so much that all their previous reservations about the Communist Party and their reluctance to participate in collective organizations dissolved. We were poised for the final leap. Over the last hurdle would be the paradise promised in the *Communist Manifesto*. No one was surprised when the order came that from then on there would be no private land or hearth. Any vestige of self-interest was to be renounced. All production instruments, including land, tools, and animals, were to be turned into public property. Everyone would be working on communal land as farm laborers and eating at the communal canteen. The ultimate goal of Communism, 'From each according to his ability, to each according to his needs,' was to be achieved with a single proclamation from the central government!

"The entire Xiamen Island, except for the downtown area belonging to the Xiamen municipal government, was lumped together to form a commune, called the Frontline Commune because of its strategic location directly facing the Quemoy Islands occupied by the Nationalists. Under the commune were about fifteen brigades. Lin Village and Hilltop Village were combined to form a brigade, called Lin Brigade. Hopping Toad Wu became the secretary of the brigade party branch, while his brother Wu Ming served as brigade head. Under the brigade were production teams, three teams each in Hilltop Village and in Lin Village. Each team had a formal team leader appointed by the brigade party committee. The three newly appointed team leaders in Lin Village were Hong San, nicknamed Opium Hong for his alleged opium addiction before the Liberation, of the first team; Lin Xiang, nicknamed Dark Skin, of the second team; and Lin Leshan, called Thunderbolt by villagers for his loud voice and hot temper, who led the third team. These three were younger than the Wu brothers and were cultivated by the Party as leaders of the next generation. Among these three, only Opium Hong was from a truly poor background. He used to be an actor in a local opera troupe and was illiterate. The two Lins, Dark Skin and Thunderbolt, were from Lin lineage but belonged to the middle peasant classification. Both of them had had some education and were supported by the Lins.

"In the early days of the communization movement, an attempt was made to make the commune and brigade large. The slogan then was 'First Big, Second Selflessness!' (*ida, ergong!*). The idea was that if we could expand the size of the collectives continually until the entire nation became a classless commune, we would then be able to accomplish the socialist transition in a single stroke and become a true Communist society.

"The thing that impressed peasants most under this new rural collective organization was the availability of white rice, which was cooked dry[1] and seemed to be in unlimited supply in commune canteens. Most peasants in southern Fujian had eaten mainly sweet potatoes as their staple. It was only during important festivals, such as New Year's or weddings that ordinary peasants would cook dry white rice. But now, the peasants were happy to discover that the public canteens provided white rice congee for breakfast, and dry white rice for lunch and dinner. The government's slogan in promoting communal organizations then was that peasants should open up their stomachs and eat as much as possible. Not only were people told to eat more and better food, but all these canteens also competed to provide better food for the people. Even schools served free meals for students. The kindergarten in this village, for instance, not only provided rice congee for pupils in the afternoon as snack, it also supplied fruit, which peasant children never dared to dream of before, to supplement the congee. Anyone who had reservations about the new policy, or anyone who did not enjoy a full stomach at every meal, would be criticized for lacking faith in Communism.

"Alongside this new collective agriculture was an emphasis on industrial development. Every collective unit, either the brigade or even a production team, was encouraged to establish its own backyard steel furnace. In Lin Village, a steel furnace made from bricks was erected by villagers under the direction of a village blacksmith in mid-1959. At that point Chairman Mao issued a slogan: 'Surpassing Great Britain and Catching Up with the United States.' (*chaoying, ganmei*). The idea was that if we could drastically increase our steel production, the basis of modern industrial society, we would become a first-rank world power within a few years. I don't remember exactly how the idea was phrased; I only remember the goal at that point: If we increase our steel output by several percentage points per year, we should be able to out-perform Great Britain in seven years, and be on a par with the United States in fifteen years.

"At that point everyone seemed to be caught up by this frantic socialist devotion. Nobody had any doubt that we could achieve these goals. Was it not true that we had already entered the final Communist stage when we organized these rural communes? Was it not true that after we had organized the communes we had unlimited supplies of rice? A paradise materialized through the guidance of the Party and Chairman Mao. As a new nation with newly reformed citizens, we were to chart our own future course and realize the Communist dream.

"I was a true believer then, a second-year student in junior high. I believed that if everyone followed Chairman Mao's direction faithfully, that is, if everyone contributed and added some grams of steel to the village steel furnace, we should be able to realize the goal and surpass all nations in this world. I had several classmates who shared the same view with me and, together, we decided to commit ourselves to this noble cause. We didn't want to be part of the most popular activity of the other peasants then: donating their steel utensils, such as cooking pots, iron hoes, and even window rails to the public furnace. We thought that collecting scrap metal or bomb shells in the field for the furnace a task beneath us. We were the first generation of educated people in the post-Liberation era. It was only because of Chairman Mao and the Party that we were liberated from the feudalistic, blood-sucking landlords. The Liberation brought to us our rebirth, an opportunity for higher education, and the aspiration to serve the nation and all humankind. We should express our appreciation to the Party, to Chairman Mao, and to the state through more creative acts. We should invent new ways to increase steel production.

"My classmates and I did a lot of experimenting. We went to the rocky hills south of the village to investigate the geological composition of the area for possible iron ore deposits there. We collected various kinds of stone chips and melted them in our privately built miniature furnace. Of course we didn't produce anything, for there was no iron ore in this area.

"The next task we engaged in was collecting sand along the beach. Either because of oil contamination from the discharge of ocean liners or because it actually contains mineral ore, the beach sand in certain areas around the island looked black. We collected this black sand for our experiment. I don't know what happened, but after smelting the sand in our furnace we did produce a few steel chips. We reported our findings to our school and were praised in the school's morning assembly for our dedication to the socialist cause.

"As I look back at those early years, I don't believe that any sober-minded human could have engaged in such wasteful, meaningless activity as we did during the Great Leap Forward years.[2] Since the goal of the backyard furnace was so simplistic and neat, namely to increase the volume of steel output by a certain percentage over a certain duration, everyone seemed to have developed a belief that this production goal was sacred. Peasants were led to believe that if the volume of steel production could reach the government's target, China would automatically turn into a Communist paradise. You cannot imagine how easily the masses were fooled by simplistic political slogans. If all that was needed was a few grams of steel to enter the paradise, most ordinary peasants were prepared to make the sacrifice. Chubby Lin, the son of a rich peasant, donated his iron frame bed to the public furnace. The bed, which had cost over RMB$100 when new, was melted down to a chunk of steel with no practical use. Scrap metal was collected and fired to red hot in the furnace. It was then hammered into square blocks with no apparent use. Nobody questioned the purposes of this madness. Perhaps there were people who had reservations about these activities, but they never dared express them. Who could afford to be considered disloyal to Chairman Mao and to the Party?

"Probably the most devastating effect the Great Leap had was in agriculture. All the able-bodied men were assigned to work in steel furnaces. After spring transplanting of the first rice crop in 1959, all the farmland in this village was literally abandoned. Nobody came to irrigate the fields or weed them or spray pesticides. By summer harvest time, only a few farmers were assigned to harvest the crop. Apparently the assumption then was that the reorganization of the countryside into communes had already solved half of China's agricultural problems. The top priority was to promote industrial output, especially steel production. Agricultural production could be handled with new technologies, made possible through collectivization.

"Several directives were issued by the central government to deal with agriculture and promote what was termed 'scientific farming.' The essence of this scientific farming was not to encourage the use of better seeds or pest control methods, but to plant as many plants in a single plot of land as possible, in the belief that this could boost production immediately. For instance, the traditional method of transplanting rice seedlings in irrigated terraces is to allow about fifteen centimeters between each hill of rice seedlings. The scientific farming method called for reducing the space between hills to only seven centimeters, thus quadrupling the number of stalks in the same plot. If a production team planted crops in the traditional manner, the higher authority would come and put a white flag along the field. This was a warning to the entire team, for the white flag implied that people in that unit cherished more white than red. On the other hand, the work unit that doubled or tripled the number of plants in a single field received a red flag to signify its dedication to the cause of Communism. Needless to day, the fields that adopted this new scientific farming lost most of their yields by the 1959 summer harvest.

"The crop failure in production units that adopted this scientific farming method contradicted the government's claims, but nobody dared to acknowledge it openly. The central government's goal then was to increase crop yields in rice paddies to more than 1,000 catties per *mou*, called *mouchan qianjing*. Under pressure from higher-level authorities to reach this production target, the brigades and teams had to fabricate their production data. One of the most common forgeries was to harvest rice from several fields in less accessible areas, and then combine all the crops in a single 'model' plot to make it look as if this densely planted field had indeed tripled or quadrupled its yield. A high-level cadre, from either the commune government or the county government, would be invited for inspection. The local officials who put up this fraudulent show would be praised by their superior as models who faithfully carried out Chairman Mao's assignment.

"To make their fraud appear plausible, the team and brigade officials had to fabricate production data on paper, too. They claimed on their seasonal reports to commune and county authorities that they had enjoyed an astronomical rate in grain production increase the preceding season. Based on these falsified reports, commune or county authorities assigned even higher procurement quotas to buy the supposed surplus rice and pork from brigades or teams. The teams and brigades had no choice but to provide the required foodstuffs to sell to the government at official prices. To meet these new procurement quotas the team and brigade officials had to dig into whatever private storage the peasants might have. This forced sale of nonexistent surplus produce aggravated food shortage problems in the countryside later.[3]

"It is funny to look back at those years. The people at the top deceived and misguided the masses, and the masses deceived their superiors, who in turn formulated new policies on the basis of fraudulent reports. It formed a vicious circle, to be exploded when only a small grain of truth emerged to pierce through those inflated political myths.

"The good days lasted for about six or seven months. During that time everyone was happy to have all the food they could eat in the canteen. But then, suddenly, there was no more food. By the fall of 1959, hunger suddenly emerged without warning and brought the entire pretense to an end. For the next twenty years the problem of hunger was part of our lives.

"Without food, the first thing to collapse in our village was the communal canteen. Peasants were told that they should return to their own families and cook their own meals with rationed food at the end of the harvest season. Each family was left to find its own food between fall 1959 and the next harvest of sweet potatoes at the end of that year. My family was lucky. A few months earlier, during that summer, when all the farmland was neglected in the frenzy of building backyard furnaces, my younger sister, who was about six or seven then, found more than two dozen huge sweet potatoes in a small stream. These potatoes were probably washed down the stream from a neglected field after a rain. Apparently nobody was paying any attention to these non-essential foodstuffs when there was an unlimited supply of rice in the canteen. My sister called them to my mother's attention. Even though there was no need to store one's own food then, since everyone could eat whatever was needed in the canteen, my mother didn't like the idea of wasting usable food. She fetched these sweet potatoes from the water, cut them into slices, and dried them under the sun for storage. These dried sweet potato slices saved my family from starving for a long period of time in late 1959.

"The human error of 1959 was followed immediately by three years of natural disaster. Children today have never experienced real hunger. They could never imagine the torment of hunger: the chronic pain in the stomach, the dizziness and emptiness in the head, and the constant craving to chew on something that is solid and edible. Just imagine what we had to eat every day then: a large cooking potful of water with only a handful of rice and a few slices of dried sweet potatoes. When you ate, you actually drank a lot of water to fill up your stomach. I still remember one morning when I was walking to school and found half of a carrot, probably dropped from a peasant's shoulder basket, on the road. I carefully wiped off the dust and put it in my pocket. Whenever I felt the cramps in my stomach in school that day I took the carrot out for a nibble. For that whole day I thought I was the happiest person in the world.

"The situation in our village during those three years of starvation was, comparatively speaking, not bad at all. Elsewhere in southern Fujian Province, especially the inland counties and in large cities, a lot of people actually starved to death. We were better off for several reasons. First of all, we are in the frontline area directly facing the enemy and can be seen with binoculars from the Nationalist-occupied islands. Our government made an effort to provide us with at least some food, so that this massive starvation would not be seen by the Nationalists and used as propaganda. The second reason for our relatively good condition was that this area was not heavily populated. Farmers could easily dig out a root plant or pick up a few greens in their fields for food.

"The death of one villager during this period can probably be attributed to hunger. This person, surnamed Li, was in his early twenties then. He was a deaf-mute and very muscular. He would do any type of hard labor for people if he was promised a stomachful of food. In 1960, when our brigade was preparing to build the reservoir, all houses in the lowland area that would be submerged under water had to be removed. The work included taking down the house beams and wall bricks and carrying them to high ground with shoulder poles. Several muscular young men were selected for the job, including this deaf-mute Li. The brigade promised to provide continuous supply of food for this work unit as long as they were working moving the houses. And indeed the food came! It was a huge pot of boiled congee with no more than two or three handfuls of rice, another handful of sweet potato slices, and a few drops of sorghum and wheat in it. Next to this pot was a wash basin full of boiled vegetable greens that villagers today feed to their pigs. A small dish of salt near this basin was for adding taste to the boiled greens. Whenever the workers felt hungry, they dropped their work and came for a bowl of this watery congee. While they gulped down the congee they also picked out a few pieces of green leaves, dipped them in salt, and swallowed them.

"I remember this so well because my old house was in the lowland and had to be torn down. I didn't have school that day and came to watch the work team. Every few minutes the workers stopped their work for this precious food. And then a few minutes later they had to find a private place to urinate. Everyone was so hungry and feeble that the work seemed to drag on forever, except for Li, who seemed to be unaware of the deceptive nature of the food he had been consuming. He was still working at his brisk pace, carrying baskets full of bricks or tiles with his shoulder pole. He probably didn't realize that he had used up all his energy after only a few hours. It was around noontime when deaf-mute Li signaled several of his co-workers to remove a heavy wooden house beam and place it on his shoulder. They did. The weight of the beam must have overwhelmed him, for he fell to the ground and died.

"Because of this insufficient nutrition level, a lot of people became ill easily during this period. Edema was the most common symptom, even among my classmates. All four limbs, but especially the legs, would be swollen like inflated balloons. The remedy for edema was rice chaff, a by-product of brown rice and used today only to feed pigs, mixed with a spoonful of brown sugar, a precious item then, and a few pieces of gingerroot. This mixture was stirfried in a wok and was to be eaten once or twice a week, depending on the person's income level, to cure edema.[4] Even though this remedy was a much better food than the watery congee of sweet potatoes we had everyday the harshness of the rice chaff was hard on the digestive system. Stomach ache became a constant problem when edema subsided. There was always blood in our stools. Bowel movements caused acute pain.

"My best memory about this period was an old man who claimed to be ill and went to see the village traditional doctor, Lin Fen. Doctor Lin examined him and told him that he was not sick, but he lacked oil in his stomach. Without vegetable oil or animal fat to lubricate his body organs, all his intestines were tangled up or stuck together. Doctor Lin told him to find either a slice of pork fat or a drop of vegetable oil to be added to his cooking pot as medicine. But the old man said that he was too poor to afford either one of those two. So Doctor Lin told him to bring his cooking wok over to the doctor's house that night. Doctor Lin had a kerosene lamp that he occasionally used at night. When the old man brought the wok over that evening, Doctor Lin laid it over the lamp for a few seconds, returned it to the patient, and said, 'Now that the wok has the smell of oil, rush home and use it to cook a dish for your hungry stomach.'

"During those few years, money meant very little to ordinary people, for there was virtually nothing to buy. The value of our currency was very low. People who lived in Xiamen City paid RMB$.20 or .30 per catty to buy rotten cabbage leaves. Today, even our hogs wouldn't eat that kind of rotten cabbage. There was a saying in Xiamen City then: 'Cabbage leaves wrap cabbage leaves for lunch, and leaves of cabbage wrap leaves of cabbage for dinner' (*wucan caibaocai, wancan baocai bao baocai*). To change the taste of cabbage some housewives salted the cabbage leaves first and then sundried them, making what was considered a real delicacy.

"Another indicator of the low value of our currency then was the high price of ration coupons. For instance, the rice ration coupon issued to city dwellers today entitles them to buy rice at government supply stores for RMB$.18 per catty. If you buy the same quality rice in the free market it would cost RMB$.25 per catty. The difference of 7 cents reflects the current value of a one-catty rice ration coupon in the free market. But during the starvation years, the value of a one-catty rice ration coupon went up to RMB$.60, sometimes even .70, or four to five times higher than the value of the grain itself.

"I have always been puzzled by the level of hunger in those years. We had the same amount of land then as we have now, but today there are more mouths to feed. The quality of our land has been virtually the same, producing approximately the same amount of food. But why is there such a big difference between now and twenty-five years ago? Today, my children refuse to eat those steamed rice cakes after the first day, the same way you did. We have so much more rationed rice than we can eat now that we feed it to our hogs. Imagine feeding hogs bright white rice! The question I asked was, 'Where did the food go during the Great Leap Forward? And why was there a shortage?' The government propaganda now blames natural disasters for the widespread famine in those years. It is true that weather conditions were not extremely favorable, but that was only a relatively minor part of the reason. Based on my observations I was forced to conclude that the real cause of this disaster was human error. Chairman Mao was responsible for all the sufferings that plagued our country for the next two or three decades."

Becoming a Political Activist

Ye's revelation about the years of the Great Leap Forward made a strong impression on me. To put his picture into perspective I asked, "How well did your family cope during those difficult years?"

"Life was difficult for my family during those years, but we were no worse off than other villagers. In fact, I can say villagers seemed to be better off than city people, at least in southern Fujian area. We lived close to the land and were able to pick a piece of root or tuber or a few green leaves to supplement our diet once in a while. We were hungry most of the time, but we survived. Besides hunger, another experience that affected me greatly during those years was blatant discrimination against my family because we were poor and powerless."

"Discrimination?" I asked. "By whom and for what?"

Ye drew a deep puff of his cigarette and calmly replied, "Let me tell you about two separate incidents that I remember and that best illustrate the discrimination my family endured in this village. The first incident involved my family and the Wu brothers. The building of the reservoir in 1960 forced many villagers to tear down their houses in the lowland area. There were approximately twenty families in Lin Village that had to be evacuated and resettled. The government agreed to compensate us with cash according to the value of our houses, and then build two rows of houses for us to live in later.

"In early 1960, the commune office sent an appraiser to our village to assess the value of the houses to be torn down. At that point Hopping Toad Wu and his brother Wu Ming still lived in the same house quite close to my house. Our two houses were about the same size and of similar quality. The only difference was that Wu Ming had built a small shack behind his old house as his kitchen when he divided up the family with Hopping Toad and started to cook separately. When the commune appraiser came, he decided that the Wu brothers' house was worth RMB$1,100, while our house was only RMB$210. The Wu brothers received RMB$800 more for that lousy shack! What could we say about this discrimination? Could we argue with the commune cadre about this injustice? Or with Hopping Toad and Wu Ming? No! When you are poor and powerless, you are nobody.

"My father just accepted the appraisal without raising any question. He even told me to shut up when I complained about the difference in compensation. He was afraid that the commune cadre or the Wu brothers might have overheard my disgruntled remarks and thus create more difficulties for us.

"The second incident was closely related to the first one. When we moved out of our old house in mid-1960, we rented a room from a Lin family temporarily. The row house promised to us by the government was to be completed a year later. In the meantime we had to rent spare rooms from other village families. This Lin family we rented a room from was quite mean to us. They boarded up the east window of our rented room, so that we could not see activities in their courtyard. That left us with only a window and door on the west side of the room for ventilation. You know how hot it can be in this area in the summer. Without windows on both sides of a room for air circulation, the room was virtually a steam bath. Even worse was when this family threshed and winnowed their harvested rice in the fall. They did it in front of our window, and the rice dust blew directly into our room so that my younger brothers and sister coughed and choked. Even though we paid rent for our room to this Lin family, they treated us as if we were nobody."

"But you are no longer a nobody," I half-teasingly reminded him.

"Of course not," Ye said with a mocking tone in his voice. "I sometimes wonder how fate has made fools of people. All those who treated my family badly in the past probably never have imagined that one day I would become the ruler (*tongzhizhe*) of this village. Had they known that then, they would probably have treated us better. Somehow I sense that my father seemed to have a hunch about this incredible turnaround. He told me repeatedly: 'Have you had enough experiences in which we, the poor and powerless, have been mistreated in this world? Remember, when you have power or money in the future, be nice to those less-fortunate!' I have taken my father's teachings to heart. When I gained power, I never abused the village poor. I not only tried my best to protect the weak and poor, I also actively undercut those who oppressed the less fortunate ones. And that was the main reason why I tried to preserve our brigade collective in the early 1980s when the central government pressured us to dissolve it. Poor people are better protected under the commune system."

"Are you saying that you are in favor of the communal organizations, in spite of all the suffering caused by the Great Leap Forward?" I asked.

"Well, the failure of the Great Leap Forward and the establishment of the collective communes are not the same thing," Ye replied. "The Great Leap Forward was doomed to fail because it was built upon false assumptions and flawed plans. Collective communes, on the other hand, can definitely fulfill certain practical needs that small-scale peasants are unable to accomplish individually. For instance, without collectivization, the construction of the reservoir in 1961 would not have been possible. It would be simply impossible to persuade each and every farmer whose land or houses would be inundated by water to participate in this collective effort. The construction of the reservoir took away half of our arable land, over 400 *mou*, from Lin Village. But the benefit of the reservoir was enormous. Whereas before 1961 only about one-tenth of our land here had sufficient water to grow rice, the presence of this reservoir practically made all our land irrigated. Collectivization also made mass mobilization of labor possible. For instance, we lost about 400 *mou* of farm land to the reservoir. Upon the completion of the reservoir in 1962 we decided to expand our land lots. We leveled the ground, removed the graves, redrew the land divisions, and expanded our fields to the slope of the hills. In doing so we gained about 300 *mou* of farm land for the entire village. None of those projects could have been accomplished had there been private landownership to prevent the allocation of resources for the entire village according to rational planning.

"Besides public construction projects, probably the most important contribution of the collective system was its promotion of well-being for all villagers. For instance, our village was able to build its own elementary school in 1962 after we were formally separated from Hilltop Village by the reservoir and formed a new brigade, called the Lin Brigade. The money for school building materials came partially from our brigade coffers, and construction labor came from our collective labor. In addition to the school, the public health care system was also made possible under the collective system in 1968. Without the collective organization of the brigade, it would be very unlikely that any individual peasant family could afford to send its son or daughter for medical training.

"The basic structure of the communal system was established throughout China in 1958. The three-tier system of commune, brigade, and production team was firmly developed then, even though in later years the locus of power shifted from one level to another due to policy changes. In general, a team is composed of about thirty to fifty families, and is the basic accounting unit. All land previously owned by team members was lumped together to become public property. Except for 5 to 7 percent of farmland that was reserved as 'private plots' for individual families to grow vegetables for their own use, the remainders constituted the main source of income for all team members. Each team had five partially to totally paid officials to run its daily affairs: a team head, an accountant, a treasurer, a work-point recorder, and a storagehouse keeper. Labor was divided among these five officials as follows: The team head made decisions on production plans for the entire team and assigned work to individuals; able-bodied men and women worked the collective land and received work points on a daily basis according to the length of time worked and nature of the work. Their accumulated work points were recorded by the work-point recorder; at the end of a season all team earnings were calculated by the accountant, and then divided up among all team members according to their accumulated work points. The team members claimed their cash or grain from the team treasurer accordingly. That was how individual families got paid."

"Did individual farmers pay their own taxes? Or how did the higher-level authorities, such as the brigade and commune administrators, generate revenue to fund their operations?" I asked.

"The flow of revenue obviously was from the bottom to the top," Ye explained. "Several teams made up a brigade, and several brigades made up a commune. A team contributed a certain portion of its income to the next higher level of administration, the brigade. The two major categories of funds from teams to the brigade were the 'public welfare fund' (*gongyi jin*), which accounted for about 3 percent of a team's net income and was used mainly to pay for the aged, infirm, and servicemen's families; and the 'public accumulation fund' (*gongji jin*), about 5 to 7 percent of the team's net income, used to pay for public works involving the entire brigade, such as building a village road or an irrigation channel. The public accumulation fund was also used to pay the salaries of the six brigade officials who took charge of the brigade's day-to-day business: the brigade Party secretary, the brigade head, the public security head (who also doubles as commander of the local militia), the clerk (who also serves as the brigade accountant), the brigade treasurer, and the head of the women's league. The first four officials work full-time and are paid with work points comparable to the highest-income farm laborer, or fifteen work points per day for thirty days per month. The last two brigade officials, namely the brigade treasurer and the head of the women's league, are part-time officials. They are paid at the second highest level at twelve work points per day, and eight to ten days per month. They are paid less than the other four because the nature of their work doesn't require them to work that much, and also because these two positions are generally occupied by women."[5]

I posed the question I had been waiting to ask, "Now, if the communal organizations were of practical benefit for peasants, why did the Chinese government want to abolish them?"

"The biggest weakness in our collective system," Ye answered, "is of course, motivation. When peasants saw that rewards were not directly linked to work, or that their work would be calculated through the collective pools before reaching them, they worked only halfheartedly. We have several sayings here to describe the kind of indolence practiced by peasants under the collective system. The first one is 'The hunting gun will shoot the first bird who sticks its neck out' (*qiangda chutouniao*). The more ability you have, the more work will be assigned to you. Since everyone would be receiving the same amount of reward at the end, why should anyone work any harder than the next person? Another saying is 'Three hills of chives are worth more than work points in the collectives' (*sanfen jiucaigen, shengguo suangongfen*). This means that if you have three hills of chives in your private lot, you will water it more frequently, put in more night soil as fertilizer, and sell it on the free market. The return from these three hills of chives would bring in more income to you than working for the collective, which would calculate your work points everyday, and reward you at the end of a season on the basis of accumulated incomes.

  · "In general, Chinese peasants are extremely selfish and short-sighted. They are more interested in immediate gains and tangible profits than in long-term interests. Their primary concern is their family.[6] Under unusual circumstances, such as the Great Leap Forward, they could be motivated and rallied for a long-term project, but with enthusiasm for only a short time. Once the initial effort failed, the peasants pulled back and refused to invest any more. And that was what happened in all these collective organizations after the failure of the Great Leap Forward. The peasants were forced to stay in the collectives after the disaster years. In doing so, they marked time while assigned to work on collective land or projects. They distrusted the allocation system and believed that their rewards were not commensurate with their work. They saved their energy to work on their private lots after work hours. That was why the collective system was doomed to fail, but nobody dared to point this out to the authorities. That was also why under the collective system, from 1958 to 1978, we made very little improvement in our living standard."

Joining the Act

5 I was often amazed by the seemingly inexhaustible social connections of Ye. He knew many important people in the commune, the district, and the city offices on whom he could call in time of need. When Lin Qishan, my landlord, who hauled bricks in a used truck, was arrested by traffic police for speeding in Xiamen City, both Lin and his truck were detained by the police. At that point the city had just issued a set of strict regulations to improve the chaotic traffic conditions in downtown Xiamen. The traffic police were ready to enforce these new laws on early violators to set an example for others. It seemed that Lin Qishan would be heavily fined, and perhaps even spend a few weeks in jail.

Early that evening when Ye learned about Lin Qishan's arrest, he acted promptly. He called upon Lin Qishan's brother, Lin Qifa, who also owned a truck, to give him a lift to Xiamen City. Later that evening Ye brought back both Lin Qishan and his truck safely. There was no jail sentence, I was told later, not even a fine.

At that point I had come to understand the internal politics in Lin Village better, and was able to figure out Ye's motivation in currying favor with Lin Qishan. Lin Qishan's brother, Qifa, was a Party member with good standing. He was serving as the public security head of the village, the number-three position after the Party secretary and the brigade head. Lin Qishan was an army veteran also with good Party standing. These two Lin brothers were looked upon by most Lin lineage members as their spokespersons and were thus quite influential. P.S. Ye at that point was plotting to oust the formal village head, Li Dehai, in a fierce power struggle. He thus had to count on these two brothers' support. This was one reason that P.S. Ye took an active interest in my rental arrangement with Lin Qishan, and intervened on his behalf.

The next morning when I asked Ye what he had done to secure Lin Qishan's release, he shrugged and replied lightheartedly, "Just visited a couple of my old friends in the city."

Other similar incidents occurred several times during the first few months I was in Lin Village. Each time Ye was able to pull strings and solve the problem. He must have ways to cultivate favor with those officials, I speculated. And yet I hardly saw him venture outside Lin Village. How did he socialize with those people? Why would they do things for him if he remained in the village? I kept those questions to myself and determined to pin Ye down when I had the opportunity.

The opportunity came one day in early March 1985, when two visitors came to see Ye. One was the president of Jiangtou Agriculture Bank, and the other one the principal of Jiangtou Middle School. To entertain the visitors, Ye asked Hopping Toad Wu to cook a big noon meal with seven or eight dishes. I was invited to this luncheon too. During the meal, by listening to their conversation, I gradually figured out the purpose of the visit. The Agriculture Bank and the Middle School were neighbors in Jiangtou Township. The bank was expanding one of its buildings and wanted to appropriate an unused lot from the Middle School for that purpose. The school principal agreed to let the bank use the lot under one condition: The bank would donate money to the school to build a new classroom. The bank considered the request exorbitant, and made a counter-offer to build a basketball court instead. The two seemed to be unable to resolve their differences, so they wanted Ye to be the mediator.

"But why Ye?" I asked them both. "And why do you think he can be an impartial third party in this matter?"

"Ah, good questions," the bank president replied. "We came to seek his advice because Ye is our old comrade and both of us trust him."

"But I assume that there must be many Party members in Jiangtou Township," I insisted. "Why do you take the trouble to come here?"

"Oh, I've confused you," the bank president said apologetically. "When I said that Ye was our comrade, I didn't mean that he was a Party member. He was our comrade because we were all in the same work team (*gongzuodui*) in previous political campaigns. We were all activists during the Four Cleanups."

I couldn't recall what Four Cleanups was or when it occurred among China's numerous political campaigns at that point and felt that I should lay the issue aside for the time being lest I become too inquisitive and impolite to the guests. But it seemed that the bank president really enjoyed remembering those days and continued to speak: "It must be more than twenty years ago now, right?" he turned first to Ye and then to the school principal. "Remember those days, when we were still in our early twenties? How much energy and dedication we all had in those political campaigns!"

His remarks appeared to be contagious, for the same eagerness and enthusiasm seemed to have caught Ye and the school principal. They joined in the conversation and talked about specific incidents that impressed them the most, then discussed specific individuals and their whereabouts now. By the end of the hour-long meal, when they seemed to have rekindled their old friendship and were in a jovial mood, Ye made a suggestion.

"Well, it seems that you two don't really have hard feelings toward each other. The arguments you have had are in the interest of your institutions, not for personal gain. May I make a proposal to resolve your conflict? First, the school will allow the bank to use the land for expansion. Second, since a new classroom as compensation for the land seems to be too high for the bank, I suggest the bank donate a basketball court to the school, plus a new set of student desks and chairs for one classroom. How would this sound to you both?"

"It sounds fine with me," the bank president responded loftily, "and I trust your arbitration."

"What about you?" Ye turned his sharp, demanding eyes toward the school principal.

"Well," the school principal tried to say something but then seemed to change his mind. "If he says fine, I can go along with this suggestion too, for old times' sake."

"See, I know there is nothing that can't be resolved among old comrades!" Ye said expansively. "Let's toast the agreement. And we even have Professor Huang here as our witness, too!"

I was impressed by Ye's adroit manipulation of friendship and timing to solve this problem. But even more intriguing was the revelation of Ye's early political career, which he had never told me about. He was an activist, worked in a work team, and was involved in a political campaign called Four Cleanups. This was a useful lead to explore the extensive political connections that Ye had. So when the two visitors left in satisfaction, I seized the opportunity to quiz Ye: "So you were part of a work team with these two men. And what was a work team?" I decided to throw out my questions one by one.

The Four Cleanups

Apparently ready for my questions, Ye returned to his seat and lit a cigarette for the conversation. "A long time ago I was actively involved in political campaigns. During that period I worked in many places in southern Fujian Province. I also took up a number of trades in those campaigns and established good personal connections with many local cadres. A true, durable friendship is one that develops when people suffer through real hardship together. These connections, once a liability, have now turned into political capital. Sometimes I find it ironic that my life can be twisted in another direction so quickly."

"What was the nature of these political campaigns? And how did you get involved?"

"Don't be impatient," Ye jokingly chided me, "and let me explain to you how I became involved in politics."

He settled himself comfortably in a rattan chair and stared at the roof beam as if in deep reflection. "I graduated from Jiangtou High School in 1963. At that time there were two options for country kids like me if they didn't want to farm or live in the countryside for the rest of their lives. The first option was to take the college entrance exam. If you could be admitted to a college, you were able to transfer your household record from the countryside to the city where the university was located, the first step in changing your classification from 'rural' to 'urban.' When you graduated from college, you would be assigned a job by the government, most likely in a government enterprise, and most likely in the city, with good pay and job security. Then, your classification in the household registration would be permanently changed to 'urban.' This option was of course my first priority. I took, but failed, the college entrance exam that year. There were very few colleges in China then. Only one out of every twenty or so high school graduates from the countryside was able to pass the rigorous national college entrance exam. With poor facilities and underqualified teachers, the chances for students from the country to pass this exam were small."

"What was the other option you were considering?" I asked.

"The second option for country kids like me was to join the military."

"Why the military?" I thought that traditional Chinese social values always ranked servicemen only slightly above bandits.

"Because it offered the opportunity to move out of the countryside," Ye replied. "The military service was for four years, so the servicemen could learn a number of skills, such as reading and writing for the illiterate, or driving and machinery operation for the literate. If a person performed well in the military, he would be initiated into the Party as a member. Party membership is a lifelong certificate for government jobs. When a Party member was discharged from the military, he most probably would be assigned to a city job. A non-farm job plus city living was the main incentive for country youth to join the army."

"But you didn't join the army either, right?" My intuition told me that Ye had never served in the military, even though at one point he was commander of the brigade militia.

"Yes, you are correct," Ye replied in a sour tone, "I never joined the army. Since there were so many country boys who wanted to join every year, only a small fraction of the volunteers were accepted. There were several considerations in the selection process. First was the person's political background, including his family's class standing, preferably tenant or middle peasants, and his loyalty to the Party. The second criterion was physical condition; only those in good health were chosen.

"I failed to pass military selection because of my slightly handicapped foot," Ye explained with a bit of embarrassment. "The injury occurred in 1953, when I was in third grade. I was swinging on my school playground when I accidentally lowered my left foot to touch the ground. I didn't have shoes on. Actually, I never wore shoes before I graduated from junior high. Anyhow, the bare bottom of my foot brushed against the sandy, hard ground and part of the flesh under the heel was scraped off and I bled a lot. Later I discovered that my left foot is slightly shorter than my right one, so I could not run as fast as other children. This problem cost me the opportunity to join the army.

"With these two options not available, the only alternative I had was to return to Lin Village. At that point our village had already been separated from Hilltop

Village because of the construction of the reservoir. We became an independent brigade, called Lin Brigade. Since Hopping Toad Wu and his brother were both promoted to work at the commune office, Opium Hong, who used to be head of the first production team, was appointed Party branch secretary for this brigade in 1962. Thunderbolt Lin, the former head of the third production team, was appointed the brigade chief.

"Since the newly constructed reservoir had physically separated Lin Village from Hilltop Village, it was difficult for children from our village to attend school there. Since these two villages had become two independent administrative units, paying financial subsidies to the school became difficult. Opium Hong, the new brigade branch Party secretary, decided to establish a school in Lin Village with our own funds.[1]

"When I returned to work in our village in 1963, I was assigned by Opium Hong to go to Jimei Teacher's Training Center for one month of special training; and when I finished, I began to teach at the village school. There were only three or four teachers then. We had to teach almost all subjects, including mathematics, language, and music, from kindergarten level up to fifth grade. In a small school, you have no choice but to teach all subjects. I taught for one year in this school, and most of the village young people now in their late twenties were my students in that year.

"In September or October of 1964, a new political campaign was brewing in rural China. It was the Four Cleanups Campaign (*siqing yundong*), which was a part of the Socialist Education Campaign (*shehui zhuyi jiaoyu*).[2] The purpose of this campaign was to re-educate or to weed out incompetent cadres in lower-level rural government units. Fifteen years had passed since the Liberation and the national leadership began to suspect that a lot of the original rural cadres had become corrupt since they held power for so long. The failure of the Great Leap Forward also contributed to morale and discipline problems among rural cadres. Three out of these four major 'cleanups' involved the rural political apparatus: local cadres or unit officials stealing public goods, accepting bribes, and abusing the work-point system. The last 'cleanup' was aimed at the impure elements, such as the sons or daughters of former landlords or rich peasants who might have sneaked back into the Party or cultivated friendships with rural Party cadres, thus regaining their lost power.

"The idea for this campaign came from then National Chairman Liu Shaoqi's wife, Wang Guangmei. In 1963, she collaborated with the first Party secretary of Hobei Province, Lin Tie, to carry out a campaign in a commune called Taoyuan Commune, in that province. Wang and Lin lived in this commune for a short while to investigate wrongdoing. Once they established good, trusting relationships with the peasants, Wang and Lin mobilized them to investigate petty crimes committed by the commune cadres. In 'struggle sessions' organized by Wang and Lin, the cadres were herded to stand trial on the podium while the peasants came forward to press their charges against them. Cadres who committed severe crimes were punished and removed from office, and new cadres were elected to replace them. The campaign was hailed by the newspaper as a great success and was thus selected as a model, called 'Taoyuan Experience' (*Taoyuan jingyan*), for the entire nation to follow. This campaign's method was to select a group of young activists, principally those with good class standing and education, for short political training. Then they were sent to the countryside, generally not their own home district, as 'work teams.'[3] The work team would seize political power from the local administration, such as the brigade or team offices, and then investigate the corrupt officials."

"Does that mean all of China was organized for this political campaign?" I wanted to clarify the magnitude of such a political movement.

"It seems so," Ye replied. "I don't know whether Tibetan or Inner Mongolian autonomous regions also had this campaign. But as far as the rest of the country was concerned, in early 1964, it was completely organized for this campaign. At the national level was the statewide organization, headquartered in Beijing, to coordinate campaigns in all provinces. In Fujian Province, First Party Secretary and Governor of Fujian Ye Fei was the commander of this socialist education troupe (*shejiao zongtuan*). Below that, every prefecture and county had its branch office to coordinate the campaign. The prefecture or county government ordered communes to organize the young activists, who received training in the prefecture or county headquarters, and then were assigned to work in another county or prefecture to prevent favoritism in their own hometowns.

"When this campaign was organized in our Frontline Commune, Baozhu, my future wife, and I were among the first twenty-two young activists selected for the task. I was proud of myself and Baozhu. We knew very well then that the Party had selected us with a special purpose in mind. After the old, corrupt cadres were weeded out, we would become the next generation of leaders in the countryside. I was deeply appreciative because it not only gave me the opportunity for higher education, which would have been simply impossible under the old feudalistic regime, but it also gave me a second chance after I had failed the college entrance exam and the military recruitment process.

"First, we, the new recruits, were gathered in Jimei Township, the headquarters of Xiamen Rural District. After a short political indoctrination, during which we were taught the reason for this campaign, its significance, and the methods to be used to carry it out, Baozhu and I were assigned to Longhai County, on the mainland close to Xiamen Island. The twenty-two young activists from our commune were mixed with activists from other counties and then divided up into smaller work teams, between five and seven per team, and were assigned to different brigades. As a worker in this campaign, I received RMB$27 per month, which was a huge sum of money then. My team was assigned to seize political power in a brigade in Longhai County. Once we arrived in that brigade we spread ourselves out to live with the poorest peasant families. We were required to practice the 'Three Commons' (*santong*) with our host family: We shared the same diet, living accommodations, and work loads as our hosts or hostesses. In return, we paid this family RMB$.30 per day for food. And we were prohibited from going out to market towns nearby to buy supplemental food. The rationale was that if we didn't live completely like a poor peasant, we would not be able to develop full identity with them. Without that, we would not be able to gain their full trust. We would then be unable to find out the suffering they endured at the hands of corrupt cadres.

"Most of the work team members in Longhai County had come from Quanzhou and Tongan counties to the north. An average work team was not large, only six or seven people per brigade. Because the number of people in a work team was small, we had to carry out our tasks very cautiously. We had to first cultivate friendships with the poor peasants, so that we could count on their support. The first task we carried out in this brigade was to establish a Poor Peasants Association (*pinnong xiehui*). We worked closely with these poor peasants, digging out their 'bitterness,' and then used the information they furnished for further investigation. We planned our strategies step by step. We had to be exceedingly careful, for at that point the central government seemed to believe that the entire rural administration had either been completely corrupted or been infiltrated by class enemies. If we acted too audaciously, we might subject ourselves to counter-attack by the corrupt rural cadres and former landlords.

"Most of these campaign activists were high school graduates and in our late teens or early twenties. We were all dedicated, idealistic young activists then. We were assigned the most important mission of the country, namely to correct the wrongs of the past. All of us were highly motivated and carried out the order from the Party exactly, line by line and word for word.

"Spiritually, we were all prepared for the task. But materially and physically we were not. Living conditions were just too harsh for us. Eating daily with the poorest of the poor caused our health to deteriorate. Even in 1964, two years after the end of the 1959–1962 famine, poor peasants in Longhai County still had very little food to eat. Every meal was the same: watery congee with a handful of rice and sweet potatoes. There was simply no solid food to fill the stomach. A teammate and I in the same brigade found a way to cope with this constant hunger. Each of us bought a few cents' worth of sugar in a nearby market town. We put this sugar in paper envelopes with small teaspoons and carried them in the inner pockets of our shirts. Whenever we felt dizzy from hunger we went to a hidden corner and swallowed a spoonful of sugar.

"We had to do this surreptitiously. It wasn't illegal, for there was no law against this practice, but we knew that this was not an acceptable practice from the Party's viewpoint. To do so would have set us above the poor peasants. The two of us were defeating the goal of this entire campaign if we couldn't even endure the day-to-day reality of the poor peasants. We would probably have been discharged immediately from the work team had our practice been detected by other teammates. We kept this sugar gulping a secret, but one day we almost got caught. It was a hot summer afternoon and our work team was having a meeting in a small, closed room at brigade headquarters. We shut all the windows because we didn't want the content of our discussion, planning for a struggle session against the brigade Party secretary, to be heard by villagers who might pass by. The closely sealed room soon became steaming hot. Both my friend and I had small envelopes of sugar in the inner pockets of our shirts. Our body heat began to melt the sugar, but there was no way we could remove the packages to discard them. We didn't dare to excuse ourselves from the meeting and to go back to our boarding house to change our clothes, for that would be suspicious. For two full hours the dripping sugar mixed with our sweat and smeared all over our shirts and underwear. Whenever I remember this hilarious episode I always laugh.

"Living with these poorest peasants taught us many good lessons. The poor peasants generally don't pay attention to proper social courtesy or politeness; they are always straightforward. In our work team there was a young woman who boarded with one of these peasant families. She was a very diligent worker and often went out to conduct investigations. Sometimes she was so absorbed in her work that she missed lunch or dinner at her boarding place. When she returned her host or hostess would ask if she had eaten. Out of politeness she answered yes. And the peasant would think that since she said she had eaten, there was no need to prepare food for her. She would go hungry for the rest of the morning or afternoon. But then, when she went out to participate in farmwork with her host family, she fainted from hunger.

"You know," Ye turned to me and said in a serious tone, "the moment I was mature enough to participate in actual political campaigns was also the moment I lost much of my faith in politics. Several incidents occurred during the Four Cleanups Campaign that made me begin to question the means used to pursue our goals. The goal of this particular campaign wasn't bad. A lot of the original rural cadres were less than desirable and had indeed become corrupt. But in carrying out this campaign, many overzealous work teams often exceeded their authority. They encouraged members of the newly established Poor Peasants Association to attack the previous landlords and local cadres, even though they were not much better than those old cadres. Thus, there was a new reign of terror in the countryside, creating more friction at the village level.

"I still remember the first struggle session my teammates and I organized in that brigade. We used the brigade meeting hall to set up the podium, and to enhance our authority in the face of possible counter-attacks by former brigade cadres and landlords, we invited a high-level cadre from the prefecture government to come as an observer. The presence of this high-level cadre, we reasoned, would discourage any attempts by the former cadres to disrupt our meeting.

"The work team members and our superior from the prefecture office were seated on the podium. We ordered the Poor Peasants Association members to discuss past abuses of the five bad elements: the landlords, the rich peasants, the counter-revolutionaries, criminals, and rightists. We decided to attack the five bad elements first, to set an example for the villagers and to intimidate anyone who dared to challenge our authority. Members of the five bad elements were brought up to the podium and forced to kneel down facing the crowd. There was a middle-aged woman among the bad elements. The high-level cadre from the prefecture signaled a poor peasant to come and asked him at close earshot: 'Is that a "landlord's wife" (*dizhupo*)?' The poor peasant answered: 'Yes, cadre,' went up to that woman, and pressed her head down to the floor throughout the struggle session. At the end of the meeting the high-level cadre asked this poor peasant, 'Why did you force that woman's head down for so long? I thought that this campaign was supposed to avoid unnecessary physical abuse.' The poor peasant answered: 'But, cadre, I thought you had given me the order to force her "head down" (*dizhetou*)!' You see, this high-level cadre was from northern China, and his accent in spoken Mandarin was barely understandable. With poor peasants with limited education and ability to understand directives from the central government, abuses were inevitable.

"Another incident I remember during the Four Cleanups period involved a middle-aged man from a former landlord's family. He was very well educated and was the manager of a trading firm in Xiamen City before the Liberation. After Liberation he went back to his old home in Longhai County. Since he was not involved in land tenancy before the Liberation, he was not executed like his father or brother. But he was still classified a rich peasant, thus a potential class enemy. One day he drew a painting on his folding hand fan of a bird flying back to its empty nest. He also wrote a poem on the fan about a bird who had left its nest for some time, and decided to return. When it returned, all its family members had disappeared."

"What does this painting have to do with the political campaign?" I was unable to see the point in P.S. Ye's narration.

"Its implication, of course!" he replied impatiently. "The fan was seized by a poor peasant and brought to the work team as evidence of treason. The peasant insisted that the empty nest in the painting demonstrated this person's dissatisfaction with the Communist government and must be a metaphor that expressed this person's discontent with the misfortunes that had befallen his family. He was apparently protesting the justice dispensed by the people on his landlord father and brother."

"But how could anyone have taken this type of accusation seriously?" I protested.

"Of course not you and me." Ye replied sternly. "We know that you cannot accuse someone of a crime by implication, but reasoning during a political campaign is different. To create 'high tide' in the campaign, activists would cultivate special rallying points to generate enthusiasm among the people. The work team was elated by this peasant's accusation. What a marvelous, new political awareness was developing spontaneously among the poor peasants! They were learning to penetrate the veils of the counter-revolutionaries. This initiative was to be encouraged and cultivated at all costs.

"A special struggle session was organized to announce this new finding. The poor fellow who drew the painting was dragged up to the podium for his trial. That evening he was severely beaten by a few activists, some of whom probably seized this opportunity to settle old scores with his family. Had the work team not intervened in this savage beating, he would probably have been killed that night. The work team intervened because it considered this person's crime not serious enough for a death sentence. After all, the purpose of punishing this person in public was to flex the muscle this work team had. The saying here is 'Killing the chicken to scare the monkey' (*shaji jinghou*), so that those who intended to resist the work team would think twice before they planned anything foolish."

"What happened to this poor fellow at the end?" I was curious.

"I didn't know exactly what happened to him after this struggle session." Ye stretched his arms and yawned. "I only heard that a few months after this episode he escaped by swimming over to Quemoy, the Nationalist-occupied island. With all his political stigmas he had no future here. His defection, even though shameful, might have given him a new lease on life.

"Well," my friend looked at his watch and said, "it is almost two o'clock now. Why don't we take a break and continue this talk later?"

The Campaign

The next morning I went to Ye's house after breakfast. I was eager to continue our conversation about his involvement in political campaigns.

Ye was in the kitchen, helping his wife, Baozhu, prepare pig feed, chopped sweet potato leaves mixed with dried sweet potato slices boiled in a large pot. Baozhu greeted me and then fell into complete silence as she always did. The proper role of village women, at least in public, was to be submissive to their husbands. That Baozhu played quite well throughout my stay in Lin Village. She was unassuming and never joined our conversation unless I asked her a question directly. But that morning, I thought, Baozhu's presence would be a blessing, for I could clarify some issues regarding the Four Cleanups with her too.

I purposely asked both of them, "Did you see each other during the Four Cleanups?"

Baozhu pretended to pay no heed to my question and kept stirring the pot of pig feed. It was Ye who responded.

"During the first year of the Four Cleanups Campaign, I rarely saw Baozhu. We worked in the same county, but in different communes. She was assigned to the Third Commune of Guankou Township. Transportation between the two localities wasn't good, and, besides, we were all busy with our important political mission. We did manage to see each other when I went home to Lin Village and she to Mudhole Village during holidays. Whenever I had the opportunity I went back to see my family and gave them the money I had saved from my job to help support them. I told you before that I received RMB$27 per month as a work team member. I paid RMB$9 each month for food with my boarding family. I would spend another $2 to $3 per month for other essentials, such as soap, cigarettes, and, yes, sugar. In general I saved about half of my salary to give to my father because at that point my family was very large. My youngest brother was born in 1963, so I had six brothers and one sister. It was very difficult for my father to earn enough work points to feed the family, so most of my younger brothers didn't have the opportunity for higher education. They had to start working early to supplement the family income."

"How often did you return to Lin Village then?" I asked.

"About once every month," Ye replied. "Since I came home frequently during the Four Cleanups, I came to know well the impact this campaign had in Lin Village. The work team assigned to this brigade immediately seized power from Opium Hong and Thunderbolt Lin, the brigade Party secretary and brigade head. A Poor Peasants Association was organized under the initiative of the work team. Before the work team arrived, Thunderbolt Lin cracked a joke about them. He said that since the work team members would be participating in farm work side-by-side with villagers as required in the 'Three Commons,' perhaps we should make a few extraordinarily large honey buckets for them to carry with shoulder poles. This would really test the work team 'city kids' to see if they could work like us. The joke was later reported by a peasant to the work team when it began to investigate misconduct by brigade officials. A struggle session was organized against Thunderbolt. He was beaten during the meeting and removed from his post as brigade head."

"Who else in Lin Village was subjected to attack during this campaign?" I asked.

"Almost all brigade and team-level officials." Ye helped scoop out the pig feed from the cooking pot and pour it into large buckets while answering. "But probably the most severe punishment engineered by the work team in Lin Village fell upon the Wu brothers. Both Hopping Toad and his brother Wu Ming were working at the commune office in Jiangtou when the campaign began. They were ordered to return to Lin Village and were subjected to scrutiny by the villagers. With Hopping Toad's questionable wheeling and dealing before the Liberation, he was quite vulnerable. He was a constable during both the Nationalist and the Japanese occupation periods. That alone immediately put him in the category of 'historical counter-revolutionary' (*lishi fangeming*). Also there was his not-so-glorious history of serving in the Nationalist army as a draftee before defecting to the Liberation Army. What was his motivation for this defection? To serve as a spy for the Nationalists? All these questions were raised, so it became a serious political case."

Baozhu quietly carried out the two bucketsful of pig feed with a shoulder carrying pole, and left Ye and me to continue the conversation in the kitchen.

"What happened to Hopping Toad was an ironic twist of fate," Ye said with a detectable trace of vengeance. "He was put in solitary confinement for several months and forced to make a confession. Since he was illiterate, he couldn't even write his own confession. He was beaten regularly, for his verbal confession didn't satisfy the work team. They were hoping for a major breakthrough in this case: the uncovering of a major hidden spy ring left over from the Nationalists and headed by Hopping Toad Wu. Hopping Toad probably never thought that he would endure this kind of humiliation and torture after the Liberation. He was so desperate that one evening he tried to commit suicide in his cell by hanging himself with his belt. Luckily he was discovered by the guard and saved. And strangely, after this torment Hopping Toad mellowed considerably. Even though he can still be very abrasive and arrogant today, you should see how he looked and acted before his imprisonment. The pendulum has indeed swung very far for him.

"There was a major injustice in our village during the Four Cleanups that was to remain unresolved until the last few years. This incident involved a Lin family, whose oldest existing family branch (*fang*) now is Lin Da, that used to be medium-sized landowners. Lin Da had four brothers. When their father retired during World War II, these four brothers divided up the family land into equal portions with approximately 20 *mou* (or 1.3 hectares) each. Lin Da was a hard-working person and carefully managed his share of the property."

Ye added a few pieces of dried twigs and branches to the hearth, poured water from a jar nearby, and added fresh chopped sweet potato leaves to the cooking pot as he prepared another pot of pig feed for morning. While he worked he continued the conversation. "The third brother, Lin Shan, had a reputation as a good-for-nothing going back to his youth. He was married then, the same as Lin Da, and had a wife and two children living off the share he received from his father. Lin Shan always abhorred any kind of physical labor. When he received his share of 20 *mou* of farm land, he hired his wife's younger brother to work the land. Then he had an adulterous relationship with his brother-in-law's wife, and the two ran off to Xiamen City. He very soon abandoned the wife of his brother-in-law and spent most of his time in Xiamen City gambling and visiting whorehouses. When he ran out of money he mortgaged a portion of his land to Xiamen merchants for cash. When World War II was over in 1945, Lin Shan had lost all his land and had become a drifter in Xiamen City."

"What happened to his wife and children then?" I asked the obvious question.

"Back in the village," Ye stirred the pig feed with a large wooden spatula and responded to my question, "Lin Shan's wife and two sons were in jeopardy when the land upon which they lived was sold. As a married-out daughter, Lin Shan's wife could not return home. The only option she had was to commit suicide. She was saved when her sons noticed her abnormal behavior and alerted

Lin Da, the most senior person in that generation. Lin Da then took his sister-in-law and nephews to live with his family. They worked on Lin Da's land and the two boys were literally brought up by Lin Da.

"By Liberation time, Lin Shan had returned to Lin Village. He was landless and classified as a poor peasant. He didn't wield any political power in this village initially, because the Wu brothers maintained a power monopoly in Lin Village. Later on, during Land Reform, Lin Da didn't have any trouble in the classification of peasants. Even though he had over 20 *mou* of farmland, his family was also large. Besides Lin Da and his wife, there were Lin Shan's wife, Lin Da's three sons and two daughters, plus Lin Shan's two sons. For ten people to share 20 *mou* of land, this family was considered average and received a middle peasant classification."

"What was the injustice done to this family that you mentioned earlier?" I was unable to understand why Ye discussed in such detail Lin Da's family land and composition.

"Class labels were of great importance to peasants before 1978," he replied ironically. "Lin Da's easy life was ended by his younger brother Lin Shan. The Four Cleanups and the establishment of the Poor Peasants Association in 1964 gave Lin Shan an opportunity to seize power. He became an activist in this new organization and began to point his finger at anyone he didn't like. He was actively involved in interrogating Hopping Toad Wu. After that, he began to demand a re-examination of his brother, Lin Da, and his class standing. Lin Shan insisted that his brother should not be labeled a middle peasant. He argued that Lin Da was actually a rich peasant. Lin Shan pointed out that during Land Reform Lin Da had 20 *mou* of land for his family of seven, that is Lin Da, his wife, three sons, and two daughters. The other three people living at Lin Da's house, including Lin Shan's own wife and two sons, were not part of the family. They were actually Lin Da's long-term, hired farmhands. With these three hired laborers, Lin Da's exploitation level exceeded 25 percent and so he should be classified as a rich peasant."

"But that was not right!" I exclaimed.

"Of course not," Ye said cynically. "The entire village was shocked by Lin Shan's accusation. How could Lin Shan accuse his own brother, who helped save his wife and sons when they were desperate? How could anyone be so ungrateful and disloyal, the complete opposite of what village people had always believed in? Even Opium Hong, the deposed brigade Party secretary, mumbled in disbelief: 'If the charity done by Lin Da to save his sister-in-law and nephews by putting them under his wings could be redefined as exploitation against them, there can be no justice in the universe!' Public opinion was against Lin Shan, but he had the backing of the work team. With their help, Lin Shan, the new activist, had his wish come true. His brother Lin Da was reclassified as a rich peasant. A new potential class enemy was identified."

"How long was Lin Shan in power?" I asked. "How long did the Four Cleanups last?"

"For about two years, until the Cultural Revolution broke out to replace the Four Cleanups," Ye replied. "In the meantime, Lin Shan also pointed his accusatory finger at his cousin, Lin Boting, the chubby one. Since Chubby Lin had been classified as a rich peasant during Land Reform, he had been subjected to all sorts of abuse whenever there was a political campaign. He meekly accepted his position and tried to make the best of it. Chubby Lin had some cousins and in-laws living in the South Seas who often sent him money or packages of food or goods. Perhaps intending to improve his relationship with the village cadres, or perhaps to show them that there was no contraband in those gift packages, Chubby Lin always sent part of the things he received to the brigade officials, to be shared chiefly with the Wu brothers in the early days and then later on with Opium Hong and Thunderbolt Lin. During the Four Cleanups, Lin Shan claimed that Chubby Lin's gifts to these cadres had been a malicious attempt to gain personal favors from them and was, in fact, a form of bribery. The long-term effect of Lin Boting's act was to corrupt these cadres, Lin Shan declared, so that the Party could be converted to an instrument of the feudalistic landlords. Chubby Lin was tried by the masses in several struggle sessions, and was punished by being forced to do the harshest and dirtiest labor in the village, such as sweeping the village sewage or public outhouses."

At that point Baozhu returned with empty buckets for more pig feed. I seized this opportunity and asked them both, "How long did you stay in Longhai County during the Four Cleanups? What did you do precisely?"

Baozhu remained nonchalant and completely ignored my question. Ye seemed to assume that I was directing my question to him, so he responded.

"I was a work team member in a rural brigade in Longhai County for about one year and then in late 1965 was assigned to a new post as a campaign worker for the Socialist Education Campaign in a grain storage facility in Haicang Township. Living conditions improved quite a lot in this new job. At least I had rice congee, even though still watery, for my meals. There was another person, whose family name was Huang, who was also assigned to this job. This Huang fellow, a big fat guy, was a political commissar in the People's Liberation Army. In the army all these political commissars enjoyed high status and thus special privileges. He probably never expected to live under such difficult conditions. Every meal he ate eight or nine bowls of rice congee. You see, when there is no grease in your food, your appetite increases enormously. We always ate at the same table apart from the other workers. My stomach was not as big as this Huang fellow's and so I did not eat as much as he did. Sometimes when I was quite full, I had to pretend that I was still eating. If I dropped my bowl and chopsticks, Huang would also stop immediately. Nobody asked him to do so. But since the goal of this campaign was to rectify previous misconduct of cadres, everyone had to be on guard about his or her excessive behavior."

"How long did you work in Haicang Township?" I asked.

"Only about two months," Ye replied. "In January 1966 I was reassigned to Jimei Township, which faces Xiamen Island on the mainland side. My main task then was to implement the socialist education campaign in township enterprises. Most of the young government-enterprise workers were recruited from primary school and had very little political education. To promote their socialist consciousness, we had to organize them and indoctrinate them in the political system. The most effective organization was the Communist Youth League. By organizing activities to attract young people, we reached out to these otherwise neglected youth and directed them to the correct path of life.

"During the day I worked in a township enterprise, such as a department store as a salesman or a canteen as a cook. I worked, ate, and lived like other workers in that enterprise. The insistence on the practice of 'Three Commons' allowed me to the gain confidence quickly of the other workers. At night, I led these youth in a study group, either to learn reading or writing, or to study theoretical works of Marx and Engels, or to review government directives. Sometimes I organized recreation activities for them, such as a ball game or a chorus for singing revolutionary songs. Once the youth in this enterprise were mobilized and a branch of the Youth League organized, I moved on to another enterprise."

"Was that how you were able to establish close friendships with many local cadres?" I began to understand the extensive social connections Ye had.

"Yes, and it was the most memorable time in my life." His eyes shone with pride and satisfaction. "I dedicated myself completely to the task, and was able to see the fruits of my labor in a month or two. Working in different enterprises also helped me to learn about different trades. Life was full of fun when working with youngsters.

"I still remember one hilarious incident from this period. To instill 'socialist consciousness' among the young people, we were instructed in our activists' manual to organize an activity called 'Reminiscing Bitterness, Thinking Sweetness' (*iku, sitian*). The purpose of the activity was to familiarize youngsters with the harshness of life for the masses before the Liberation, and to compare that with the good life, the sweetness, that the Communist Party had brought to them. What we did normally was to identify an old-timer who lived a poor life before 1949. If this person's living conditions improved significantly after the Liberation, we would invite him to come and talk to the youngsters about the past 'bitterness' and the current 'sweetness.'

"In Jimei Township then, there was a retired serviceman from the army. We knew that he was from an exceedingly poor farm family in north China. Because of his family's poverty, he was sold to a rich family as a servant. As a servant he was mistreated most of the time and not given much food or clothing. Whenever he made a mistake doing his household chores, he was severely beaten. He finally ran away from this family to join the Liberation Army. When I met him, he had retired with a regular monthly government pension and enjoyed a life of leisure. This veteran would be an ideal person for the youngsters to hear from. So I organized a 'Reminiscing Bitterness, Thinking Sweetness' meeting and invited this veteran to give a speech. He came and gave very graphic descriptions about the difficult life he experienced before the Liberation. There was no food, no clothing, and no shelter to cover his head when he was a child. He was beaten often by his master, the master's wife and son, and other senior servants, when he was sold to that rich family as a servant, and so on and so forth. Then he began to talk about the good life after the Liberation, depicting the improvements made in the early 1950s. Everything seemed to be working out well, I told myself. The youngsters should easily pick up the message hidden in his speech. I was proud of myself for another mission accomplished.

"But then, to my astonishment, this old fellow didn't stop as he was supposed to! He began to describe the difficult time he experienced after the failure of the Great Leap Forward: how much hunger he had suffered during that period, and how many people he had seen die. I tried to stop him. But since he was invited as a guest speaker, and he was an honorable retired serviceman, I did not want to be rude. I looked at the audience. By then the youngsters had also realized the blunder this veteran was making, and listened with amusement. I saw that several of the young people were actually making a great effort to conceal their laughter. I began to feel like laughing too. When the meeting was over I reported this incident to my superior, and he also appreciated the humorous situation."

"How many jobs did you have during that period?" I asked.

Ye counted to himself on his fingers and replied, "During the latter part of 1965 and the first few months of 1966, I worked in six or seven different enterprises. This work experience gave me the opportunity to meet many people, especially young, low-ranking Party cadres. These connections, my intimate acquaintance with those cadres who are the heads of many local offices now, have turned out to be my major political capital. Also, because of my hard work and success in this socialist education campaign, I was admitted to Communist Party membership in March 1966. I was wholeheartedly grateful to the Party for this extraordinary honor. I, the son of a poor downtrodden peasant, was accepted into the Party! Imagine, I was considered an equal of those few who passed this test, and was considered part of the backbone of the Party for the next generation! I might have reservations about some of the abuses and terror tactics used in this campaign, but I should have complete faith in Chairman Mao and the Party to provide the correct guidance for our actions. There were perhaps hidden reasons for abuses or terrors that I was too immature to understand."

"Was Baozhu admitted to the Party then?" I asked.

"Yes," he replied. "At that point there were approximately 120 veteran activists from the Four Cleanups Campaign who were granted Party membership in Xiamen Rural District, including Baozhu, my future wife. All of the 120 new Party members were gathered in Jimei Township, the district headquarters, waiting for assignments to our next regular job. The Four Cleanups Campaign had been successfully completed. We, the chosen few, were on our way up. We would have a bright, rewarding future, with only the sky as the limit. Needless to say, none of us was aware that a new storm was brewing on the horizon, and that our lives would soon be completely turned around. The distant thunder of March 1966 warned us of the unfolding drama of the Cultural Revolution."

Ye dropped his voice at the end of his sentence, as if exhausted from our long conversation. Or perhaps he was trying to avoid an unpleasant subject that had always been off limits to outsiders. I was unable to detect any emotion on his face, for the kitchen where we sat had few windows and was not lighted. I decided to end my investigation for the day.

Return Home

6
My research in Lin Village progressed smoothly during the first four months of my residence there. I had become acquainted with many villagers who would invite me to their house for special social occasions or drop by my flat to chat with me about their problems. By March 1985, when I was quite confident that I had established good enough rapport with most village families and that I understood issues that the villagers were concerned about, I decided to conduct a systematic household survey to collect information that could be analyzed later. I designed a set of questionnaires that included questions on family life, finance, farming, marriage, ancestral worship, and value orientations. Of the 200 families in Lin Village, 40 were selected following the one-in-five random sampling procedure. During those household visits I had intense, face-to-face meetings with these village families with structured questions. It was then that I came to realize that there were still many villagers that I didn't know due to their low visibility, and I had not realized some of the problems they faced. The following incident was one such example from my field notes.

A Peasant's Story

April 12, 1985: Visited Lin Fen's family as scheduled. When I pulled out the questionnaires and asked Lin Fen questions, an old woman with gray hair and wearing a traditional bluish blouse and black slacks emerged at the doorstep. She called to me in her coarse voice, "Can I interrupt for a minute? I have an urgent appeal to make to you." Lin was apprehensive for a moment, but pretended to ignore the woman. I was quite sure that Lin must have tipped off this woman about my visit so she could come talk to me. It was quite apparent that unless I dealt with this woman first, I would be unable to continue my interview with Lin Fen. So I replied, "What do you want to talk to me about?"

"You see," the old lady grumbled, "I used to have 120 grams (about four ounces) of gold in the form of a necklace and two rings. During the Cultural Revolution we were told by the government to turn in all traditional things to the commune office. Most other villagers defied the order by burying their

87

valuables in their houses or in the field. But my late husband and I were honest. We took all the gold ornaments, 120 grams total, to the commune headquarters in Jiangtou Town. I even have a receipt to prove it." She searched in her pocket and produced a yellowish, wrinkled paper with a few characters scrawled on it.

"What can I do for you then?" I asked politely.

"Well," the old lady scratched her scalp and said, "I heard that the Cultural Revolution was over, and that the government had returned things that were confiscated to their proper owners. But I never received my gold ornaments back! I went to the commune office several times, but the cadres there said that this receipt wasn't written by the official in charge then. They wouldn't return my gold because they insisted this receipt was a fake."

I took the receipt from her and looked at it carefully. It was just a sheet of paper, probably torn from a student notebook. The poorly written characters did state that a gold necklace and two rings were received by an individual, whose signature was illegible. There were no official red seals, used by all Chinese government offices, on this receipt. There was not even a date on it. Apparently the old lady and her husband had given the gold to an impostor who pretended to be an official in the commune office. It was a mistake that must have been committed over and over by many peasants. During the chaotic years of the Cultural Revolution when political power shifted from one faction to another frequently, it was quite likely that someone had preyed on this illiterate couple's ignorance and had taken their gold. I felt sorry for her but there was nothing I could do. I returned the paper to her and said, "It seems that what the commune cadres told you was correct. This receipt appears to be a fake."

The moment I said that I saw tears stream from the old lady's eyes. She mumbled, "But what can I do now? You must be able to help me! I know you can! I know you are sent down by Chairman Mao to investigate injustice done to us poor peasants! Please report my case to Chairman Mao. He is the only person who cares about us poor peasants!"

I didn't know how to respond to her. For one moment I almost laughed out loud. In her eyes I was sent down by Chairman Mao, who had died in 1976, almost ten years before! Then I became depressed. How could Chinese peasants, even today, be so ignorant to be fooled by almost anyone, and to be totally uninformed about events outside of their immediate village?

Cultural Revolution

When I later told P.S. Ye about this incident, he had exactly the same mixed reactions as I did. He at first laughed and said, "Chairman Mao is resurrected from his tomb ten years after his death to take care of this old lady!"

Then he turned sullen and mumbled, "Didn't I tell you how ignorant the Chinese peasants can be? They know nothing about the outside world, not even who is the current national chairman. They bow to anyone who seems to have the slightest amount of power. They never dare to challenge the authority or question the legitimacy of government policies. The only way to correct the injustice they have suffered is to appeal to the almighty Chairman Mao!"

"Was the Cultural Revolution really so bad that even a harmless, ignorant peasant woman couldn't avoid becoming its victim?" I asked Ye.

"Not really," he replied. "First of all, this old woman and her late husband are exceptional cases. As far as I know, most other villagers were smart enough to disobey the government order by hiding their valuables. The fact that this couple turned their gold over to just anyone who happened to be in the commune office that day shows how dumb they were. Second, my advice to you is don't believe everything you read in the newspaper. Our government now blames all problems on the Cultural Revolution. This is definitely an overblown exaggeration."

"Are you suggesting," I inquired, "that there was minimal damage done to the countryside or to the peasants during the Cultural Revolution?"

"No," he replied impatiently, "I wasn't saying that there was no damage done to the rural areas or to country residents. I myself was a victim of the Cultural Revolution. But I want to make it clear that, comparatively speaking the Cultural Revolution caused no more harm than many other political campaigns in rural China. To city dwellers, the Cultural Revolution was a true nightmare. But less so in the countryside."

"In what sense were you a victim of the Cultural Revolution?" I followed up on his new topic.

"Well, this is a long story." By then Ye had become used to my persistence in asking questions that interested me, and decided to satisfy my curiosity about the Cultural Revolution. "From an official viewpoint, the Cultural Revolution began in March 1966, the month I was admitted to the Party. When it first started, nobody in Fujian was sure what was going on at the national level or which way the wind was blowing. There was one directive after another issued from the central government. We were asked to study those documents carefully. From all those documents with conflicting messages, we knew a big political storm was brewing in Beijing, but couldn't be sure of its exact nature. Even after Marshal Lin Biao issued his 'May Sixteenth Document,'[1] we still couldn't figure out the riddle and didn't know how to respond."

"What were you doing then?" I asked.

"I was waiting for my job assignment along with 120 other new Party members in Jimei Township, the headquarters of Xiamen Rural District. But the local Party leadership didn't know how or where to assign us. After May 1966, conditions became increasingly chaotic. Communication between the local and central governments became irregular. Local officials didn't know which faction in the central government was actually in power. Without clear indications from the top, local Party leaders just sat back and waited, not wanting to choose the wrong side.

"In July 1966, the Jimei Township Party leadership decided to keep me in the township office to run the Communist Youth League. It was a big promotion for me, to be able to move my residence registration from a village to a township. Before this new assignment was made official, however, external events, beyond the control of the township Party leaders, caused confusion and uncertainty. A civil war seemed imminent. Factional fighting was spilling out from Beijing to provincial capitals. With the entire national Party paralyzed, there was simply no way to make my new assignment official! Besides internal conflicts, there were external threats as well. In southern Fujian, Nationalist gangsters were fueling this chaos by parachuting agents and weapons into the remote hills to stir up trouble.

"An interim assignment for me, the Jimei Township Party leadership decided, was to run a state farm called Xu Village owned by Xiamen Rural District in Bantou Township area. Xu Village is in a remote corner of the district, bordering Tongan and Changtai counties in the hills. Many junior high graduates from Xiamen Rural District had been assigned to this state farm, and a branch of the Communist Youth League had been established there. My mission was to run the state farm, to lead the Youth League, and to prevent the Nationalists from using the chaos to establish a guerrilla base there. I worked in Xu Village for four or five months. During this period I had the youngsters burn down the natural forest and clear brush. We then planted tea trees in the hills as a cash crop. We watched anxiously from this relatively isolated haven in the hills the turmoil that was unfolding in China. With my future in suspension, there was nothing to do but wait.

"By early 1967, I don't remember whether it was January or February, the situation in China became clear. By then the Red Guards had seized control of the country. National Chairman Liu Shaoqi was purged and denounced as a revisionist traitor. All the policies implemented by Liu became questionable. We, the young activists who participated in the Four Cleanups Campaign organized by Liu Shaoqi's wife, Wang Guangmei, were considered the descendants of Liu's wrong ideology. New directives issued from the central government demanded the disbanding of young activist groups recruited during the Four Cleanups, and ordered us all back to our original home villages immediately.

"But because of my good track record during the Four Cleanups, the Party secretary of Jimei Township, a man named Huang Bingfu, who is currently the deputy director of Xiamen City's Office of Education, asked his superiors to let me stay on and work in the township government. I was the only one out of those 120 selected to stay. But this request was denied, despite his repeated arguments with his superiors. Orders from the central government were clear, Huang's superiors told him. All those young activists recruited during the Four Cleanups and Socialist Education Campaign were children of revisionist Liu. They should be sent back to the countryside and be re-educated by the masses.

"We were given RMB$50 per person as severance pay and ordered to return home immediately." Ye lowered his voice and stared at the ground as if in despair. "That was the major turning point in my life. For a while I was very depressed. It seemed that the bright future I was anticipating suddenly evaporated. I was to be condemned to live in the village for the rest of my life. All sorts of questions came to mind: What would become of me back in Lin Village? Would I be subjected to the struggle sessions and tried by the masses? Then what? Would I be tilling the soil and carrying nightsoil with shoulder buckets like other ordinary peasants? The only consolation was that Baozhu was also ordered to return to her home, Mudhole Village. This would be the time for us to plan our future, if we survived this ordeal.

"I returned to Lin Village in March 1967. The situation in Lin Brigade then was better than I had thought. The year before, with the conclusion of the Four Cleanups and the withdrawal of the work team from Lin Village on May 1, 1966, the original brigade administration had been restored. Opium Hong resumed his post as the brigade Party secretary. Thunderbolt Lin took back his old job as the brigade head. Only Hopping Toad Wu and his brother, Wu Ming, lost their commune-level jobs permanently. They were the true victims of the Four Cleanups."

"Did the Wu brothers return to Lin Village too?" I asked.

"Yes, they did," he replied. "But with the Four Cleanups Campaign denounced as the wrong policy, under the Cultural Revolution campaign the Wu brothers felt that they could vindicate the wrongs done to them and recoup their lost power. To do so they would have to bring the two brigade officials, Opium Hong and Thunderbolt Lin, under their control. A new round of conflict was brewing in Lin Village, which somehow coincided with the factional fighting among the Red Guards in other parts of China."

"What precisely were you doing when you returned?" I interrupted.

"Initially," he turned to me, "I had no regular job assignment. Opium Hong asked me to temporarily replace the brigade accountant, who had died shortly before my return. I worked there for about eight months. During that period a major disaster befell my family. As a Communist, I have never been superstitious. But during that year I felt that my life seemed to be out of my control and that the whole world was collapsing on me.

"It was that my younger brother, Ye Jiade, drowned. He was three years my junior, and had had mental problems since early childhood. He was twenty-one years old when he died. Since he had a mental disorder, he was not assigned to work in the production team and spent most of his time roaming around the countryside. One day he saw a girl and followed her to the country outhouse."

The moment he mentioned the outhouse I knew the nature of the incident. Even though general living conditions in the countryside have improved significantly in recent years, as seen in those opulent two-story buildings, peasants still rely on traditional outhouses. It is normally a pit in the ground surrounded by a waist-high stone wall. When using the outhouse one had to be careful not to fall into the pit, and also to be careful not to expose oneself to passersby. Although the smell of a typical outhouse, with the mixture of ammonia and spoilage in the pit, was more than I could tolerate, villagers liked it because they could easily scoop out the nightsoil from the pit and use it as fertilizer. As expected, Ye continued his narration: "This young woman didn't cover herself well when she went to the outhouse. My brother saw her and was fascinated. He followed her all day long. When he returned home he claimed that he wanted to marry her. But who wanted to marry an insane person? Full of disappointment, my brother began to roam around not only during the day but also at night. Apparently he fell into an unused well one evening and drowned. My entire family was saddened by this loss. I concluded that it was my destiny to suffer all these misfortunes in one year.

"By late 1967, I was assigned to a regular job as the brigade clerk. I was to take charge of the brigade paperwork, such as transmitting directives from the higher-level offices to the teams, and drafting reports for the brigade office to the higher authorities. By then, because of my involvement with the brigade-level administration, I was again in a position to know about the internal village and regional politics associated with the Cultural Revolution. But because of my precarious position as a follower of the defeated policy of Liu Shaoqi, I was careful to maintain a neutral position in the internal conflicts.

"As a bystander, I began to fully comprehend and appreciate the absurdity of political campaigns in China. Always concealed by a rather fanciful and idealistic, but also simplistic, slogan, a few politicians fanned the frantic zeal of young people. But hidden in these empty promises was actually personal greed of those few struggling for power. Unwittingly, the youth were fooled by an idealistic image drawn for them by the few at the top. They sacrificed their time, energy, and sometimes even their lives, for an unrealistic doctrine. As I witnessed the zeal and madness of the Cultural Revolution I began to wonder if I myself was one of those unwitting youth in the previous campaign. Then I began to question whether the Communist movement in China had been a historical mistake."

I was shocked by his frankness, but was fascinated by his keen observations. I asked him, "Are you saying that the Cultural Revolution, as a political campaign, was essentially similar to other campaigns, such as the Four Cleanups, in entrapping innocent youth in China?"

"That is precisely what I told you earlier," Ye said with conviction. "As a political campaign the Cultural Revolution probably had less impact on the countryside than the Land Reform or the Four Cleanups. Our newspapers today often depict the Cultural Revolution as the wellspring of all evils in China. They blame the Cultural Revolution for a lack of discipline among youngsters, for rampant corruption among Party cadres, and for the destruction of our cultural legacy. Some of these accusations might be true, especially with regard to problems in cities and the violent abuse of high-level cadres. But in rural China, this is certainly an exaggeration. The Cultural Revolution was a city event, and the main targets of the Red Guards were intellectuals and high-level Party cadres. Peasants participated in the Cultural Revolution or allied themselves with specific external factions mainly to reap the benefits of intermittent fighting in the cities. The Four Cleanups was quite different because it targeted rural cadres and certain segments of the peasantry.

"If we compare the actual practices of these two campaigns, we can immediately see that in rural China, the Cultural Revolution was merely a continuation of the Four Cleanups. To put it another way, we might say that the Cultural Revolution gave those who were defeated and humiliated during the previous campaign a chance to settle their old scores. Resentments and hatred in rural China had been cultivated and bottled up so much in previous campaigns that they could be ignited and exploded with a minimum inducement."

"But wasn't it true during the Cultural Revolution that many practices were carried to extremes, such as physically attacking cadres or burning old books?" I remembered those horror stories reported in the West about the extreme cruelty and absurdity of the now infamous Cultural Revolution.

"Ha! Exaggerations!" he snapped. "Let me give you a few examples. Today, a lot of people say that sending high school graduates to the countryside for re-education by the poor peasants was a practice developed during the Cultural Revolution. It is not true. This policy was actually developed and experimented with during the Four Cleanups. It was then that junior high and high school graduates were being regularly asked to 'volunteer' their services in the countryside. Another example is the slogan of 'Breaking Down the Four Olds' (*posijiu*),[2] the watershed causing the massive destruction of our cultural legacy. Today the Red Guards take the full blame for committing those atrocities. Again, it was an exaggeration. In rural China, the destruction of whatever was considered feudalistic or superstitious began during the Four Cleanups, if not earlier. It was during the Four Cleanups that work teams and poor peasants confiscated all ancestral tablets and statues of deities from peasant households and burnt them in public.

"Similarly, public humiliation and trial of Party cadres and government officials by the masses did not start during the Cultural Revolution, but the Four Cleanups. During the earlier campaign the rural cadres suffered, but the Cultural Revolution punished city and high-level functionaries. It is only with this comparison in mind that you can gain a complete picture of the pending conflicts in Lin Village as the Cultural Revolution began."

"Were there Red Guard factions in the village during the Cultural Revolution?" I asked.

"Not really genuine factions," Ye sighed with relief. "They were associated with external factions. The two major factions of the Red Guards in the Xiamen area during the Cultural Revolution were Ge Lian (United Revolution) and Chu Lian (Fostering Revolution).[3] Chu Lian was the original Red Guards organization in Xiamen City, and for a while controlled the entire municipality. Participants in this faction were mainly students, factory workers, and city government workers. Ge Lian was a splinter group from Chu Lian and relied upon support from the military, police, and peasants. Ge Lian's main base was the suburbs of Xiamen City and neighboring villages. Since Ge Lian was pro-military, agreeing with peasants' attitudes, it was more popular in our village. However, during the height of the Cultural Revolution, our village had people associated with both of these factions. The brigade administration, including Opium Hong and Thunderbolt Lin, were for Ge Lian, the dominant faction in the countryside. On the other hand, the Wu brothers were linked with Chu Lian. They joined the opposite faction not because they shared Chu Lian's beliefs, but because they tried to oust Opium Hong and Thunderbolt Lin through the support of Chu Lian."

"Did these two factions fight often?" I inquired.

"Not really," he answered. "They didn't fight in our village. They mainly participated in battles organized by Ge Lian and Chu Lian in or around Xiamen City. The biggest battle between the two occurred August 23, 1967.[4] The battleground was Lianban Village, immediately outside Xiamen City. Many young people from Lin Village went to help Ge Lian with firearms in that battle. Immediately before the war the central government had ordered the confiscation of all firearms from Red Guards to prevent factional fighting. All the weapons used by Xiamen Island's local militia and the Red Guards had been seized by the army, except for those in the two brigades, Hecu and Wutong, directly facing Quemoy, a Nationalist-controlled island. To prevent the Nationalists from staging an attack, the government didn't lock up weapons used by the militias of these two brigades.

"Weapons from these two brigades turn up later during the battle and were used mainly by Ge Lian, based in the countryside. As for Chu Lian, there were rumors that it had seized large quantities of firearms from Xiamen police and city garrisons. Rumor had it that Chu Lian sent its women to steal the firearms. They allegedly surrounded a police station or a military garrison and stripped off their clothes. The policemen and soldiers didn't dare face these nude women and fled. After Chu Lian obtained its armaments, it prepared to attack the Ge Lian headquarters in Lianban Village. Ge Lian armed the militia with firearms from Hecu and Wutong brigades. Some of our villagers associated with Ge Lian also dug up the firearms they had buried when the army came to search for illegally possessed weapons. They fought a fierce battle in Lianban for two days, using not only small firearms such as rifles or pistols, but also heavy machine guns and armored vehicles."

"Did you go to see the actual fighting?" I asked.

"Not on your life," he replied jokingly. "But I went to Lianban after the battle was over. It was awful: burned out trucks, blood stains, and corpses lying all over the street. Apparently Chu Lian was badly defeated and lost a lot of people. Most of these Chu Lian victims were teenagers, probably high school students. Some even carried slings in their pocket. Many Chu Lian people were also captured by Ge Lian. They were so young that you wondered whether they really understood what they were doing. One villager told me that when he interrogated a Chu Lian youth about why he had joined the battle, the lad said he didn't know he was coming to fight. He said that he was told in school that there was an interesting activity in Lianban area that day and was sent over in a truck with his other classmates, who happened to come back to school to read the wall posters. I was sad that people so young and so innocent could be used for personal political ambitions."

"How did the fighting between these two factions in Xiamen affect village affairs?" I changed the subject.

Ye responded, "While the intermittent warfare between Chu Lian and Ge Lian in Xiamen area waged for almost two years, the conflict in Lin Village also intensified, chiefly between Opium Hong and Thunderbolt Lin on one side and the Wu brothers on the other. The Wu brothers, to expand their influence, allied themselves with some of the less-than-desirable elements in the village, such as the woman Zhang Lingzhu, nicknamed 'the Witch' for her alleged ability to perform witchcraft. Another equally notorious person in the Wu brothers' group was Gao Dalou, the Black Barbarian, Wu Ming's brother-in-law."

The name "the Witch" brought to my mind a woman that I had accidently come across the week before. Early one afternoon as I was walking along the shore of the reservoir, I suddenly saw a house at the edge of the village that I had never noticed before. To find out who lived in this relatively isolated house I knocked on the door and found a fiftyish woman with two little girls she said were her granddaughters. She invited me into the house to have freshly brewed tea with her. Once I sipped the tea she began to pour out all her complaints against virtually all the residents of Lin Village. She made all sorts of accusations about prejudice against her and her husband: The Wu brothers in the past had oppressed her family because it was new to this village; P.S. Ye looked down upon her because she and her husband were from poor tenant families before the Liberation; all their neighbors stole crops from their private lots; her son was falsely charged and arrested by commune police; and so on and so forth. With all these problems, she claimed, her family decided to build their house in this isolated corner away from other villagers. It was in this house that I first saw displayed openly three statues of deities on a central altar in the living room. Later I asked other villagers and found out that this woman's name was Zhang Lingzhu and that she claimed to know witchcraft but was distrusted and despised by almost all villagers.

"Who is this 'Black Barbarian'?" I had never heard this name before and was curious about how he got this nickname.

"Black Barbarian is of Malaysian stock," Ye explained. "Malayan people generally have darker skin than the average Chinese. That was why the villagers called Gao Dalou 'Black Barbarian.' Gao was adopted by Wu Ming's father-in-law when he lived in Malaya in the 1930s. Gao was brought back by his adopted father to Lin Village when the old man returned here. That was how Gao grew up here."

"How did the two factions fight in Lin Village? I thought you said that they mainly participated in external fighting?" I pressed for clarification.

"It is true that these two groups didn't fight openly in our village," Ye admitted. "But they fought indirectly or clandestinely. For instance, in order to curtail Thunderbolt Lin's power, the Wu brothers plotted to eliminate one of Lin's right-hand men, Lin Lihou. Lin Lihou was Thunderbolt's paternal cousin and also his chief liaison with the Ge Lian faction. In the village, Lin Lihou was head of the agricultural production crew for the second team. In this capacity every morning he had to check the water-pumping station belonging to his team to make sure that adequate water had been pumped for all the fields. Knowing that Lin Lihou would be coming to the pumping station in early morning, the Wu brothers sabotaged the water pump's electrical wiring. The pump was running, but the metal parts were also fully electrified. When Lin Lihou came to inspect the water pump he would most likely lay his hand on the pump, and he would be electrocuted by the 220-volt electricity."

"Was this murder plot successful?" I asked, even though I knew it wasn't because I had seen the name Lin Lihou in the household registrations.

"Yes, and no," Ye purposely increased the suspense by slowing down his narrative. "It was unsuccessful because Lin Lihou was not killed. Instead, it killed an unintended victim, Chubby Lin."

"Chubby Lin!" I exclaimed in disbelief, for at this point I had developed quite a lot of sympathy for this 'victim' of the Land Reform. "But how?"

"It was in late 1967," Ye dropped his voice as if in sorrow, "a cold and dark winter morning. It was so cold that Lin Lihou decided not to go to the field. Instead he sent Chubby Lin, the common servant for all cadres, to check the water-pumping station for him. Chubby was gone for two or three hours and failed to return to report his work. Lin Lihou became suspicious, so at noon he went to the station to check. There he was, Chubby Lin, electrocuted when he laid his hand on the pump. When he fell, one of his legs was tangled up with one of the pump belts. The belt kept on running, grinding off the flesh of his left leg all the way down to the leg bone. It was a grotesquely bloody scene. A few men who went to see it threw up right on the spot. Lin Lihou was saved, for Chubby Lin died for him. For Chubby Lin, perhaps this tragic end was better than living like a non-person, abused by almost everyone in the village.

"This case was never formally solved. There was no witness who could prove that the Wu brothers had sabotaged the water pump. It was not until five or six years later, when the Wu brothers' faction developed internal conflict, that Witch Zhang began to tell everyone within earshot how the Wu brothers did it, but by then it was too late to do anything about it. Since Chubby Lin belonged to the enemy class, meaning his life was considered valueless, the Wu brothers were not charged with any crime.

"The next plot designed by the Wu brothers against Thunderbolt Lin came a year later, in late 1968. This time Hopping Toad's brother-in-law, the Black Barbarian, was used as an instrument of attack. At that time our brigade was raising several horses to be used for hauling carts and for plowing. The horse stable was right behind Thunderbolt Lin's house. Black Barbarian was skilled in fixing horseshoes and was assigned to tend the brigade horses. One evening he stayed in the stable until well after dark. When nobody was around, Black Barbarian banged his head against the wall and cut his body with broken glass. He then called out for help. When other people arrived, they thought Black Barbarian was badly injured because of the blood stains and bruises all over his face and body. He told the supposed rescuers that he was attacked in the dark when he was working with the horses. He claimed that since it was dark, he didn't see clearly who the attacker was. But, he said, the height and size of the person suggested Thunderbolt Lin, the brigade head. When this incident was reported to the commune government, Thunderbolt was removed from his office as punishment."

"But there was no proof that Thunderbolt Lin was actually the attacker!" I protested. "How could the commune office make such a decision based on such flimsy evidence?"

"Who told you that decisions made by our government must be based on justice or truth? The truth is that most policy decisions are probably made on the basis of political expediency, not other criteria," Ye replied cynically.

"But what was the political expediency involved in firing Thunderbolt Lin?" I insisted.

He seemed to be prepared for my question. "It was because, in late 1968, the Chinese government had decided to curb the Red Guards and to restore order in China. Heavy punishment was dispensed among local cadres who were accused, or even suspected, of being involved in factional fighting. Apparently Thunderbolt Lin was used to set an example for other rural cadres in our commune."

"That means the Wu brothers escaped punishment again," I remarked. "But how did people later find out that the Wu brothers and Black Barbarian were involved in this entrapment of Thunderbolt Lin?"

"Yes, how did we know that the Wu brothers planned this 'bitter flesh intrigue' (*kurouji*, literally meaning self-inflicted injury to attract sympathy)?" Ye repeated my question. "Again, from the mouth of Witch Zhang when she split with the Wu brothers and revealed all their previous plots and plans. But in 1970, two or three years before her revelation, Thunderbolt Lin had died from cancer of the liver, a common disease in this area. Since Thunderbolt was not around to press charges against the Wu brothers, this case was quietly laid to rest. With Thunderbolt removed from office in late 1968, the commune administration appointed Lin Xiang, nicknamed Dark Skin, who used to be the head of the second team, as the new brigade head. So even though the Wu brothers were finally successful in removing Thunderbolt Lin from office, the appointment of Dark Skin Lin, another member of the Lin lineage, prevented the Wu brothers from gaining any real power in this village."

"Was there any other incident during the Cultural Revolution that had significant impact on village life or on individual villagers?" I asked.

"Definitely." Ye was apparently not annoyed by my endless questions and replied, "How could it be otherwise? The Cultural Revolution was one of those maddening periods full of internal conflict and hatred characteristic of our recent history. Political fanaticism can be very contagious. Living in an environment full of continuous factional fighting made most people cruel and irrational. Even Opium Hong, normally a mild person, became bloodthirsty and inflicted wounds on other people. Let me give you an example.

"It was in early 1967, when the first Mao button appeared in the Xiamen area. Opium Hong received one from the commune administration and pinned it on his jacket. A villager named Hou Hannan saw this peculiar thing and called out jokingly, 'Hey! Opium Hong, what kind of dog tag are you wearing on your jacket?' Opium Hong would have ignored him had this remark been made at any other time, but the Cultural Revolution had turned everyone into lunatics, and had made Chairman Mao the demi-god. Insult the savior of all China? Opium Hong ordered Hou Hannan's arrest and banished him to tend the brigade cattle in the cowpen.

"When Hou Hannan worked in the cowpen," Ye continued, "there was an unruly cow that created a lot of trouble for him. Cursing the cow, Hou picked up a shoulder carrying pole and hit the cow on its back, as most other peasants would have done. Hou's fate was probably running against him at that moment, because the cow dropped dead. The case immediately became serious. Hou Hannan not only insulted Chairman Mao by calling his button a dog tag, he also purposely destroyed public property by killing that cow. He was no longer a common criminal but a class enemy, one who tried to discredit and destroy the great socialist motherland by damaging its public property.

"Hou Hannan was subjected to public struggle sessions in the village and was then sent to a labor camp in western Fujian, about 200 kilometers from here, to perform hard labor. In that camp there was a kind of sisal plant being grown experimentally. The camp was also experimenting with a fiber-cutting machine to harvest the sisal. The machine had sharp blades and a lot of people in the camp were supposedly injured by operating that machine. Hou Hannan was no exception. He lost his right hand while serving his term there. If you look, you will notice that he does not have his right hand."

Ye's Marriage and Family

A few days after my initial conversation with Ye about the Cultural Revolution, I was able to do a follow-up interview with him on his life in Lin Village during that period. As usual, I sat with him in his dining room with a pot of hot tea and a pack of Marlboro cigarettes I had bought in one of the friendship stores in Xiamen City. I asked him, "When did you marry Baozhu? Immediately after you began your job assignment as brigade clerk?"

"No, not that fast," he laughed. "I had to save up some money for this event. I married Baozhu in October 1968. As I mentioned before, Mudhole Village and Lin Village had been historical enemies, and we were the first couple to overcome these feudalistic obstacles. Baozhu's mother and brother had been against us from the very beginning, as was Thunderbolt Lin before he was removed as brigade head. Opium Hong, the brigade Party secretary, was neutral on this issue, for he was not a member of the Lin lineage and bore no grudges against the Chens in Mudhole Village. The argument I used to defend my marriage was that the conflict between Mudhole Village and Lin Village was mainly between the Chen lineage and the Lin lineage. Since I was not a part of the Lin lineage, I was not bound by this inter-lineage animosity. Most villagers agreed with me. And after Thunderbolt Lin was fired, the new brigade head, Dark Skin Lin, raised no objection to this marriage. Baozhu and I had a rather quiet, low-key wedding ceremony. It was planned that way for several reasons. First of all, both Baozhu and I belonged to the class of repudiated cadres who, at that point, were targeted by the Red Guards. Second, the Cultural Revolution was destroying every vestige of the past. A conspicuous wedding would have invited criticism from the brigade or commune cadres. And third, both families were too poor to afford anything luxurious."

"But were you supposed to have an engagement ceremony before the formal wedding?" I remembered what I had learned in rural Taiwan during my childhood, and tried to check this out.

"Oh, yes!" he seemed to have been awakened, "how could I have forgotten about the engagement ceremony? But we were very untraditional even in our engagement ceremony, which occurred two months before the wedding. During the engagement, called *tiding* here, the custom prescribes that the future groom carry a boxful of gifts, normally candies, red rice cakes, a piece of cloth, and so forth, to the bride's family on a predetermined day. We had selected August 28 for our engagement because the almanac indicated that it was an auspicious day for such an activity. The week before, however, I received an order from the Party to attend a meeting that day in Xiamen City's Lujiang Mansion to study new directives issued from the central government. I couldn't disobey a Party order by not attending the meeting, for I was still a Party member. But then I also had planned the engagement ceremony. I went to the meeting that morning and tried to get sick leave from the head of my unit for that afternoon. At first he refused. But when people told him that I was supposed to be at my own engagement that afternoon, he let me sneak out for two hours. I rushed home on my bicycle, picked up the gift box for Baozhu's family, rushed over to her home for a cup of tea, and then rushed back to Xiamen City for the remainder of the meeting.

"For my wedding too, there was something quite non-traditional. I was sure the village elders wouldn't like it at all. The local custom here dictates that the day before the wedding the groom should visit the bride's home and stay overnight so that he can lead her back to his home early next morning before daybreak. When the groom arrives at the bride's home, he is to join the bride in the living room of her house. There the bride's family lays a large round bamboo sieve in the middle of the room right in front of the ancestral altar. On the sieve are two chairs, a washbasin full of water, a mirror, a hair comb, and a towel. The couple is directed by the matchmaker or an older woman to sit on the chairs. They use the towel and the water in the washbasin to clean their faces. The matchmaker or the older woman then combs the groom's and the bride's hair individually, mumbling a few auspicious phrases to wish that this couple tangle their hair together for the rest of their lives. This ceremony is called *gongshou* (combining two heads) in our local dialect. Only men who have gone through this ceremony are considered to be adults. Those who haven't are always regarded as children, even when they live to be one hundred years old. But for my wedding I didn't go through this ceremony. Neither Baozhu nor I cared much about this particular ritual. Similarly, Baozhu's family didn't care what we did or didn't do, for her family was against this marriage.

"Early the next morning when I took her back to my home," he said jovially, "I carried her on my bicycle. In the past the bride was carried to the groom's home in a wooden sedan carried by four porters. In the remote hills of western Fujian people use wooden wheelbarrows. Nowadays young people hire a taxi from Xiamen City, even when the wedding is of two neighbors. And, in the past as well as today, when the bride travels from her natal home to the groom's home, the groom should always carry a sieve or an umbrella to cover her head. This is to shield her from the heavenly god (*tiangong*)."

"Did Baozhu carry a sieve or umbrella over her head while riding on your bike?" I thought this would be a rather amusing scene.

"No, how could I ask her to do that!" Ye laughed. "We didn't follow a lot of the traditional practices in our wedding. For instance, when Baozhu arrived my home, she didn't go through the standard ceremony that most other brides have to go through, such as stepping on a piece of ceramic roof tile to crack it when entering the house, or walking over a small stove with open fire to purify herself, or kneeling and bowing to her new parents-in-law. All those rituals are symbolic. But my father was an open-minded person. He said that since Baozhu was a high school graduate and a Party cadre, we should excuse her from all the feudalistic practices. My parents always liked Baozhu for her diligence and filial piety. Even today, my mother has never had an argument with Baozhu over anything."

"But did you have a wedding banquet when she arrived your home?" I asked.

"Yes, of course," he confirmed. "My family prepared three tables of food on my wedding day to entertain guests, mainly our kin and close friends. This was of course quite modest compared with the fifteen to twenty tables people prepare for a wedding nowadays. But in those days we were too poor to have anything fancy. Besides, in 1968, several spinoff political campaigns from the Cultural Revolution were still going on, such as investigation of the 'hidden historical reactionaries' and 'capitalist roaders.' We had to be very careful in our behavior, so we wouldn't be accused with those labels."

"Was Baozhu's family involved in the wedding ceremony in your home?" I was curious whether this marriage had served as the bridge between not just two families, but also two hostile villages.

"No," he replied. "The local custom here prescribes that the bride's and groom's families hold their ceremonies separately. Three days after the wedding banquet in my house, I accompanied Baozhu back to her home. According to the local custom, her family should have given a banquet in my honor. This is called *nuxu zhuo* (literally, son-in-law's table) in the local parlance. Since her family was not enthusiastic about this marriage, they prepared only one table with fewer than ten guests. After this banquet at her house, the entire wedding ceremony was completed."

"What did Baozhu do when she moved to Lin Village? I suppose she was the only female high school graduate in the entire village then?" I asked.

"Yes. With her qualifications, both a high school graduate and a Party cadre, Baozhu could have taken whatever job she wanted," he said with pride. "But the only trouble was there was no job vacancy in this brigade. All brigade-level positions were filled. As a newly entered outsider, she couldn't just brush some old cadres aside and take over their jobs. But luckily, the year before our marriage the government launched a program to train 'barefoot doctors' to serve the rural masses in southern China. This program was expanded to southern Fujian Province at the end of 1968. In our village, Baozhu was selected by Opium Hong as one of three trainees for this program. The trainees attended special training sessions, from three months to eight months long, at the commune hospital. During those training periods they received work points from the brigade at the level of skilled farm workers, about twelve work points per day. When not attending training sessions, she stayed home promoting public hygiene or family planning for a fixed number of work points per day. Besides working as a trainee for the barefoot doctor position, she also worked in the field as a regular brigade member and raised pigs as a family sideline. She was a great help to my mother, doing household chores, and her salary was a big relief to the burgeoning family."

"When did you have your first child?" I pointed at A Sai, who was sitting quietly, listening to our conversation.

"A Sai came in late 1969," Ye replied, "my father's first grandson. It was a really joyous moment of my life. While celebrating A Sai's arrival, I also felt

Baozhu, P.S. Ye's wife, in her clinic

sadness for my younger brother who had died three years earlier. He had no male issue to carry on the 'incense and fire' for his line, and to provide sacrifice for him during important festivals. His branch of the family was ended forever. I consulted with my father and suggested that A Sai be adopted by my deceased brother as his heir, so that A Sai's future sons would be able to carry on this branch of the family line. My father appreciated my suggestion so much that he burst into tears. You see, in this part of China, it is the parents' obligation not only to provide proper upbringing, education, means of living, and a wedding for the sons, but they must also make sure that the sons have male issue to carry on the family line. By allowing A Sai to be adopted by my deceased brother, I solved the major problem or, perhaps we can say, guilt that my father had after my brother's death."

Ye's explanation made me realize that in spite of the government's effort to change traditional social values, they neverthless persisted. But then I also noticed that A Sai, who was fifteen years old then, didn't seem to be normal. He seemed to be unusually quiet, not like other adolescents his age. He also seemed to be slow, in both his speech and actions. I suspected that he was slightly mentally retarded, but had never had the courage to ask Ye. Since our conversation was about A Sai now, this gave me the opportunity to verify my suspicion.

"Has A Sai always acted like this?" I asked cautiously.

"No," Ye lamented, "A Sai was a chubby, lively little baby. He was the joy and pride of everyone in the family. But the hand of fate didn't spare him. In early 1970, when he was only a few months old, both Baozhu and I were busy with our work. Baozhu had just started her second medical training session. I was re-assigned by Dark Skin Lin, the new brigade head, to take charge of household registration for the entire brigade. I spent a lot of time working in the brigade office compiling old records, which were not in good order. During our absence, my mother, who really adored her first grandson, took care of A Sai.

"One morning as I left for work, I noticed that A Sai had a little fever. I didn't pay much attention to it, thinking that it was probably just a common winter cold. That afternoon I returned home and was surprised to discover that A Sai's body temperature had gone up so high that I could barely lay my hand on his forehead. My mother, who is basically illiterate, was trying to reduce the temperature by feeding A Sai boiled cold water mixed with crystal sugar. Crystal sugar looks like ice, and in the traditional medical remedy is considered to contain the 'cold' (*han*) element to reduce body heat. But I knew instantly that there was something more wrong than just high fever. I wrapped A Sai up in a quilt and rushed him on my bicycle to the commune hospital in Jiangtou where Baozhu was attending her course. The doctor's diagnosis was that A Sai had contracted meningitis. Even though early detection saved his life, the long high fever he suffered that morning damaged his brain. A Sai was permanently retarded.

"Certainly A Sai's illness defeated our original purpose of having him produce sons for my brother. Since he is retarded now, he may not be able to find a spouse and have his own son in the future. Both my father and I were quite saddened by this tragedy. My father consoled me by saying that perhaps the heavenly god (*tiangong*) didn't want my deceased brother to continue his line. If this was fate, then we had to accept it. As a Communist, I don't believe this was fate. We peasants suffer so much because we don't have good education and don't have good medical facilities. That is why when I came to power in this brigade I made my first priority the building of a good clinic and providing comprehensive medical insurance for all villagers, regardless of wealth or need. Even after we disbanded the commune and brigade collectives in 1984, I still insisted that medical coverage for all villagers under the old insurance policy be preserved."

After Ye made this strong, emotional statement, he seemed to retreat a bit from his self-confident mood and continued the conversation in a hesitant tone. "Sometimes, however, I wonder if my father's beliefs about fate in everyone's lives has some grain of truth in it. One harvests what one sows, as the old saying goes, and that is almost predestined. Perhaps what we, the Party cadres, did in the past two or three decades has been so excessive that we, as a group, have been condemned.

"Look at Opium Hong! Both of his sons are like idiots. When these two boys were looking for wives through matchmakers, other villagers jokingly remarked that girls wanted to marry into Opium Hong's family not because of the two boys, but because of Opium Hong. Thunderbolt Lin, our former brigade chief,

A family portrait: P.S. Ye, his wife, Baozhu, and their three sons

died from cancer of the liver at an early age, despite his good health and good looks. A few years after Thunderbolt's death, his only son, a young man in his late teens, was killed in a work-related accident. My younger brother had a mental disorder first, then drowned in a well. Now my first son will have to carry the stigma of retardation for the rest of his life. What can I say? Perhaps there is justice in the universe after all. Luckily after A Sai my wife bore me two more sons. These two are both very bright and in good health. They are at least some guarantee of my family's future."

Security Head

7 Daily life begins early in Lin Village. Long before the first ray of sun lightens the distant coastline five kilometers to the east at around five o'clock on a summer morning, an observer can feel the stir of life in the still dark houses. Women are generally the first in the family to arise. Quietly dressing and washing herself with water from well water stored in large ceramic jars in the open courtyard, the housewife dashes to the kitchen to heat up for breakfast leftover rice gruel and dishes from the night before.

Coal clumps are a timesaving innovation used to start the family hearth in the morning. Villagers claim that processed coal dust was introduced to this area in the early 1980s. The brigade purchased incompletely burned coal dust from an electricity power plant in Xinglin—a byproduct to be discarded—and transported it back to the village to be resold to individual households. Since the coal dust has residual burning power, it can be used again for household cooking. In their spare time housewives mix the coal dust with water and clay, and press the mixture into cylindrical tubes with honeycomb holes in the middle using a simple cast-iron mold. After these beehive coal clumps are completely sun dried, they can be burned slowly overnight in the hearth. Without this device, village women claimed, they had to get up much earlier to start the stove using rice husks with dry twigs or leaves—the latter two having been laboriously collected in the hills.

When the breakfast is ready, the housewife awakens those family members with regular jobs in village factories, who eat and rush off to work. If the housewife has some spare money, she may be tempted by street hawkers who peddle a variety of breakfast supplements that they load into large wooden boxes and carry on the backs of their bicycles. The peddler who sells fresh bean curd is from Jiangtou Town some five kilometers to the west. Another peddler, who sells a kind of elongated fried dough, comes from Hongshan Village, about one kilometer to the south. Fresh fish, shrimp, and oysters are brought over from Hecu Village along the coast. Each of them has a unique way to hawk his merchandise while negotiating through the narrow village alleys. The bean curd hawker calls out most clearly: "Fresh bean curd!" once every two or three minutes. On the other hand, the fried dough peddler just squeaks out a high-pitched "Gi-iap!" once in a while. No matter what words or tones they use, villagers all know by instinct which voice is associated with which product. The housewife may stop the hawker when he passes by and purchase her desired goods for the family.

By six o'clock most village men start their daily work. Since many villagers operate trucks or hand tractors, the morning rush hour in the village is filled with rumbling noise from all the diesel engines. With their husbands or adult sons or daughters off to work, the housewives turn their attention to their hogs and fowl. They chop sweet potato stems and leaves into small pieces and boil the mixture with rice rinse water carefully stored in a ceramic jar from the night before. Sometimes spoiled food or unwanted leftovers are also dumped into this large cooking pot for the hogs. Chickens and ducks that generally roam around freely in and around the house are given a few handsful of unhusked rice and vegetable leaves.

Once the animals are fed and cared for, it is time to wake up the children for school. Since the village elementary school has only kindergarten to fifth grade, children above fifth grade have to go to Jiangtou Town middle school by either walking or biking, and it is at least a twenty-minute bicycle ride. Adolescents must be awake by 7:00 A.M. in order to make their morning school periods beginning at 8:00. Then, by 7:30, the youngest of the house, those attending elementary school, should be dressed and fed and ready for school. After eight o'clock, when the rushing and shuffling around the house is over, the scene quiets down. The housewife will either be on the way to the family field to farm, or to the village wells or a nearby brook for her daily clothes washing.

The relaxation of government control in the countryside since the late 1970s has injected much energy and dynamism into village life. Villagers claim that they work much harder than they used to under the collective system. Truck drivers now own their own trucks, and the more time they put into their work the more income they earn for the family. The direct reward from work creates a good deal of enthusiasm among villagers in their daily work patterns.

The only group of people who remain unaffected by this bustling seems to be brigade-level officials. Each morning they gather in the brigade office to discuss village business that demands their immediate attention. Most of these gatherings are quite informal. They sit around the sparsely decorated room filled with office desks and chairs, and sip tea or smoke cigarettes or read the newspapers. Party Secretary Ye tells the brigade head Li Dehai that the brigade must file a report on last year's grain production to the commune administration. Or the head of the brigade Women's League, Hou Lingli, tells all those present about the recent meeting she attended at the district office about a new birth control campaign to reduce the birthrate in the village by another two-tenths of a percentage point. She points out that the brigade will have to devise a new policy to carry out this campaign.

As brigade officials talk informally, some villagers might wander in to report an incident that just occurred, or to complain about an inconvenience caused by the road construction on the village thoroughfare, or just to gossip. The brigade clerk might go off with a villager to check on the electric poles that supply village needs. Or the brigade chief might drift out to receive a truckload of chemical fertilizer assigned by the government to the village. Although the brigade-level officials seem to have daily duties, they generally defer important decisions to Ye.

As the de facto ruler of Lin Village, Party Secretary Ye behaves like a benevolent county magistrate, the so-called father-mother official, of imperial China. In that capacity he literally wrote the laws and ordinances for villagers, presided over their litigations, and dispensed justice in whatever way he saw fit. My close association with Ye gave me a rare opportunity to observe how conflicts were resolved, and justice maintained, in the countryside. The following incident reveals not only the nature of rural jurisprudence, but also the way the villagers resolve conflicts in contemporary China.

Ye Settles a Dispute

May 2, 1985: A sunny and pleasant day, warm but not humid. I was sitting in Ye's kitchen chatting with him when a village woman, Wang Xiuhua, came in. She said she wanted to press a charge against her paternal cousin, Wang Wenshan, head of the first production team, because he slapped her on the face. According to the village ordinance (*xianggui minyue*), she insisted, such misconduct should be punished with a fine of at least RMB$10. Ye asked her why Wang Wenshan had slapped her. Was there an argument before the incident? Xiuhua said she had an argument with Wenshan about spreading rat poison around her house. Wenshan had purposely spread the rat poison close to Xiuhua's chicken coop. Fearing that the poison might accidentally kill her chickens, Xiuhua tried to stop him but he refused to listen. In the ensuing argument Wenshan was overwhelmed by his rage and slapped her on the face.

Ye deliberated for a moment and asked Xiuhua plainly, "Do you know that spreading rat poison was an assignment given to us by the commune office? Do you know that Wenshan was carrying out a government order to benefit all villagers by killing off the rats?" Xiuhua said that she fully realized that, and had no objection to this practice. The only complaint she had with Wenshan was that he spread the poison too close to her chicken coop. Wenshan shouldn't have slapped her for that, she insisted.

Ye deliberated again for a few minutes and told Xiuhua to go home. He assured her that he would fully investigate the case and then reach a proper decision. After she left, Ye turned to me and said: "Xiuhua hasn't told me the full story. I can't see why Wenshan would slap her if she only asked him not to spread the rat poison close to her chicken coop. Why don't we go and pay Wenshan a visit?"

We walked to the eastern edge of the village, where the first team is located, and found Wenshan at home. He seemed to be anticipating our visit, because he had already prepared a pot of freshly brewed tea. When Ye burst into Wenshan's living room, he sneered and ridiculed the latter, "I never realized that you were such a brave, strong man who can beat up a woman, especially when she is not your wife but your cousin!"

Wenshan seemed to be embarrassed. He welcomed us by gesturing us to sit in the two rattan chairs in the living room. He poured tea in two cups for us and meekly protested, "But I didn't do it on purpose. Xiuhua spread malicious rumors about me. That was why I slapped her."

Wenshan explained that when he, as head of the first production team, received the assignment from the brigade office to spread rat poison around the team area, he decided to contract the task to a poor family. The team still had some operating funds left, and there was a poor family, a widow with two children, in the team that needed assistance. So he paid this widow RMB$5 to spread the poison. When this woman spread rat poison around Xiuhua's house, Wenshan said, Xiuhua came out and intervened, accusing the widow of trying to poison her chickens. The widow stopped her work and reported this incident to Wenshan, who went to investigate. He told Xiuhua that the widow was carrying out an assignment given to them by higher authorities, and that killing rats would benefit everyone in the team. Xiuhua insisted that the widow purposely and maliciously spread the poison close to her chicken coop. Xiuhua then began to challenge Wenshan by asking him why he had given the job to the widow. She accused Wenshan of carrying on an affair with the woman, so he embezzled team funds for her. Wenshan said that it was at that moment he lost control of himself and slapped Xiuhua.

After listening to Wenshan's side of the story, Ye nodded in satisfaction and instructed Wenshan, "You go and tell Xiuhua that I have come to investigate this case. Under normal conditions I would fine you RMB$10 for your misconduct according to the village ordinance. But in this case, since Xiuhua was the one who provoked you while you were carrying out public business, I will suspend the punishment. Tell Xiuhua that she deserved the slap on the face. If she complains again, I will slap her on the other side of her face."

On the way back to Ye's house I asked him why he seemed to be favoring Wenshan's side over that of Xiuhua. On what basis had he come to such a conclusion? Ye glanced at me and laughed, "You have to know them well, including their personalities and behavior patterns, to know who is telling the truth. Wang Wenshan, for example, is a capable manager of his team, so he has been elected team head since 1978. But he also has the reputation of being a truly henpecked husband. His wife openly flirts with many village men, but Wenshan never dares to interfere because he is afraid of women. On the other hand, Xiuhua has been known to have a very long tongue. She manufactures rumors about almost everyone that she comes across, and spreads these fabrications relentlessly. Wenshan wouldn't dare attack Xiuhua unless extremely provoked. Of course I will not punish Wenshan. What he did would only help build up his self-confidence. To me, this incident is settled."

Internal Conflicts in the Village

I was very interested in law and order issues in the village. In the absence of a formal police force, how were villagers able to maintain peace? What instruments did the Chinese government use to exercise control in the countryside? And what role did the Party play in such matters? To satisfy my curiosity I managed to have several lengthy discussions with Ye during the last two or three months of my fieldwork. In one of our discussions in late May 1985, I deliberately asked Ye a direct question, "What are the main types of internal conflicts in Lin Village? And how do villagers resolve these conflicts?"

He thought for a moment and replied, "I have never thought about this question before. But now that you ask and I reflect on the nature of past conflicts in our village, it appears to me that prior to 1970, most seemed to be politically related. A lot of personality clashes had their beginnings during political campaigns. But after 1970, the number of politically related conflicts declined. On the other hand, other types of conflicts, such as theft, adultery, and gambling increased to replace them."

"What might have been the reason for this change, in your opinion?" I encouraged him.

"There are probably several reasons," Ye, still thinking, replied. "The decline of political fervor among Chinese after the tumultuous Four Cleanups Campaign and the Cultural Revolution was almost inevitable. The 1969 suppression of the Red Guard factions made people realize how ridiculous these political campaigns had been and how foolish they had been to have been used by officials struggling for power. As a result, people lost interest in politics and devoted their energy to production. The turning point seemed to be in 1970.

"This is not to say that we, the country people, could stay completely immune from political campaigns. During the early 1970s, the ripple effect of the Cultural Revolution was not yet complete, for there were still minor political campaigns periodically instigated by the central government, including the Cleansing the Class Ranks (*qingli jieji duiwu*) campaign in 1969, the Criticize Lin Biao, Criticize Confucius (*pilin, pikong*) campaign in 1973, and the Anti-Deng [Xiaoping], Counter-attack Rightist Trend (*pideng fanji youqingfeng*) campaign in 1976. But these campaigns had limited impact in the countryside. They were mostly city events and involved principally high-level Party cadres. The peasants seemed to have become apathetic. They had lost faith with the Party."

"What about Party cadres?" I asked. "Did they share the same feelings?"

"Yes," Ye confirmed, "even the rural cadres, after the continuous flip-flop of government policies and after their repeated humiliations in public during struggle sessions, had similarly lost their steam. They reacted half-heartedly to new campaigns, and they minimized attacks against alleged 'class enemies' of the Party. They had learned their lessons quickly and clearly: Today you may be the prosecutors and judges of the 'class enemies,' but tomorrow you may be on trial yourself. To save your own skin tomorrow, you should be nice to your fellow villagers today.

"In Lin Village, even the Wu brothers seemed to have gradually mellowed and had abandoned their ambition to recoup lost power after 1970. It must have become apparent to them that past efforts had been futile. After the removal, and subsequent death, of Thunderbolt Lin, whom they considered their major adversary in any power struggle, a new young cadre, Dark Skin Lin, was appointed brigade head by the commune Party committee in 1969. Dark Skin had graduated from middle school and was supported by the Lins. The Wu brothers must have realized that since they were illiterate and past the age of forty-five, they stood little chance of being reappointed to administrative positions at any level.

"Another factor contributing to the reduction of internal fighting in Lin Village was the split of the Wu brothers' faction, which, as I mentioned earlier, included several less-than-desirable characters in the village. Witch Zhang and her husband used to be close allies of the Wu brothers, so close in fact, that they acted like dogs in a pack. When they applied for building lots from the brigade administration to build new houses in 1970, these three families, Hopping Toad, Wu Ming, and Witch Zhang, applied for adjacent lots in the northwestern corner of the village."

"But why did they split up?" I asked. "Was it merely because the Wu brothers ceased to be interested in regaining their political power and found no use for their allies?"

"No," Ye replied, "it was not for that reason. The faction split in 1972 or 1973, when they began to build their houses and argued frequently. Witch Zhang's house is at the farthest corner of the village, and the path from her house to the village passes through the boundary between the Wu brothers' houses. Witch Zhang asked the Wu brothers not to build their houses too close to each other, so that there would be room for a cow-drawn cart to pass through. The Wu brothers promised to comply with her request. But when they built their houses the next year, they were extremely close to each other. The Wu brothers did what was in their best interests. Building lots allotted to villagers were quite small, so everyone had to make maximum use of their allowed space to build as large a house as possible. But what they did in building large houses had inadvertently narrowed Witch Zhang's passage so much that even a person with a shoulder pole and two baskets would have difficulty passing through. Witch Zhang was furious and openly broke with the Wu brothers. Then Witch Zhang began to gossip to any villager within earshot about all the malicious plots and plans engineered by the Wu brothers. To most villagers' relief, the breakup of the Wu brothers' faction reduced the possibility of political conflict within our village."

"Now," I asked, "were you suggesting that the end of political conflict in the village in the early 1970s was directly linked to the increase of other types of problems, such as adultery, gambling, and theft? What is the cause-and-effect relationship between these two types of conflicts?"

"Well," Ye was slow to respond, seemingly searching for the proper words, "superficially you may say that once political conflicts ceased, other types of problems increased. But I am not saying that one was the direct cause of the other. Their relationships are probably indirect."

I could not follow his line of reasoning. Seeing my perplexed expression, Ye volunteered the following explanation: "Before 1970 the villagers were much more involved in politics and were also poorer. But when the Cultural Revolution ended in 1969,[1] the villagers were no longer unified by their devotion to the cause of Communism. They were more interested in personal material gain. They devoted most of their time to their private plots. They became cynical about anything political. Living conditions improved somewhat in the early 1970s, clearly at the expense of public spirit. That was how inter-personal conflicts increased. Improved living conditions seemed to be directly responsible for the increase in victim crimes in our village."

I still had problems with Ye's explanation, for there seemed to be a few pieces missing. But I decided to pursue this issue from another angle. "In what ways were the living conditions improved here in the early 1970s?"

"The change came gradually. Not that we had become rich as we are now. We were still far from that. What was considered prosperous then was to have enough sweet potatoes to eat every day, and a dry rice meal once every three or four days. But even that was a major improvement from the years of starvation of the 1960s. Production levels in this area increased considerably after the construction of the reservoir, which turned most of the dry land in the vicinity into irrigated fields and rice terrace. In 1969, Dark Skin Lin, the new brigade head, in response to the 'Learn from Dazhai' campaign, mobilized all the village able-bodied workers to perform large-scale construction work. The task was to level the surface of all farmland belonging to our village, and to redraw the land divisions to maximize the size per unit. Family graves previously scattered all over the private fields were dug up and relocated in woods around the rocky hills or around the lake. A few families grumbled that these resettled graves interrupted their family geomantic composition (*fengshui*). But most other families, with fresh memories from the Four Cleanups and Cultural Revolution, remained quiet. Boulders that protruded in the middle of a field were chipped apart and removed. Boundaries that had zigzagged through the fields and had provided a narrow path for peasants and their animals were straightened and broadened.

"Because of these improvements, in late 1969 our brigade was designated a vegetable production area by Xiamen City's vegetable company. This company, which is actually a city government office, assigns vegetable production quotas to designated brigades in the suburbs. The company then collects the vegetables from producing brigades and delivers them to government-run vegetable stores throughout the city. Every year the vegetable company instructed us what to grow in which seasons. In return our brigade received from the company fixed cash payments, rationed chemical fertilizer and pesticide, plus rationed rice at a government-posted price. After we had satisfied the vegetable production quota for the company, we could sell the surplus vegetables in the free market, which, by the early 1970s, had become increasingly visible. This arrangement was definitely a big improvement for us. Whereas in the past we could grow only sweet potatoes and eat them as staples, now we could have more rice for our meals. The increased cash income was also a big improvement, allowing the villagers to purchase things they wouldn't dare to think of before, such as a bicycle, a radio, or a wristwatch.

"My family's financial condition also improved considerably during the early 1970s. Baozhu and I, my three brothers and sister, plus our children, still resided with my parents as a large family. My father and mother worked full-time and earned adult work points in their work team. My second younger brother next to the deceased one, Qinghui, joined the navy in 1970. He was twenty-one years old then and had a primary school education. To join the military was considered the best choice for him. Both Baozhu and I also worked full-time, drawing our regular income from the brigade office. I was the brigade clerk and Baozhu a trainee to become a barefoot doctor. I didn't demand the division of the stem family or didn't move out and set up my own household as many villagers would have done because I knew the heavy burden my father was carrying. He had spent a major portion of his meager income to support me when I attended school. He raised my brother, Jiade, to twenty-one years of age; but Jiade died and never reciprocated (*huibao*) my father. Even though Qinghui had joined the navy, the military stipend was low and my father had to send him money occasionally to supplement his salary. There were two younger sons and a daughter still in school who relied upon my parents to feed them. By staying in the stem family Baozhu and I could contribute our income to the family pool, thus reducing my parents' burden. Also as a stem family we could easily cut corners in our expenditures. It was through this joint effort that my family was able to start building our new house in 1972.

"The biggest dream of all peasants in this part of China is to build a house. Not just any house, but a big one, big enough for the parents, their sons, sons' wives and grandsons, and great grandchildren. To have a three-generation family living under the same roof and eating out of the same cooking pot is still the ideal for most villagers. Building a large house is also costly. It takes long-term planning and saving, plus long-term building. Take our new house as an example. The ground level was built with stone slabs purchased from quarries in and around Xiamen Island. We had to find ways to haul them to the construction site after purchasing them. Then we had to buy sand and cement for the foundation and red tiles for the floor. The way we do it here is, if you have spare money, say RMB$200 in a year, you use it to purchase 20 cubic meters of stone slabs, if the price per cubic meter is RMB$10. When you and your family members have spare time, you work together to haul these slabs to the building site piece by piece with shoulder poles, or several pieces at a time if you use a hand tractor. Then you wait until the following year when you have another RMB$200 left to buy cement, sand, and floor tile. You start to dig the ground, lay the foundation of the house, and use the stone slabs to build the wall, probably waist high.

"In the third year, you purchase more stone for the wall, and hopefully by then you have enough stone to complete the ground-level outer walls and the walls between rooms. During the next year, the fourth one, you purchase long, broad, and thin stone slabs to cover the house. These slabs are also used temporarily as the roof for the ground level. When this is done, the building looks like a rectangular box and the family can move into this half-finished house. During the next years, the family still has to save more money to buy bricks, cement, and steel to build the second floor. Since the ground level of the house is built with solid stone slabs, the second floor can be built with less expensive materials such as bricks.

"To cut costs, most of the villagers use their own labor in the initial stages of construction, such as hauling stones, digging the foundation, and so on. But later they have to hire professional masons for more delicate tasks such as laying the tiled floor or erecting room divisions. The second floor is an even more difficult task. It takes more skill to lay bricks than stone slabs. Carpenters are also needed for doors and windows. Putting up the main beam of the house is not only difficult, it may also affect a family's fortune. Only experienced construction workers can be entrusted with this responsibility. All this adds up to a large sum of money, so a family has to spend between five and ten years building a new house."

"What was the single most important reason for your family to build the new house?" I asked. "Practical needs? A public show of your prosperity?"

"Probably a mixture of both," Ye answered without hesitation. "As I told you before, my original house was small with mud walls and a thatched roof. It was hastily built by the government to accommodate those families who had to be relocated after the construction of the reservoir. It only had three bedrooms; my parents and younger sister used the first one, my three brothers the next, and my wife, children and I the third. It was just too crowded for our family in that small house. By that point we also had some savings. So we selected a vacant lot behind our mud house and in 1972 applied for permission from the brigade office to build a new house. And little by little over five years we built the house. Even though by today's standards this house is not particularly glamorous, it was one of the few two-story buildings in this village when it was completed in 1977."

With this background information clearly laid out, I thought it appropriate to change the conversation back to the original topic: internal conflict in Lin Village. I asked Ye, "When did you become involved in dealing with local crimes?"

"When I was appointed the commander of the brigade militia (*minbing yingzhang*, or commander of militia battalion) by Opium Hong in 1975," he answered matter-of-factly. "As the head of the local militia, I also had the double assignment of head of brigade public security (*zhibao zhuren*). I looked on this assignment with amusement. I had never served in the army, and thus had no experience with the military. The only reason I was appointed to the post was because it was important and had to be filled by a reliable Party cadre. There weren't many qualified Party members in the village who could fill this position at that point. The neutral position I had taken during the Cultural Revolution also made me an acceptable person to all factions in this brigade. My nomination was swiftly approved by the commune's Party branch and my life seemed to be changing for the better.

"From my personal viewpoint, this new assignment was important in my career development. First of all, it showed that the stigma I carried with me from the Four Cleanups was no longer considered a serious flaw by higher-level authorities. The fanaticism of the Cultural Revolution had subsided. Criticism and attacks against Liu Shaoqi and his policies seemed to have been carried to the extreme by the Red Guards. Almost all Red Guard factions had by then been condemned by the central government. Cadres in my generation, previously condemned as followers of the revisionist line of Liu Shaoqi, were being given a second chance by Party leadership. If my assessment of the situation was correct, then I still had an opportunity to move up within Party leadership and move out of the countryside.

"This assignment was important to me for yet another reason. It put me in the inner core of the brigade power structure. The brigade administration consists of six salaried positions: brigade Party branch secretary, brigade head, security head (also in charge of local militia), clerk (who also doubles as accountant), treasurer, and head of the women's league. The actual power holders are the first three: Party secretary, brigade head, and security head. Important decisions are made by these three, and they are all on the same pay level.

"As commander of the brigade militia, my chief responsibility was to organize training sessions for local youth according to schedules set up by regional office. Local militias throughout the entire rural district of Xiamen Island constitute a division and include the division headquarters, a division commander, and his staff. The division command office worked out training schedules for all the brigades under its command, and sent out instructors, regular army officers, to conduct the training. My duty was to see that all village youth in the right age bracket went to the military training classes. During those training periods they received their regular daily work points from their teams as compensation. Whenever there was an emergency, such as a typhoon, a flood, or any other major disaster, the local militia was alerted and assigned to relief tasks by the brigade Party secretary or the commune administration.

"I didn't enjoy this part of my assignment very much. Since I had never served in the military, I didn't know much about military affairs. Worst of all, people made fun of me because of it. For instance, whenever a new militia division commander was assigned to this district, he would make an inspection tour of all brigades under his command. While inspecting our brigade militia unit, he would ask me which army unit I had served in. When I would say I had never served in the army, he would first doubt me and then burst out laughing. 'How could we entrust the duty of training our local militia to a non-military man? This is not a local opera troupe!' I felt humiliated each time this happened.

"I had more fun serving as village security head. My duties included investigating crimes in the village, punishing culprits when caught, and executing orders issued from Opium Hong, the Party secretary. While serving in this capacity I was able to develop a deeper understanding of the nature of crimes in the countryside. I also dispensed justice with total impartiality, so I established a good reputation among the villagers. Whenever I said something, the villagers heeded it because they knew I meant it. I know many villagers were afraid of me and accused me of being a local tyrant. But they also trusted me. They knew I would never sacrifice their interests for my personal gain or for somebody else's gain. Because of the villagers' trust in me, our brigade was able to progress rapidly when I became brigade Party secretary in 1978."

"Now, tell me what type of insight you gained about village crimes when serving as the brigade security head." I steered Ye back to the topic of law and order before giving him a chance to change to another subject.

Ye seemed to enjoy this discussion enormously. "Oh, sure. Let's take theft, once the most prevalent crime in the countryside, as an example. Under the old collective system, stealing was at epidemic levels. Most incidents were petty thefts involving public property. When farmers finished their daily work assignment at dusk, they wouldn't hesitate to pull one or two sugarcanes from the fields to chew as they walked home. Or when they realized they needed an additional sweet potato or two for dinner, they would just dig out one or two from the public field and stick them in their pockets. Since these things belonged to the public, of which they were a part, they felt no guilt in taking these items for personal use.

"The range of stealing extended far beyond farm produce. Tools in the public warehouse, lumber at public construction sites, or even stone slabs covering village roads often disappeared overnight. Whenever I caught a thief, I would either levy a fine against the culprit or order the thief to perform public labor, such as sweeping the village streets. Sometimes I reported more serious cases to the commune administration for them to handle. Generally I preferred to handle petty crimes internally, for commune officials dispensed harsh punishment against criminals. To maintain harmonious relationships within the village, it was better to deal with the problems ourselves. The only theft case I did report to the commune concerned a petty thief who sought revenge after I punished him for his misconduct.

"This case involved Witch Zhang's son, A Hui. My conflict with Witch Zhang started almost immediately after I was appointed head of public security. I had never liked Witch Zhang, even as a child. She and her husband had moved to Lin Village shortly before the Liberation and worked as hired farm hands for some wealthy farmers. After the Liberation they gained prominence because of their poor-peasant status. Her husband was given a job in the commune's supply co-op in Jiangtou Town, the commune headquarters, and moved steadily upward until he became the store manager. I didn't like Witch Zhang, not so much because of her association with the Wu brothers, but because of her personal characteristics. She is abrasive, argumentative, and licentious. She slept with many villagers, old and young, including her daughter's suitor, a village boy half her age. Her husband acted like a boar (*zhugong*), literally a male swine chasing after women. Few village women talk about sex openly. But Witch Zhang often bragged about how her husband carried on with her every night like a boar.

"A few years ago, Witch Zhang's husband had an affair with a female worker in that supply co-op where he at that time worked as an accountant. We wouldn't have known much about this disgraceful affair had Witch Zhang kept quiet. She began to complain to other women that her husband no longer acted like a boar at night and that she suspected there was another woman involved. One day her husband told her that he would be staying in the store late that night to check on the accounting books. Witch Zhang went over to her husband's store in Jiangtou that evening and sneaked in. There they were, her husband and the female worker, on the warehouse floor behind the store. Witch Zhang picked up a broom and swung the broomstick at their bare bottoms. Her husband screamed and fled, but she severely beat the other woman. After this episode, Witch Zhang bragged to other women that the liaison between her husband and his mistress had been broken by her swinging broomstick, and that her husband acted like a boar toward her at night again.

"Witch Zhang gained her nickname because she was very superstitious. She keeps several statues of local deities in her house and regularly offers food and incense to them. She claimed that she could enter a trance and be possessed by one of the deities in her home. While in a trance, she said, she could exercise spiritual power like a witch (*tongji*, literally a child shaman). She uses this alleged skill to intimidate other people. But most villagers believe that she is a fraud. Had she really had that ability, she would have applied it to the Wu brothers long ago.

"My conflict with Witch Zhang's family started with her son, A Hui. In 1975, when I began my assignment as the brigade security head, the city vegetable company assigned our brigade to produce half a million catties [or 250,000 kilos] of cabbage during the months of August and September. The brigade administration divided up the production quota among all five teams, and the teams reserved sufficient land to produce the required cabbage. Each team also assigned its best farmers to tend the cabbage field, making sure that it would produce enough cabbage to meet its quota.

"Everything seemed to be working out well, except for the bad weather. The excessive heat of July killed a lot of the cabbage plants prematurely, and it seemed we would be unable to fulfill our production goal. To remedy the situation, we in the brigade administration decided to appropriate the cabbage grown in private lots to make up the shortage. Since the private lots constituted one-tenth of all arable land in the brigade, and most farmers grew cabbage in their private lots with better yields than those from the public land, we should be able to turn out enough cabbage to meet our production quota. We anticipated resistance from the villagers, for because of the drought and poor vegetable production that year, they could sell their cabbage at a much higher price in the free market than the city would pay. But then we reasoned that it would be important for the brigade to keep its promise to the company. The long-term profit and security provided by the company to our brigade far outweighed the short-term gains of a few farmers in the free market.

"We announced our decision through the village loudspeaker system one evening in early August: From the next morning on, all cabbage produced in private lots should be turned over to the brigade office, which would then ship it in bulk to the city vegetable company to meet the production goal. We explained the reason and significance of this act, and its long-term versus short-term benefits and costs. I declared that no villager would be allowed to take cabbage to the free market from the next day on. Anyone who disobeyed this order would be fined RMB$10.

"To make sure that everyone complied with this new rule, I stood in the village main thoroughfare at four o'clock the next morning. I caught several villagers trying to sneak to the free market with cabbage from their private lots, and fined them RMB$10. Most of those caught pleaded for special permission to go to the market or begged for my clemency in waiving the fine. But when I insisted and threatened to turn them in at the commune office, they all complied, except for A Hui, who was headed to the market carrying two baskets of cabbage on the back of his bicycle. He argued vehemently, like his mother. He asked me why I didn't levy a fine on his neighbor, Hopping Toad Wu's son, who had carried two baskets of cabbage to the free market the day before. I told him that it was because the new regulation took effect that morning. I couldn't punish Hopping Toad's son for what he did before it was declared illegal. A Hui then retorted that if I didn't punish Hopping Toad's son for selling cabbage in the free market the day before, I couldn't punish him for the same act now. He then began to accuse me of maliciousness against his family. He irritated me so much that I almost beat him up. Finally I took him to brigade headquarters and locked him in the detention room for one day.

"About two or three months after this incident a theft occurred. This time it involved a few pieces of lumber used by the brigade administration when we remodeled and expanded the primary school. Lumber has always been in short supply in this area. The government assigns only two cubic meters of wood to the entire brigade each year through the government supply store. That amount of wood wouldn't be enough even to make caskets for all those who died in the village in a year. Villagers who want to build houses or furniture have to purchase their own lumber in the free market, which automatically means exorbitant prices. After the construction of the school, the remaining lumber was carefully locked up in the brigade storage house for future use. A few days later, the window of the storage room was broken and three or four pieces of the best lumber were stolen. It was the first time that anyone had ever dared to steal things from the storage room in the brigade office compound. I did a little investigating around the village that day and learned that A Hui was the prime suspect. A few villagers told me that lately they had seen A Hui loitering around brigade headquarters late at night. Hopping Toad's oldest son said that he heard someone hauling things through the narrow alley in front of his house late the night before and saw A Hui's silhouette in the darkness. Even more damaging was the fact that Witch Zhang was building a new addition to her house.

"The next day I searched Witch Zhang's house. I spotted immediately the lumber stolen from the brigade storage room, ready to be used in their construction. At first Witch Zhang denied that the wood was stolen. She claimed she had purchased it on the free market. But she couldn't tell me where or from whom she had purchased the wood. Furthermore, I called over the carpenters who had worked on the school building, and they all identified these pieces of lumber as belonging to the brigade. I charged Witch Zhang a fine of RMB$50, and she grudgingly paid it. After that she began to spread rumors that I had intentionally sought out her family, for I was in alliance with either the Wu brothers or with Thunderbolt Lin's younger brothers. She also hinted that she would seek vengeance against me.

"And revenge she did seek. In early 1976, my family grew watermelon on our 0.7-*mou* private lot as our spring crop. Watermelon can be grown in early spring, and its price is generally good if we can harvest it by early summer and sell it in the free market. We took good care of the crop and, by early April, the melons in our lots were as large as my fist. We were anticipating a huge profit when the melons ripened. We could use the money to continue construction of our new house.

"Early one morning in April, a neighbor who went to work in his private lot before daybreak rushed to my house and told me that he found all my melon plants had been uprooted. I went over to my lot, at the western edge of the village, and couldn't believe what I saw: Every single hill of watermelon plants was carefully pulled out and laid next to the hole. The act was different from ordinary theft, which did occur quite frequently during the watermelon harvest season. Village families who didn't grow watermelons in their own private lots might send children out to their neighbors' lots on a hot summer night to fetch a few melons to kill the heat and quench their thirst. But this incident was certainly different from normal petty theft. It was an act of revenge.

"I reported this case to the commune immediately and a policeman was sent over to investigate. He found a few footprints in the field and made plaster samples of them. He then inquired if there had been threats against me by any villager. The only threat was made by Witch Zhang, as most villagers confirmed. The police took the plaster footprint samples to Witch Zhang's house, and they matched A Hui's feet exactly. A Hui was immediately handcuffed and taken to the commune prison.

"The commune Party secretary was furious about this case. He told me that any vendetta against Party cadres on duty should be severely punished; otherwise common citizens would have no respect for officials and the Party. He thought about charging Witch Zhang's family a fine of RMB$3,000 to compensate my loss, and putting A Hui in jail for fifteen years for his counter-revolutionary acts. I thought for a while and told him that the RMB$3,000 fine as compensation for my watermelons sounded all right, but, I inquired, could the jail sentence be reduced to three months instead? Fifteen years in jail would be too long. This would only breed more hatred in Witch Zhang's family. After that fifteen years in jail, A Hui would be back in the village, a full-grown adult. Since I would most likely be living in Lin Village for the rest of my life, and would be coming across Witch Zhang or A Hui once in a while, I would rather see grounds for reconciliation with them rather than further animosity. To live harmoniously with your neighbors is more important than maintaining public discipline.

"Apparently my rationale convinced the commune Party leader, who finally agreed with the reduced sentence I proposed. When A Hui was released from jail after his three month sentence, I was asked to sign him out as his guardian. I was responsible for correcting all his future misconduct. Even though I had done this great favor for Witch Zhang by reducing her son's jail sentence, she never expressed any appreciation to me. Even now she still spreads rumors about me. She accused me of embezzling public funds, stealing public construction material to build my own house, and assigning good jobs to my brothers. But what can you do with a person like Witch Zhang?

"The most bizarre theft case I handled in my capacity as the brigade public security head involved the stealing of village women's underpants. For a while I received many reports from village women that the underpants they hung out to dry in the sun in their courtyards were stolen. I thought that perhaps it was the act of petty thieves who stole these underpants and sold them in Xiamen City's free market. But then I found out that I was wrong! One day I was working in the field with several villagers, fixing an irrigation ditch. We needed a couple of extra spades so we went to a small storage house the brigade had built in the middle of the field. Amidst bags of chemical fertilizer and rice seeds for the next season's planting there was a small space left and carefully concealed under some rice straw. I asked a villager to pull away the straw. There they were, all the underpants lost in the village during the previous year. I was completely bewildered. Who would have done such a meaningless thing? If the thief didn't steal those underpants to sell, what did he want with them? Since you probably know more about psychology than I do, can you tell me what type of person who might have done such a ridiculous thing?" Ye turned to me with his question.

My insight told me that this was probably a case of sexual deviation, and told Ye so. But I pointed out that since I had no formal training in psychology or psychoanalysis, it would be unwise for me to speculate who might have been responsible for such an act. Ye accepted my explanation and grumbled that he would pay close attention to village teenaged boys, since they were probably the ones engaging in this prank.

More Village Crimes

My next interview with Ye about village crimes came shortly after the previous one. This allowed me to continue our discourse about what we had discussed in our earlier interview. This meeting took place in my flat, and I opened the conversation with a question. "What are the major types of crimes in this village in addition to theft?"

"They are gambling and sex-related crimes (*nannu guanxi*, literally man-woman relationships, including both fornication and adultery in the Chinese context)." Ye seemed to have thought about this issue a lot, and was more ready to answer my question than he was the last time.

"Gambling has been a real headache for me, especially in the past three or four years as our economy has greatly improved. The villagers seem to be addicted to gambling. They gamble with money when they have it, or gamble with cigarettes when they don't have money. They gamble during the Chinese New Year, when peasants traditionally gather together for a few games. They also gamble during other festivals, such as after a wedding party or a god's birthday banquet. They gamble with *majiang*, poker cards, dice, or Chinese chess. Mostly men gamble. Women generally are busy from dawn to dusk with household chores so they don't have time to gamble. Some older women do gamble, especially those who can rely on their sons and daughters-in-law to take care of them.

"My policy with regard to gambling is that I will not interfere with old folks who have nothing to do during the day and get together for a few games that involve only a small sum of money. Older people in the countryside have few recreational activities. They don't like to watch television because almost all the broadcasts are in Mandarin, a language they don't understand. They are too old to go to Xiamen City for shopping or movies. It is natural that they play a few games to pass their time. I intervene only when they develop arguments over bids or cheating.

"Gambling among young adults is a different matter. They gamble until late at night and spend the next day yawning. They don't do their assigned work properly. Worse yet, gambling causes family discord when the husband loses money. Wu Hanlin, who is Wu Ming's oldest son and whose nickname is Mustached Wu, is a typical addicted gambler. He is a smart young man with a lot of potential. But if he can't find a place to gamble during the week, he becomes restless. In the beginning when I caught Mustached Wu gambling, I fined him. But I soon realized the fine would not discourage him from future gambling. He paid the fine grudgingly, and then went on to the next gambling gathering. Once Mustached Wu lost several hundred dollars so he stole his wife's gold bracelets, part of her wedding dowry, to pay his debts. When she found out about it she argued with him. He beat her severely and left the house. She tried to hang herself but was saved by her mother-in-law, who was watching her carefully after the argument.

"When I heard about this incident I called Mustached Wu over and lectured him for two hours. I told him that he was a coward and only dared to beat up his wife. I couldn't do anything about it. I could only fine him for his gambling, which wouldn't break his bad habit. But if he continued gambling, I warned him, his wife would eventually be successful in committing suicide. When she died I would charge him with wife killing and lock him up for the rest of his life. It would be too late for him to beg for my mercy then. That was the only time that Mustached Wu showed signs of repentance. He solemnly swore to me that he would never gamble again. He promised that if I ever caught him gambling again, he would chop his the little finger on the left hand as a measure of self-punishment. After that he quit gambling for about six months. But then it all returned. Now Mustached Wu is afraid of me, avoiding me, because he still owes me the little finger on his left hand."

"Do you think that the increase in gambling in this village is directly related to the improved living conditions in recent years?" I inquired.

"Yes," Ye said. "When the Party loosened its grip on peasants, they were able to devote more time and energy to improving their production. With more money to go around and less concern about feeding their stomachs, the peasants turned to gambling and other type of crimes, such as sex crimes, which have also become common in the countryside since the early 1970s. The peasants are not like city folks in that we have a more flexible attitude toward men-women relationships. There are many dark corners at night in the countryside that village boys and girls can use for their secret rendezvous. Since this is a mixed-surname village, many village boys do marry village girls. Unlike city people, we peasants don't care much about pre-marital or extra-marital relationships, as long as such relationships do not disrupt our brigade's annual birth quota or cause family discord. For instance, Opium Hong's daughter went through two abortions before she married a village boy. Everyone in the village knew it, but nobody considered that a disgrace, as city people would.

"Another example is the fifth team's former team head A Ho and his wife. A Ho is a strong and handsome man, also a veteran of the Liberation Army and a Party cadre. He has everything going for him, except his impotency. In contrast, his wife is a very demanding woman, always wanting sex. She began to flirt with village men even before she married A Ho. Once she found out that he couldn't satisfy her, she openly slept with other men. Her mother was living with A Ho's family. Even this old woman helped her daughter in setting up liaisons at night. Whenever A Ho returned home at night, this old woman would tell him to go and sleep in another room away from his wife, for the wife would be busy entertaining other men. Poor A Ho would sheepishly obey.

"Peasants also openly make sex jokes. The boldest fellow in this regard is Lin Fucheng, or Tuxedo Lin, named for the vintage tuxedo he inherited from his father, which he wears daily. He lives in the second production team. In the early 1970s his team had a woman agricultural head, who supervised all agricultural work in the team. One day Tuxedo Lin was working alone in a field of Chinese white radish, called *luobo*. He picked a big one and stuffed it between his legs. When the woman supervisor came, Tuxedo Lin lay under a tree moaning. The woman commanded: 'Tuxedo, why are you resting there? Don't be lazy!' 'Help me, help me!' Tuxedo Lin called out to the woman while holding that gigantic radish under his pants. 'Look at it here! I have a reverse *yang*.[2] I need help!' 'What can I do?' the woman superviser asked. Half opening his eyes, Tuxedo Lin said, 'Give me a massage there.' The woman, apparently embarrassed, hesitated for a moment and said to Tuxedo Lin, 'Why don't you just stay put and I will go to your house to get your wife. She should be able to help you better.' After she left, Tuxedo Lin laughed all the way to where the other team members were working and told them the story. They all had a hearty laugh that day.

"I don't interfere in these incidents as long as they pose no threat to public security, although I know that in cities any deviation from the normal marital relationship would be investigated by the police, and if proven, the offenders would be arrested and jailed. The only criminal man-woman relationships that I dealt with in my capacity as brigade security head involved either charges pressed by one of the related parties in a triangle relationship or rape. I can give you two examples to illustrate my point.

"The first case involved Thunderbolt Lin's widow, Xiulan. After her husband's death in 1970, Xiulan had liaisons with several village men. Around 1980, she developed a clandestine relationship with a village boy, Hou Qiang, the youngest brother of Hou Hannan, the unfortunate guy whose hand was cut off while serving in a labor reform camp. At that point she was already close to fifty years old, while the boy was not even twenty-five. This affair was very well concealed so that no other villager knew of it. Xiulan was living in the old house with her youngest daughter, A Mei, who was twenty-one then and worked in a factory in Jiangtou Town. Whenever A Mei had night shifts, Xiulan called the boy Hou Qiang over to sleep with her.

"One summer day in 1980 A Mei was working a night shift and rode to work on her bicycle in the late afternoon. Xiulan also decided to go to Xiamen City to visit her natal home. She left in such a haste that she forgot to inform Hou Qiang about her absence. Around midnight Hou Qiang sneaked into Xiulan's house as he had done before. The funny coincidence was that that night A Mei had a headache and decided to take the night off. When she returned home she found Hou Qiang hiding in her mother's room. A Mei screamed, and Hou Qiang fled.

"The neighbors came and reported the case to me. The next day when Xiulan returned home from Xiamen, the story of Hou Qiang hiding in her room the night before had spread all over the brigade. To save face, Xiulan came to see me and claimed that she wanted to press a charge against Hou Qiang for attempted rape of A Mei. What else could Hou Qiang be planning by entering her house, she asked. It was a convincing argument, at least superficially. But Xiulan didn't know that I had interrogated Hou Qiang earlier that morning and he made a full confession about the secret liaison he had with Xiulan.

"I took Xiulan to my office and gave her a lecture. I said how could she do such an immoral thing as entrapping a youngster like Hou Qiang? She was twice his age and already a grandmother to her son's children. If I passed her charge against Hou Qiang on to the commune public security office, Hou Qiang would probably be sent to a labor reform camp for five to ten years. Would Hou Qiang's long prison term ever bother her conscience? Would she ever be ashamed of her licentious behavior and her entrapment of a youngster? At first she pretended she didn't understand what I was talking about. She denied that she had been involved with Hou Qiang. But when I recited a few details about their relationship that Hou Qiang had related to me earlier, she began to sob and, finally, confessed to making a false charge.

"After I talked to Xiulan I called in Hou Qiang. By then he had also learned of the rape charge that Xiulan had pressed against him and was scared. I told him that Xiulan's charge was dropped. He was saved at least momentarily. But I wanted him to make a full confession to me as to how many other relationships he had with village women. You see, this Hou boy is tall and handsome. Many village women could be easily taken by him. He confessed that he had caressed eight girls and women before, but had sexual intercourse with only two, including Xiulan. I told him that he should be more careful in the future. If he was caught again, I would report him to the commune public security office.

"The second sex crime case I handled was also related to Thunderbolt Lin, this time his younger brother Lin Leshui, nicknamed Playboy for his indulgence in leisure activities such as gambling, drinking, women, and so on. When his brother Thunderbolt was still alive and was serving as brigade head, Playboy Lin had already begun to be presumptuous in the village. For a while he was after Witch Zhang's daughter. When she rebuffed his advances, Playboy Lin threatened to kill her entire family with the rifle and hand grenades that Thunderbolt kept for the local militia.

"I tolerated Playboy for a while when I had first assumed my post as the brigade security head. Thunderbolt had just died a few years before and I didn't want to be too harsh with his brother. So when Playboy's first sex crime was reported to me, I let it pass and didn't take any action. That case involved the wife of a village hoodlum named A Wai. This hoodlum became a drifter during the Cultural Revolution and left the village to live in Shanghai. A Wai was involved in several robbery and rape cases there. He was later arrested and sent to a labor reform camp in Qingliu County, western Fujian Province, for twenty years. His wife, a rather nice-looking woman, stays with her in-laws in Lin Village. One evening Playboy climbed into her room and tried to rape her. Her screams woke up her father-in-law, who came to her rescue and caught a glimpse of Playboy in the candlelight. When he came to report the case to me the next morning, I told him that there should be more witnesses for the charge. He was an old man, and he could have made a wrong identification because of his poor eyesight.

"Privately I warned Playboy to be more restrained in his flamboyant behavior. I had been protecting him only for the sake of his deceased brother, who enjoyed high esteem among villagers. If Playboy continued his misconduct, I would have to turn him over to the commune security office. He sneered at my remarks and just turned around and left. Privately, I was preparing for the worst, which did come two years later.

"There was a poor family living at the northern edge of the village. This family had a grandmother, her forty-year-old daughter-in-law, and a granddaughter about eighteen. The old woman's son died from cancer of the liver a few years earlier. Without a male adult laborer earning work points in their team, this family couldn't earn enough to feed themselves. It had been a local secret for several years that for RMB$5, a man could go to visit this family at night and sleep with the forty-year-old widow."

I was totally unprepared for this disclosure. From all the reading about China I had done in the West, the indication was that, after 1949, the government had completely eradicated prostitution. I decided to clear this up with Ye: "Are you saying that there is a prostitute even in this village? I thought all prostitution had been wiped out in China!"

"Ha!" Ye squawked, "that is what our government wants you to believe. There are prostitutes in every major city or town in China. It is true that the government takes very stern measures against prostitutes. There is a female labor reform camp in Qingliu County in western Fujian for arrested prostitutes. There are always seven to eight hundred prisoners there. Judging from the existence of this camp, it is clear that our government was never able to wipe out prostitution in China.

"In 1977, Playboy married a nice-looking girl from the neighboring village of Hongshan Brigade. The marriage apparently didn't change his bad habits a bit. One evening he was hanging around with several of his cronies, gambling and getting drunk. One guy made a remark about the village prostitute and Playboy claimed that he had never visited there before. Half drunk, he stood up and declared that he would go to visit that family.

"As he stumbled away, his friends thought that he was merely making up a pretext to go home and sleep with his wife. But Playboy didn't. He went to the house at the edge of the village, climbed over the wall, and sneaked into the room where he thought the woman was sleeping. He had gone to the wrong room, however. It was the little girl's room instead. When he tried to mount her, the girl screamed. Both the grandmother and widow came in and caught Playboy with his pants down. He was so drunk that he couldn't even run away when I was called over. There wasn't anything I could do but report the case to the commune office. Playboy was sentenced to the labor reform camp in Qingliu County for ten years.

"The funny thing about this case was that after Playboy's arrest, his wife stayed with her in-laws in Lin Village. In late 1984, after the breakup of the collective, she purchased a hand tractor and hired a young man to drive the tractor for her as a business. The tractor operator was from Tongan County and lived with her family. I was sure that there was more than just an employer-employee relationship between them. One day I called this tractor operator over and gave him my advice. I told him that he should be more discreet about his behavior while living in this village. If there should be anything wrong with him, I would have to report him to the commune office, which meant that he would most likely be sent to the labor reform camp in Qingliu County. I said that it would be very funny if he did end up there, for when he, the hoodlum A Wai, and Playboy got together and compared their crimes, Playboy would say that he was arrested for attempting to rape A Wai's wife while A Wai was in prison. The tractor operator would then say that he got into trouble because he had a relationship with Playboy's wife while Playboy was in prison. They could then call each other playmates for trying to sleep with the same set of women.

"For most of the minor sex crimes reported to me, I charged the offenders a fine. In addition, I also ordered the men involved to perform the public service of cleaning the village sewer ditches. Isn't this what they were doing when they made advances to other women? This kind of public humiliation is very effective in keeping the villagers in line.

"There were several men in this village who seemed to have an extremely strong urge to chase women. One was Black Barbarian, the man of Malaysian stock, and whose sister married Wu Ming. Black Barbarian had his own wife, who left him a long time ago. He claimed that he could perform Malaysian magic to solve problems, and many women went to see him when they had physical or family problems. Perhaps Black Barbarian did know some magic. I heard that he could read charms to put people to sleep. While the woman was under hypnosis, he made love to her. Sometimes he gave money to village girls to let him 'play' with them. Once a seventeen-year-old, skinny village girl was sick. When her parents took her to the commune hospital, she gave birth to a child. She didn't even know that she was pregnant. Later we found out that Black Barbarian had played with her a few times and gave her RMB$1 or $2 each time. I was furious about this incident and sent Black Barbarian to the commune prison for two years.

"Another village man, whose name I shouldn't tell you, was even worse. He made demands on his wife almost every night. Sometimes when he returned home from work while his wife was still cooking in the kitchen, he wanted to do it right on the kitchen floor. The poor woman always looked frail and tired. When she refused him, he became crazy. One evening their neighbors heard the woman crying and screaming and they sent for me to intervene. When I arrived I found their house locked. I called the man's name, but he refused to answer. I could hear him smashing bowls and dishes on the ground and banging benches and chairs against the wall. The woman was crying aloud. After a while the man dashed out of the house like a wounded bull. I didn't dare stop him. I rushed into his house and found the woman. I couldn't believe what I saw. To punish his wife for refusing him, the man had stuck a broken glass tube into her vagina, cutting her badly. She was bleeding and couldn't move. I had to call several men to carry her to the brigade clinic on a stretcher. My wife, Baozhu, had to remove the broken glass piece by piece with a pair of surgical forceps. I fined this man RMB$50, knowing that this would only restrain him for a couple of months.

"One major problem with my job as the brigade security head relates to my size. I am short and don't have much muscle. Most other adult men in this village could easily beat me up if they chose to do so. When I intervene in a fight or other domestic conflict, I have to act cautiously to prevent the fighting parties from directing their anger against me. Once a village woman had a fight with her mother-in-law. They both had sticks and were beating each other with all their strength. To stop them, I had to step in between them. When the first blow came I shielded my head with one arm. I was hit on the right elbow. When the second blow came from the opposite direction, I was too slow to react and was hit on the shoulder joint. The pain caused me to fall, and that scared these two women. They stopped their fighting immediately to look after me.

"Sometimes I have to act boldly in dealing with certain individuals. Around 1977, the government began to tighten up the number of children a peasant family could have. The new limit was two. I normally stayed aloof from family planning and birth control campaigns, for they should be handled by the head of the Women's League in the brigade. Only when a family disobeyed the birth regulation or refused to pay fines, I, the security head, would then become involved to enforce the laws. There was a family in the first team who had been unruly in the past. The family already had two children when the wife became pregnant again. Hou Lingli, the head of the Women's League, tried in vain to persuade the wife to have an abortion. I had no choice but to go over and take that woman by force to the commune hospital. When I arrived at their house the husband stopped me at the gate and refused to let me take his wife. He accused me of being selfish, for I had three children, all sons, while he had only two, both girls. He threatened that if I forcefully took his wife for an abortion, which meant that I would cut off his family's 'incense and fire,' he would seek revenge by killing me and my children and sever my family line too.

"Frankly, I was quite scared and didn't know what to do. I debated with myself for a while and decided that I couldn't let this kind of challenge go unanswered. It was a cold winter day. But I took off my jacket and replied, 'What do you want to do with me? You want to kill me? Come and fight first. I don't care about getting killed. If you should kill me, I would still have the entire Communist Party to back me up. My family and children would be taken care of by the Party. But if I should kill you, what would you have? A straw sheet to wrap up your corpse for burial like a dog! So, come over and have a fight, screw your mother's stinking vulva!'

"As I called out this challenge, I felt a burning sensation in my eyes and the sweat on my forehead. This guy probably never expected me to react so strongly. He didn't know what to do, so he just mumbled a few words and turned away. I walked past him into his house and took the woman out, without any further resistance. Sometimes you have to act in a rash and belligerent manner in dealing with villagers. This is called killing the cock to warn the monkeys (*shaji jinghou*), so they respect you."

Prosperous Years

8 Living conditions in Lin Village were frugal but adequate. I noticed, for instance, people in Lin Village all had shoes to wear in the winter. Clothing was made from sleazy cotton fabric, often with patches. But most people were well bundled up.

Villagers seemed to be well fed too. They ate three meals a day. Breakfast consisted of rice congee as the staple with a couple of side dishes of vegetables and dried fish or bean curd. Dinner was light too and was quite similar to breakfast. The major meal of the day was lunch, consisting of steamed dried rice, of which most village adults could gulp down three or four large bowlsful in a meal, several dishes of garden fresh vegetables, and the main dish of meat or fish. The diet seemed to be rich in carbohydrates and low in protein, but the villagers had other ways to make up the deficiency. Poultry and eggs were consumed in large quantities during special occasions, such as wedding banquets, seasonal festivals, and religious ceremonies, which occurred at regular intervals.

One of these folk rituals is popular in southern China. Villagers in Lin Brigade worshipped the wandering ghosts, called Lords of the Outer Gate (*menkou gong*), on the first and fifteenth days of the lunar month. On those days, most housewives purchased an additional quantity of meat or fish, or slaughtered a chicken or a duck from the flock, in order to prepare four or five dishes as sacrifice. At noon, the cooked food would be placed on a long wooden bench at the front gate of the house facing the street. The housewife lit two sticks of incense to propitiate the wandering ghosts who had to be placated with food, but who also had to be carefully kept outside the family gate. When the incense was about finished, the housewife burnt a few pieces of spirit money to send off the ghosts. The dishes would then be brought in to the dining table where family members were waiting eagerly.

Children in Lin Village appeared to be healthy. Most of them have round and pink cheeks and well-formed bodies. Promotion of public health and preventive medicine by the government over the years seemed to have paid off well: Communicable diseases such as polio, tuberculosis, typhoid fever, smallpox, and measles had all been eradicated among the younger generations. I saw only an eleven-year-old boy who limped around. Upon inquiry I found out that he had contracted polio as an infant because his mother failed to take him to the brigade clinic for his polio vaccine.

The social atmosphere in Lin Village was generally relax and congenial. Whenever several village adult men got together, they talked about how and where to make money. They compared notes on where to borrow money for investment in a family trade, or the latest exchange rate between the local currency against Hong Kong or U.S. dollars or Japanese yen. They were also well informed on the availability and costs of special consumer goods in Xiamen City's major department stores, such as color television sets, stereo systems, refrigerators, and motorcycles. Whenever a village family purchased one of these highly desired durable goods, it would instantly become a topic of gossip among villagers. They all knew where the purchase was made and how much it cost. They would also compare this purchase with a similar one made previously, and comment on the business acumen of the new owner. In a closely knit community, villagers seemed to be well informed about others' activities and income levels, and were eager to compete with one another in their ability to improve living conditions.

Like peasants elsewhere, successful young men in Lin Village also engaged in conspicuous consumption. Despite the official egalitarian doctrine, the villagers were highly status conscious. One major status symbol was cigarettes that villagers smoked and treated their guests to during household visits or social gatherings. The highest rank went to villagers who could afford genuine imported American or British brands, such as Kent, Marlboro, 555, and Winston. At about RMB$4.50 (or U.S.$1.50) per pack, the equivalent of a well-paid adult laborer's daily wage, the three or four villagers who could afford such luxuries were in their early thirties, and were definitely the village business leaders. The second-tier consumers were those who smoked imported cigarettes made from tobacco from the United States but rolled and packaged in Hong Kong. The most popular brand, Good Companion, cost about RMB$2.25, half the price of the genuine imported brand, but still quite expensive. There were about two or three dozen villagers who fell into this category. Most of them were actively engaged in non-farm trades such as trucking and manufacturing. They were older than the first group, and were more conservative in their consumption habits. The rest of the village men used locally produced cigarettes that were relatively inexpensive, about RMB40–50 cents per pack. Those who belonged to this category were generally looked down upon by the first two groups as country bumpkins who had no taste for quality goods and who lacked the ability to improve their lot in life.

Beneath the surface of tense economic competition and a desire for self-aggrandizement, people in Lin Village also engaged in gracious mutual assistance that seemed to be handed down by custom. Thus when Hou Hannan had a wedding banquet for his first son in February 1985, after the Chinese New Year, I found Hopping Toad Wu and Lin Qishan—both considered village gourmet cooks—cooking in Hou's kitchen to help prepare the banquet for eight tables of guests. Despite the cool weather, both Hopping Toad Wu and Lin Qishan were sweating while frantically washing, chopping, and cooking the endless dishes under a canvas canopy temporarily set up in Hou's courtyard. I was not surprised to find Hopping Toad Wu there, for he was retired and had nothing else to do. Furthermore, working in the kitchen gave him the opportunity to "sample" good food and a few free drinks. But it was odd to see Lin Qishan, my landlord, there. He owned and drove a truck and made at least RMB$50 per day. To help at this banquet he had to forgo his daily income. I also knew that Lin didn't care much about Hou Hannan as a person at all. When I asked him the next day why he helped, he replied with a big grin that Hou Hannan's younger brother, Hou Tong, was a sworn brother of his.[1] While he didn't care much about helping Hou Hannan, he had to help because it was his sworn brother's nephew's wedding. This kind of mutual assistance, defined by traditional social ties, seemed to be quite common in Lin Village. I often found several village families, often related by blood or marriage ties, working together to harvest rice or build a new house.

In sharp contrast to this smooth and relaxed social life in Lin Village was the ever-present political apparatus and political control, which were in direct contradiction to the traditional Confucian ideologies of governance, including rural autonomy and a laissez-faire administration. Villagers were forced to participate constantly in political indoctrination or campaigns. The presence of a tightly controlled political system was best embodied in the ubiquitous loudspeakers. Those wired, shiny, cone-shaped loudspeakers were strategically installed not only in the village, but also in adjacent fields where villagers worked. There was no escape from the system. The control switch for the loudspeakers was in the brigade office, with a half-time electrician who not only switched it on and off according to schedule, but who also carried out necessary repair or maintenance work.

Every morning at six o'clock the broadcast began. It was a routine transmission of radio programs from Xiamen People's Radio Station, consisting mainly of military music, news briefs, and commentary, all in Mandarin, the official language. The program lasts for an hour. The next hour-long broadcast came at noon, again with music, news, and commentary. By dusk, the third hour-long dosage of political indoctrination was broadcast. Villagers generally ignored the broadcast, as if it didn't exist, except for using it to tell the time of day. Once in a while brigade officials used the loudspeakers to broadcast information that concerned the villagers: A movie would be shown in the primary school at eight o'clock that night; rationed rice or chemical fertilizer had arrived for villagers to purchase; it was time for truck and hand-tractor owners to pay their annual license fees immediately; the brigade health clinic had received forty dosages of encephalitis vaccine for infants, so all those under two should be innoculated immediately. Villagers heeded those broadcasts, for most of the content had direct bearing on their lives.

Symbolically, the loudspeaker system embodied political control in rural China in yet another manner: The peasants were the recipients of messages and instructions; they were to act accordingly, not to react. It was a one-way street, from top to bottom, not vice versa.

I had mixed feelings about village life and development in China. On the one hand I was impressed by the progress being made in rural China in comparison with other developing nations. It seemed that villagers, as far as I could see, were provided with basic necessities, such as food rations, health care, and elementary education. The other side of the coin, however, was the ever-present political control, ideological regimentation, and coerced conformity to whatever Party lines were in command. It seemed to be a stiff price to pay for the material improvements the villagers enjoyed.

I expressed my observation and thoughts to Ye on an afternoon in May when he came to chat with me in my flat. He responded with laughter, "Even though you are a professor, I must say that you have missed many important observations about China."

"What do you mean by that?" I protested, feeling that Ye was deliberately trying to put me down.

"For one thing," he replied, "if you think that today's political control is tight, you haven't seen the real thing yet. You have never experienced a political campaign in China. Imagine the village loudspeakers broadcasting Chairman Mao's quotations from morning until night, non-stop, without music. Or villagers asked to repeat sentences from the little red book in public rallies, never understanding the meaning in the first place. Imagine an order from higher authorities that all village Party cadres must have regular political meetings one afternoon each week to study policy announcements or writings of Marx, Lenin, or Chairman Mao. Compared with political controls of the 1950s or 1960s, there are none today."

"Granted, I underestimated political control in China in the past," I insisted, "but I must say that living conditions here are probably much better than what one might see in India or in Africa. To me, this seems to be directly related to the tightly controlled but highly efficient administrative system that one finds in China. The fundamental contradiction then is between economic development and human liberty. In order to achieve quick development, sometimes citizens of less-developed countries, such as China, may have to forgo some of their individual freedom. The problem I weigh is how to draw the delicate balance between collective interests and individual freedom."

Ye looked at me wearily. "I don't know anything about India or Africa, nor do I know where you have picked up this great idea about the conflict between economic development and liberty. The only thing I know is based on my personal experience, and it seems to run counter to what you said. The more political controls imposed on the peasants, the less they want to work. On the other hand, when the national government shed itself of most controls in the countryside and gave peasants more free choice, they responded with greater enthusiasm and higher production. This may not be true for all of China. But in Lin Brigade, at least, as far as I can tell, it was only in the 1970s, when people realized the absurdity of political campaigns in the countryside and stopped cutting each other's throats, and when the national policy became more flexible toward peasants, that we were able to achieve genuine development. If you don't realize this point, you will never be able to understand current agrarian reform, either at the national level or in this village."

"How did this change evolve?" I asked. "Gradually or overnight? Was it initiated by the central government or at the local level?"

"Nothing is initiated by local authorities," Ye stated emphatically. "Everything has to come from the top. Policy statements issued from the central steering committee of the Party will gradually trickle down to the bottom. That is why every cadre has to read very carefully the commentary in the *People's Daily* in order to understand future directives. Ever since the reinstating of Deng Xiaoping to power in 1973, we have known that the frenetic political campaigns of the past would be over.

"The most significant development was certainly the change in local-level administrations. The Dengist policy of rural reform was to push aside those old cadres who, despite their long Party membership, were basically the last vestige of past revolutions. To promote pragmatism and local initiatives, Deng first changed leading cadres at both commune and brigade levels. In late 1975, at the direction of the commune Party committee, there was a big shuffle in brigade leadership in Lin Village. Opium Hong, who had been the brigade Party secretary for about fifteen years, was promoted from 'rural cadre' (*nongcun ganbu*) status to 'national cadre' (*guojia ganbu*). The removal of Opium Hong from the brigade administration signaled a major change in brigade politics. There was nothing wrong with Hong, but he was illiterate, even though he was a faithful follower of Party lines. He was incompetent and probably never understood what Communism is, nor did he know how to take any initiative in promoting development. He could never carry out the reforms launched by Deng after 1978."

I was confused by the terms rural cadre and national cadre and wanted a clarification. "What exactly is the distinction between a rural cadre and a national cadre? How come in one breath you said that Hong was 'promoted' to national cadre, and then you sound as though he was demoted when he was removed as brigade secretary?"

Ye seemed to be unprepared for my question about something that must have been a truism to him, and appeared to be puzzled for a moment. Then he seemed to realize my "ignorance" of China, and addressed my questions slowly. "A rural cadre is an official appointed by the Party to serve in the local office of his native home community, where he relies chiefly on local revenue for his income. A rural cadre has very little opportunity to be transferred out of his native home to another place. On the other hand, a national cadre is one who belongs to the national bureaucracy and whose assignment is determined by the central government. He draws his salary from the national treasury rather than from local revenue. A national cadre may also be transferred from one job to another, or from one place to another. This kind of transfer means he can change his household registration to the city if he is assigned to a job in the city. When a national cadre retires, he receives retirement pension from the government—a benefit not enjoyed by the rural cadre."

"It seems to me then that what happened to Hong was definitely a promotion when he became a national cadre," I commented. "But why do you seem to indicate otherwise?"

"It really depends on your perspective," Ye conceded. "For personal security considerations, most rural cadres opt to become national cadres and consider it a promotion. But this may not be true for personal career considerations. A national cadre may sound prestigious, but there are also many dead-end jobs in the national bureaucracy. A rural cadre serving as brigade Party secretary commands a few hundred people. He is the de facto ruler of the brigade. But a national cadre may have only a dozen street sweepers under his command. So the division between a national cadre and a rural cadre is not as clear-cut in prestige and power as it appears."

"Is there a distinction made between what positions belong to rural cadres and what belong to national cadres?" I asked.

"Yes," Ye confirmed. "In the countryside the division between rural cadre and national cadre generally follows administration levels. Cadres at the brigade and team levels are rural cadres. Cadres above brigade at the commune and county levels are national cadres. One common practice of our Party to reward a loyal leading cadre in a brigade, normally the brigade branch Party secretary, is to promote this person to a post in the commune, thus making him a national cadre. In the old days this promotion from rural to national cadre was considered a great honor to the recipient—recognition by the Party of one's work, plus job security and retirement benefits.

"Opium Hong was assigned to become Party secretary of the commune-run brick factory in Hilltop Village. Since Hilltop Village is only about ten minutes' bicycle ride from his house, Opium Hong commutes to work and maintains his household registration in Lin Village.

"Dark Skin Lin, the brigade head since 1968, was promoted to brigade Party secretary in 1975. Early that year I was promoted by Opium Hong from brigade clerk to brigade public security head. When Dark Skin Lin was appointed the new brigade Party secretary at the end of 1975, there was a vacancy in his former post of brigade head. I thought for a while that I might be promoted again to become the new brigade head because of my long-term Party membership and because of my high school education. But to my disappointment I was bypassed, probably due to my stigma as a participant in the Four Cleanups and Socialist Education Campaign. There were still sporadic anti-revisionist campaigns at the national level that year to prevent the implementation of Deng Xiaoping's policies. As a follower of Liu Shaoqi's revisionist line, I was probably still considered unreliable for the brigade head post. A village Party cadre, Li Dehai, who was forty-seven years old then and had a primary school education, was appointed brigade head.

"Li Dehai was a dour, humorless wimp. On the surface you might think he was nice and friendly because of his soft-spoken, sleek manner. But inside, he was a spineless bastard. Whenever a villager came to ask him a favor, he would promise it immediately without considering the long- or short-term consequences. He probably thought this would be the best way to gain popularity in the village. When he failed to deliver these promises, he would tell the villagers that it was the other brigade cadres who refused to go along with his decisions.

"The worst thing Li Dehai did was the way he handled internal conflicts in this brigade. When one of the two conflicting parties came to him and asked for his support, he would agree with him completely. But then when the opposite side came, Li Dehai would immediately turn around and agree with it. His false support for both parties often led to further aggravation of the situation, for each side would assume that the brigade administration was behind it. Maybe deep down he enjoyed watching these conflicts from behind the scenes. A sense of self-importance probably inflated his otherwise weightless and meaningless ego. For the other Party cadres, it was always an enormously difficult task to clear up the mess created by Li Dehai. Soon after his appointment as brigade head the villagers began to call him 'Double-Headed Snake' for his treacherous, capricious character."

I had dealt with Li a number of times and my impression of him fit well with Ye's description.

Ye continued, "To some extent you could say that Double-Headed Snake Li represents the typical Chinese peasant: short-sighted and self-centered, only interested in immediate personal gain. Li simply couldn't raise his vision beyond the narrow horizon of himself, his family, and his close kin. Not that he is dumb. Actually he is probably one of the smartest or, perhaps I should say, shrewdest persons in our village, always manipulating for personal petty gain at the expense of others. When we, the brigade officials, dealt with brigade issues and discussed their long- versus short-term effects, or personal versus collective interests, Double-Headed Snake always sat there listening without any opinion or expression. Deep in his heart he must have been thinking how stupid we were for wasting our time worrying about other people's business.

"In the meantime the situation in the countryside improved continuously. The arrest of the 'Gang of Four' in 1976 put an end to the remnants of the Cultural Revolution era. Some of the old pragmatic cadres who were repudiated during the Cultural Revolution began to return to their old posts quietly. I was pleased to find out that the newly appointed commune Party secretary, the deputy commune Party secretary, the commune head, and directors of several offices at the Rural District were my teammates or good friends during the Four Cleanups campaign. If these people had a chance for a comeback, I should have mine too.

"The restoration of these old cadres also brought more flexible policies back to the countryside. Brigades were given more autonomy in planning their own economic activities, such as the right to set up small-scale enterprises or to grow more cash crops for market after fulfilling government procurement quotas. More rural free markets were set up for peasants to sell their surplus produce. Our brigade purchased the first hand tractor in 1975. Instead of using it to plow the field, we used it as a transportation vehicle by attaching a cart to it for hauling goods. This hand tractor was so profitable that in 1978 the brigade decided to purchase a second-hand Liberation brand (*jiefang pai*) truck to expand our transportation team."

The Strategy of Prosperity

"My opportunity finally came in early 1978 when Dark Skin Lin was elevated to national cadre and was assigned to the post of Party secretary of the commune's Water Works Office. Whether Dark Skin Lin's new job could be considered a promotion is hard to say, just like what had happened to Opium Hong three years earlier. The commune's Water Works Office is in charge of the reservoir between Lin Village and Hilltop Village. He has less than half a dozen people under his command. He told me that the main things he does every day in his office is sip tea and read newspapers.

"I was nominated by the commune Party to fill the brigade Party secretary position vacated by Dark Skin Lin, bypassing Li Dehai. There was no opposition to my nomination at the commune level, for by then most of the key people in the commune's Party were my associates from the Four Cleanups period. My old post, head of the brigade militia, was passed on to Lin Qifa, a cadre from the Lin group. Lin Qifa is a righteous, firm person. Even though he has had only a primary school education, he is respected by most villagers. Another asset Lin Qifa has is that his wife is Thunderbolt Lin's younger sister, which gives him more prestige in this village.

"After I took over my new assignment as brigade Party secretary in March 1978, I visited the commune Party cadres to sell my reform ideas. I told them that the only way to motivate people to work is to make them see clearly that they have a share in their work. I asked for the commune's approval to conduct two experiments in my brigade. The first was a free election at the team level. All five team heads in this brigade would be elected by working team members on a one-man, one-vote basis. Since everyone in a team would have the right to vote, he should also have the right to be elected as team head or deputy team head. To implement this free-election system, I asked permission from the commune to drop two previous regulations involving team head selections. The first one was that team heads be appointed from the top: the candidates be nominated by the brigade Party branch and then be approved by the commune Party organ. The election should allow for the team heads to be decided by team members, not by somebody at the top. The second regulation to be dropped was that only Party members could be elected as team heads. There was no reason to believe that qualifications or ability to run a team were limited to Party members. The Chinese Communist Party used the term 'democratic centralism' (*minzhu jizhongzhi*) to describe decision-making procedures in China. But in the past there was more centralism than democracy. Election at the team level would tip the balance, allowing more democracy in the countryside.

"The second experiment I proposed was a bonus system. I suggested that future team heads be authorized to keep a certain percentage of the surplus from the team's production as a bonus. The team head used his discretion to reward hardworking team members with this bonus. Only by controlling this economic leverage could the team heads promote production in their teams.

"I argued persistently with the commune-level cadres to convince them of the practicality of my suggestions. I pointed out one fact to the commune cadres: 'The peasants have been cursing our Communist Party for years for bringing an incompetent administration to the countryside. If we continue to appoint team heads to run the teams, the peasants can always criticize us for all the problems they encounter. If they elect their own heads, then they will have only themselves to blame if production goes wrong.' Reluctantly my superiors agreed to let me try my ideas. In June 1978, after the first rice crop harvest, I announced these experiments in my brigade and ran the first election. The result was amazing. Whereas before the election, all five team heads in this brigade were Communist Party members appointed from the top, the election replaced all of them with non-Communists.

"I was not troubled by the results. Actually, the development was natural. The fundamental problem in the countryside is the Communist Party itself. When the Party recruits members, it picks people who are loyal, obedient, and unimaginative. These people are considered safe, for they have little personal ambition and only know how to follow Party directives carefully. But in a new situation when personal initiative and creativity are needed, these old cadres just can't adjust. So they must be replaced.

"Take the former head of the first team, a Wang, as an example. A veteran who returned to our village in 1975, he was appointed head of the first team for three years. While he was team head, their production level hardly improved. The only thing this fellow knew was to brag about how important he was in the army. He told his teammates that if he had stayed in the army he would eventually have become a battalion commander. During the 1978 election, you know how many votes he received? Zero! Even his wife and brother, who both worked in his team and voted, didn't vote for him. He came to protest to me, claiming that the election was flawed. For a person as important as he was, he should be leading the brigade, not just the team.

"I couldn't help but ridicule him. 'You think you are important, ha! Explain one thing: Why, after three years as team head, has not even a single person in your team voted for you? Are they so stupid that they allow a great guy like you to be bypassed? How come even your wife and brother didn't vote for you? If there is an election in your family, you will probably not even be elected as family head. My suggestion to you is to go home and work hard in your family. If you have the solid support of your own family, maybe next year you will be re-elected team head.'

"When I reported the election results to the commune, I was immediately reprimanded by the commune Party secretary. He said. 'Your reckless act is jeopardizing the future of our Party. Your election cost us five team head positions. What do you think we are now? We have become the opposition party in the countryside!' I was asked to evaluate my actions during that meeting. But I was not discouraged. I didn't care about offending one or two cadres, as long as what I did could benefit the majority of the brigade. I told the commune Party committee that I had just begun this election system in my brigade. If the commune administration wanted me to revert back to the old system, it would have to wait until the following year. The commune Party secretary grudgingly accepted my suggestion and warned me not be so audacious in the future. Should there be any sudden political changes, I would be sacked for my bold actions.

"By December of 1978, the national Party had its Third Plenum of the Eleventh Party Congress. During that meeting the new rural-reform policy was discussed and approved by the central government. The reform policy called for the return of more production and administrative power back to the lower collective units. My experiments in Lin Village turned out to be in line with the new policy. When the announcement of policy change was made, the commune Party secretary congratulated me for having saved my skin this time. But I was undaunted and determined to push for more changes in my brigade.

"The presence of non-Party team heads required adjustments in the brigade-level administration. In the past, things were much simpler: All team heads and brigade-level officials were Party members. When we had our regular brigade Party branch meetings, once every month, we also discussed issues involving brigade and team administration. The presence of non-Party team heads after the election forced us to change the decision-making format. What I did was to preserve the regular Party meeting, during which we, the Party members, discussed the main issues concerning the Party first, then the brigade and team administration. After we had come up with some basic understanding and completed the Party meeting, we called the team heads to join us. This was called the 'Expanded Cadres' Meeting' (*kuogan huiyi*), a forum in which Party cadres and non-Party officials gathered together to discuss and decide important issues that confront the entire brigade.

"This new system has worked quite well. These new team heads regard themselves as representatives of the common citizens (*laobaixing*), and argue forcefully from that perspective. This is in sharp contrast to the other Party cadres, who care more about following directives from their superiors and not breaching Party discipline when they express reservations about new orders. The feisty mood of these new team heads really opened the eyes of the cadres. After seeing how these new team heads act and how they argue in meetings, the other Party cadres began to act more independently and creatively. As a result, this entire brigade began to act more aggressively in diversifying our production.

"After the first election in 1978, I gathered these five new team heads together and encouraged them to invest in new activities. I told them that the small amount of credit needed for investments could be arranged through the brigade treasury. For large sums of capital, I would go to the commune's Cooperative Credit Association or the China Agricultural Bank for loans. Besides these two channels, I could also raise funds by borrowing money without interest from other government enterprises, such as the city's construction company or the food-rationing cooperative, which normally have large sums of operating capital that sit idly in their bank accounts.

"The first person to react positively was the head of the fifth team, Hou Tong, the younger brother of Hou Hannan, the one whose hand was severed in the labor reform camp. What Hou Tong did was to convince his teammates to invest 18 percent of the team's annual income in a sand brick factory for his team. This kind of sand brick was easy to make, needing only coal dust, plaster, water, and sand to mix together. Coal dust was purchased from Xinglin Electricity Company, which burns coal to generate power. Plaster was purchased from Longyan County in western Fujian Province and hauled over by trucks. Both of these two ingredients were relatively inexpensive, especially in the early days when demand was low. Even cheaper was sand. It could be hauled from along the island's coast. The only expense was transportation.

"The ingredients are poured into a tank, mixed with water at fixed proportions, and ground by an electric grinder into a fine mixture. This mixture is then pounded into rectangular or square molds with shovels and hardened using an electric hammer, operated by female workers. These half-wet bricks are then sun dried for forty days until they become as hard as cement blocks. This sand-brick factory, when completed in 1979, was one of the first two such facilities on the entire island. It was the time when government policy was relaxed and many new construction businesses were started in Xiamen City. Demand for construction material was soaring. Hou Tong's team made a lot of money from this investment. Many young boys and girls in his team began to work full-time in this factory. In order to ship large quantities of bricks from Lin Village to the customers, Hou Tong invested in a truck and several hand tractors. Many young adults in that team were assigned to work full-time in transporting the brick rather than going to the field.

"Seeing the quick success of Hou Tong's sand brick factory, other teams began to imitate it. By the end of 1979, the first, second, and third teams built their own sand brick factories. The brigade administration also set up a sand brick factory in 1980 as a brigade-owned enterprise. From 1978 to 1980, the total volume of our brigade's net production profit doubled. Our brigade surpassed Hecu in 1980 to become the highest-income unit among all eighteen brigades in this commune. It was also in 1980 that Lin Village replaced Huang Brigade in all of Xiamen Island to become the model brigade open to domestic and foreign visitors who wanted to see a successful village in China's new modernization drive.

"In early 1980 the commune administration launched a contest for its eighteen brigades. The campaign was to increase net grain production and monetary value by at least 20 percent, and to decrease the birthrate to twenty-five per thousand that year. The slogan designed by the commune leadership was 'Two Ups, One Down' (*erzeng, yijiang*). The grand prize was RMB$3,000 to the winning brigade.

"By the end of that year, only my brigade achieved above 20 percent growth rate in both grain output and cash return. When I sent Lin Qifa, the brigade security head, to the commune office for the cash award, the commune Party secretary refused to give it to him. I was furious when I heard this and went immediately by truck to commune headquarters. Do you know the excuse the commune Party secretary used? He said that even though my brigade had achieved increases in grain output and cash earning above the prize-winning criteria, our birthrate didn't go down to the required twenty-five per thousand. The birthrate in our brigade was twenty-nine per thousand that year. I argued with him by pointing out that even though our birthrate didn't go down as far as required, my brigade was still the best in the other two areas. If there was an award for those achievements, my brigade was entitled to it. He laughed and said that since no brigade had accomplished all three requirements there would be no award for the year. The commune administration could just save the money for other uses, he said. I was very angry and called him all sorts of names for cheating us all. He apparently was amused and said that I should be more careful with my language. He said I had 'iron teeth' (*tiechi*), meaning that I talked too loudly and too firmly before I understood something completely. He said that my way of doing things would be all right under the current policy, which was rather flexible. Had I acted in this manner five or ten years earlier, I would have been in real political trouble. I knew that he was giving me good advice, for I had known him since 1964 when we were in the same training session for the Four Cleanups Campaign. As my classmate (*tongxue*) he would do his best to protect my position.

"The increase in production in Lin Village during my reign has been phenomenal. In 1978, when I first took over as Party secretary, the total annual output of our brigade was close to RMB$300,000. In 1984, the last year before the breakup of this brigade, we had a total output of RMB$2,000,000. A six-fold increase in seven years! It is no wonder that this brigade has led over other brigades in this commune in per capita income since 1980."

"Now, in retrospect," I interrupted his monologue, "what has been the secret of your success? Or, to put it in another way, what factors contributed to the phenomenal growth of Lin Brigade during the past six or seven years?"

"What has been the secret of our success?" Ye echoed my question. "Some people may think that as a showcase brigade open to outsiders, our village must have received substantial subsidies from the commune, the Rural District, or even Xiamen City, just like Dazhai Brigade in north China during the Cultural Revolution. I am sure that by now you have learned that this is utterly untrue. The only subsidy our brigade receives is RMB$30 per month from the commune as entertainment fees (*jiaoji fei*) to entertain visitors. RMB$30 per month! What is that amount of money good for? It only buys ten packs of imported Good Companion cigarettes for us to use to entertain visitors. Our actual expenses from the brigade coffer for entertainment are close to RMB$300 per month.

"Speaking of subsidies to local communities, I have a lot of complaints about our government. In 1982 the rural district's director of education came to visit our brigade. I used this opportunity to ask him for funds to build a cement courtyard for our primary school. I pointed out to him how the mud court in the school yard created problems; it was dusty on sunny days and muddy on rainy days. It was not good for our image as the model brigade in this district if we couldn't even afford to build a cement court. He was convinced and promised to allocate RMB$6,000 to our brigade to build a cement courtyard for the school. Because of his promise, I used brigade money to purchase cement and hire some village construction workers. After the completion of the courtyard I began to ask for the money from this fellow. He kept on delaying by saying that his office had run out of money that year. He promised he would include the sum in the next year's budget. You know what happened the next year? He was transferred to another post in the provincial government in Fuzhou City. When I asked the new director to pay the bills, he claimed that he didn't know anything about it and wouldn't honor his predecessor's promise. Our brigade ended up having to absorb all the expenses.

"This is why I often felt ambivalent about our model-brigade status. On the one hand, it is nice to be recognized for our success. We receive two or three groups of visitors each month, including foreigners like the Japanese Youth Delegation who came to visit us in October 1984. This recognition allowed me to be elected a representative to the city's assembly council and to the provincial people's congress in 1983. But on the other hand, this model-brigade status has also meant a drain of our manpower and resources. Aside from the cost of entertaining visitors, at least one or two brigade cadres have to sit around all the time in the brigade office to meet visitors, brief them, and show them around. The worst visitors are those from the central government or from the provincial government. Since these high-level cadres have power, they think they know everything. They come around to inspect everything we do here, and criticize us for whatever doesn't meet their standards or viewpoint. My strategy for dealing with these people is that I humbly tell them that I accept their criticism and will correct the situation according to their suggestions. But once they have gone, I would just ignore their demands."

"Still, you haven't told me what factors contributed to your success in the past few years," I gently reminded him.

"Oh, yes," Ye responded apologetically. "The reason for our brigade's success, I believe, can be summed up in an ancient Chinese saying: 'Appropriate heavenly timing, locational advantage, and harmonious human relations' (*tianshi, dili, renhe*). Let me explain each of these three conditions.

"Appropriate heavenly timing (*tianshi*) refers to the dramatic change in national rural policy after 1978. The commune Party secretary was correct when he said that I would be in real trouble had I made these changes a few years earlier. The two experiments I launched in my brigade—namely, electing non-Party members to team head positions and using bonuses to encourage production— would have been considered heresy during the Cultural Revolution or the Four Cleanups era. Frankly, I think Dark Skin Lin, my predecessor as brigade Party secretary, could have done equally well had he been given the opportunity to experiment with new ideas. But in those years when he was in power, our political climate was still dominated by the occasional blowing of Communistic wind (*gongchan feng*). Had he done what I am doing now, he could have been either overthrown or 'struggled' to death.

"My rise to brigade Party secretary was timed perfectly. As I have told you, a few months after I came to power, the Chinese Communist Party had its Third Plenum of the Eleventh Party Congress. The new policy approved in that meeting legitimized the experiments I had already launched in our village. History was completely turned around in that meeting, and my brigade was taking a lead over other brigades. That became the first condition of my brigade's success.

"The second condition for our success involved the strategic location (*dili*) of this village, about ten kilometers from downtown Xiamen. Our products can be shipped to the city easily with minimum transportation costs. That was one reason the city vegetable company selected us as a vegetable production area. Similarly, our advantageous location makes this an ideal place to manufacture bricks for city construction. Brick kilns in Longhai or Tongan counties may enjoy the advantage of easy access to raw materials essential for making sand bricks, such as sand, coal dust, and plaster. They even have lower labor costs than we do. But one thing they can never compete with is our proximity to the city. Reducing transportation costs by even one cent per brick makes a big difference when you consider a truckload of three or four thousand bricks per trip.

"Our close proximity to Xiamen City also allows us to respond quickly to new conditions there. When a city construction crew suddenly discovers that it needs an additional ten thousand bricks for a project, it will phone us and the bricks will be delivered within a day. In keeping our promises to customers well this brigade has established a good reputation among the city's construction offices. I have always considered long-term reputation more important than short-term profits. Many brigades in the city's suburbs mix good-quality bricks with substandard ones to cheat their customers. I won't allow our people to do this. If we have damaged bricks we sell them at a lower price and let the customers know in advance that these are damaged products. The mutual trust established with our customers has been crucial to our continued success even though now there are many brick kilns on this island that can sell for less."

Back-Door Connections

"The most important ingredient of our brigade's success," Ye continued, "has been the last condition, harmonious human relations (*renhe*). Social relations have two dimensions, one external and the other internal. External relations are chiefly my contacts with cadres whom I knew during the Four Cleanups. Many of these young activists are now in their forties and are in charge of middle-level offices in the city, the district, and the commune. Whenever I want to have something done or need a favor from them, I can always call on them for help. Of course I have to reciprocate (*huibao*) when they need my help. Our newspaper, the *People's Daily*, recently reported that backdoor connections among various government offices and among cadres have become so complex that they are now a subject for study in itself, called 'Connectology' (*guanxi xue*).[2] This is a very perceptive observation and a fitting term. Without proper connections, you can do nothing in China. Let me illustrate how these external social connections have been used in dealing with specific problems in our brigade.

"Take lumber as an example. The government sells us only two cubic meters of lumber per year through the commune's supplies cooperative. This is definitely insufficient for construction and furniture needs in our village, especially during the past four or five years when villagers have had more savings and wanted to build new houses. I worked out a scheme involving many of my old acquaintances to solve this problem. The first person I approached was a friend from the Four Cleanups days who now works as the brigade Party secretary in Mingxi County in western Fujian Province in the hills. His brigade has a lot of nice pinewood that they are required to sell to the government's purchasing office according to annual procurement programs. The people in his brigade, however, are allowed to use surplus wood produced above the quotas to build their own houses. When they build new houses, the second-hand lumber from old houses can be sold to people in other areas. I discussed with my friend, the Party secretary, the prospect of purchasing second-hand lumber from his people. As long as his brigade can rebuild their houses every three or four years rather than the usual twenty or thirty years, their second-hand lumber is not much different from original wood.

"After I made an agreement with him about purchasing used lumber from his brigade, I discussed with our township office using surplus wood for construction. The township administration had planned to build a new office building in Jiangtou Town, but had been delayed because of an insufficient supply of wood. I convinced them to establish a trading partnership with my brigade. Our brigade would provide the necessary connections to the wood supply, and the trucks to haul back the lumber. The commune office would secure all the necessary official documents for safe passage through the roadblock checkpoints and tariff offices set up by various local government offices. The commune office would also allow us to use its bank accounts to cable the funds to the brigade in the hills once the transaction was completed.

"We have gone to Mingxi County twice in the past two years to purchase two truckloads of wood each time. Both trips have been successful. The lumber hauled back was divided equally between our brigade and the commune office. We paid around RMB$350 per cubic meter for the wood in Mingxi. The cost for shipping is about RMB$100 per cubic meter, which includes gasoline for the truck, wages to the driver and loading workers, and gifts to the checkpoint inspectors. A truckload is about fifteen cubic meters. Once our share of fifteen cubic meters of lumber was back in the village, I rationed it to villagers according to their needs. Those building a new house or those bringing in a wife to live with the family and needing wooden boards to make new beds would have the highest priority in purchase. I sold them for RMB$585 per cubic meter, so that the brigade made about $100 for each cubic meter of lumber sold. That price was still much cheaper than the free-market price of RMB$850 per cubic meter in 1984. For each truckload of lumber sold, the brigade earned RMB$1,500.

"The entire operation was completely legal. I am not stupid enough to do things against Party discipline. We did use certain personal connections and loopholes in the current regulations in our operation. But I was not afraid because I was not doing it for my personal benefit. All profits from the wood transition have gone into the brigade coffer. I didn't monopolize the wood for my personal use, either. It was true that from the second trip I kept seven cubic meters of wood out of the fifteen for my discretionary use. But I didn't use it for myself. I allocated one cubic meter each to my two younger brothers who had just gotten married and needed wood to build furniture. Another cubic meter went to my mother-in-law, that is, Baozhu's mother, in Mudhole Village. The fourth cubic meter went to my third brother's father-in-law, who lives in this village and was building a house. My sister's family and my next-door neighbor Lin Chenghu, whose nickname is Tiger and whose grandmother is my grandmother's sister, split another cubic meter for bedding boards. I kept two cubic meters for my own house. At that point I was thinking about dividing up the old family and building my own house. I didn't think there was anything illegal in my scheme. I could do it because I had all the proper connections.

"I can give you another example of the importance of proper social relationships in making our brigade successful. This example is one you can still see in Xiamen today. When Xiamen City tried to improve the chaotic traffic situation in the downtown area in early 1985, the city's Traffic Control Office came up with a plan of building steel fences along both sides of the main thoroughfares in the downtown area. Because of these steel fences, pedestrians could no longer cross the streets where they wanted to. There were designated crossing zones with openings in the steel fence, avoiding the problem of jaywalking.

"The city approved this project and asked the Traffic Control Office to build these steel fences. I happened to know the deputy director of the Traffic Control Office, an old friend from the Four Cleanups days. I convinced him that our brigade workers had the expertise to do a good job with minimum costs. In my dealings with him I found out that the supplies cooperative in the Traffic Control Office had been short of imported cigarettes. Since I know the manager of the import store in the Special Economic Zone, whose store has the authority to import cigarettes with low custom duties, I arranged to have the Traffic Control Office purchase a large quantity of imported cigarettes from that import store. I don't consider this bribery. None of us was taking graft in this deal. We were doing it for the benefit of our collectives. I was merely using my connections to set up trading relationships for two parties who otherwise would not be able to deal directly. In doing so my brigade received the contract to build the steel fence for the city.

"Even though harmonious social relationships (*renhe*) are important in dealing with outsiders, it is equally important to maintain harmonious social relationships within the brigade. My appointment as brigade Party secretary has reduced internal factional rivalries in our village. I was not in alliance with either the Lins or the non-Lins. I can relate to the Lins through my grandmother, and I can relate to the non-Lins through my grandfather. Furthermore, the neutral position I took during the Cultural Revolution made me acceptable to both the Wu brothers and Thunderbolt Lin's group. Now that Thunderbolt Lin is gone, and the Wu brothers are fading away in retirement, tension in the village has been reduced dramatically. Younger generations look beyond past internal conflicts. In developing our brigade's new enterprises I am able to have the Wu brothers' sons and Thunderbolt Lin's younger brother sit in the same room and work out plans.

"Another factor that enhanced internal harmony in our village was the change in our national policy. In 1978, during the Third Plenum of the Eleventh Party Congress, the government decided to abolish all class labels. The division between rich and poor peasants based on their pre-Liberation economic status became meaningless. Not only did the government remove all class labels, it also announced the removal of all 'hats' (*maozi*) from previous class enemies, such as historical counter-revolutionaries and rightists. This act had tremendous impact in the countryside. One of the toughest points in the countryside since the Liberation has been the division of peasants into favored classes versus those condemned.

The social stigma attached to the 'bad elements' was so strong that those so labeled encountered seemingly insurmountable problems in their day-to-day lives. They were thus bitter, and refused to participate in social activities. On the other hand, the 'favored classes,' such as the tenants and outcasts, regarded themselves as legitimate rulers of the countryside and abused their power against others.

"Let's take Lin Da as an example. After his classification was changed from 'middle peasant' to 'rich peasant' at the instigation of his brother Lin Shan during the Four Cleanups campaign in 1964, he immediately faced real hardships. During struggle sessions in a political campaign, he would be called up to the stage to be attacked along with other rich peasants. He would be assigned to carry out village menial work as punishment. His sons were not allowed to join the military. Worse yet, people treated him like a person with leprosy. His old friends and kinsmen wouldn't step on his doorstep. In 1964, his first son was already married. But he still had three younger sons. After he was classified as a rich peasant, his three younger sons were in a sense sentenced to celibacy. Who wants to give a daughter to such a bad family? Lin Da developed an ulcer and stayed home all the time if he could. He was condemned and didn't want to interact with anyone. It was only after 1978 when his label of rich peasant was removed that he recovered from his illness and resurfaced. Then his second son was able to find a wife, even though he was already thirty-six years old. Now Lin Da still has two unmarried sons, both in their early thirties. He will have to work hard to save up enough money for these two sons' marriages now that they can find wives.

"With the elimination of class labels in the countryside, a major problem has been solved. Everyone is now on equal standing. There are no more divisive forces to tear them apart. I consider this policy, the abolishment of pre-Liberation class labels, the most important contribution our Party has made to the people of China. In 1982, when we transcribed the household registers from the old record books to the new ones, we eliminated all descriptions of class origins. In doing so, we erased the last vestige of past conflicts based on pre-Liberation divisions. New harmonious social relationships now flourish in Lin Village, making reforms possible.

"More important, this new harmonious social atmosphere in our village allows us to tap potential external connections the villagers have. We began to look at the entire brigade as a single entity and pooled together all usable connections villagers have in order to help us deal with our problems. Let me give you an example to illustrate this point. When we built sand brick plants in our brigade and established a fleet of hand tractors and trucks to deliver the bricks, we needed one crucial item: gasoline. The government rations thirty liters of gasoline to each truck per month. The gasoline can be purchased at government gasoline supply stations. Thirty liters of gasoline is sufficient for a truck to run for only two days, given the high intensity of work in our brigade. If we were to purchase additional gasoline in the free market at twice the government prices, we would be unable to make a profit from our bricks.

"It happens that Hou Lingli, head of our brigade's Women's League, has a husband who works at a suburban gasoline station. Her husband, a member of the Lin lineage, informs us whenever there is surplus gasoline at the end of each month or season in his station, and we can buy it without ration coupons at the government price. Also my friends in the commune office inform me if there is more than the normal quota of gasoline shipped to this area. I send our people over to get additional ration coupons before any other brigades have the chance to do so.

"To reciprocate for Hou Lingli's husband's gasoline, the brigade not only gives her, head of the Women's League, a steady monthly stipend, but she also has an additional job as treasurer of the brigade enterprise, which includes the sand brick kiln. Since her income is directly tied to the income of our brigade enterprise, there is every reason for her husband to seek an adequate supply of gasoline for us.

"Another important connection we have is a villager's son who is a veteran of the Liberation Army and has been working as a secretary in the Xiamen City mayor's office. Through this elderly gentleman we receive information from his son in the mayor's office about new developments in the city: new building codes for city construction that might affect the sale of our bricks, new zoning regulations that might affect our brigade's production plans, or new license permits for peasants to run certain enterprises. All the information can be used in the brigade's decisions on future investments, development of new business, or setting up production goals for our enterprises. Again, for this family's invaluable contribution to our brigade I gave the old man half a stockholder's share in the brigade-owned sand brick facility when it was contracted out to me in mid-1984. This half of a share allows the old man to draw dividends annually.

"The last example I can give you of our brigade-wide connections is from Li Dehai's family. Even though I dislike Li Dehai, the Double-Headed Snake, the brigade head since 1975, I found an important connection he has that is beneficial to our operation. Li's sister-in-law, that is, his brother's wife, is working in the commune's credit cooperative. She reviews all loan applications, and loans are critical to all our economic activities. When we built the new sand brick plant we borrowed money from this credit cooperative. When an individual peasant wants to build a new house or to purchase a hand tractor, he can borrow money from the cooperative at 0.7 percent monthly interest rate, or 8.4 percent annual interest rate. Because of her critical position, I gave Double-Headed Snake half of a stockholder's share in the sand brick facility in 1984.

"The first three or four years of the 1980s have been the best years of our brigade. There was one sand brick plant for each of the teams, except for the fourth team, which owns a traditional fire brick kiln, and another plant owned directly by the brigade. These five sand brick plants employ more than two

A village boy sitting in front of a sand brick factory

Two village youngsters working on a hand tractor

hundred village youth. Besides those directly working in the plants, the transportation of bricks also necessitated building a fleet of hand tractors and trucks. The brigade selected and financed young, capable people for driving school training. Once they finished their training and received drivers' licenses, they drove trucks or operated hand tractors for the collectives. Many villagers also work in loading and unloading the bricks for trucks and hand tractors.

"Besides our success with sand brick production the brigade administration also engages in many other new economic activities that have been financially beneficial to the villagers. We expanded the brigade machine shop in 1978 by adding machine tools. With this expanded facility we were able to repair agricultural machines and seek contract work in the city. The steel fences that we put up in Xiamen City's main thoroughfares in late 1984 were processed in this machine shop. At the peak of this shop's operation it hired more than two dozen villagers. In 1979 we also built an electroplating facility in the village. The goal was also to subcontract work from larger factories in the city to augment the villagers' income. This plant had not been very successful so far.

"The brigade also purchased an electric saw in 1979. This facility is also used for both village work and outside contract work. When Xiamen City's bicycle factory exported its products and needed wooden crates for bicycles, our brigade contracted to provide the crates. The most striking success in the brigade enterprise has been the construction team I set up in 1978. We started this facility to solicit construction contracts from offices in the city. When we learn that a unit in the city is putting up a new building, we estimate the need for raw materials, such as bricks, cement, and steel. Then we add labor costs and operating expenditures. Once the total costs are tabulated we approach the unit and submit our bid for the job. Since I know many middle-level cadres in the city, I often call on them for help. Once we receive the contract for a building project we put villagers to work. We then hire additional workers from Huian County for any remaining contract work. Sometimes we also subcontract part of the construction work to crews from Huian County, such as carpentry work or electrical work in the buildings.

"The wealth generated in our brigade in the early 1980s has been mainly from industrial and service work. The change is more than obvious. As I told you before, the total net output in our brigade in 1978 was close to RMB$300,000, with agriculture providing over 90 percent of all income. By 1984, total agricultural production remains about the same, but the output from industries and services has increased more than eightyfold. The total annual revenue for our brigade in 1984 was close to RMB$2,000,000. It was after 1980 that the villagers stopped eating sweet potatoes as their staple. We have finally eliminated hunger completely from our lives.

"As our brigade became increasingly prosperous in the early 1980s, I deliberately distributed the wealth evenly throughout the village by how I assigned work to villagers. Since working in brigade enterprises means higher income than working the land, I would select youngsters from poor families to work in factory jobs first. After these poor families were taken care of, I would then distribute jobs to other average families. We tried our best to give at least one non-farm job to each village family, so that everyone would benefit from the new prosperity. This principle had also been accepted by the teams when assigning jobs in the team sand brick factories. For older widowers or widows, or handicapped persons, there was light work in these new enterprises that we reserved for them. We paid them good wages to serve as night watchmen, water surveyors to check the irrigation ditches, or cattle attendants to watch the brigade's or team's cattle. The goal of Communism is to protect the weak and disadvantaged. I take pride in doing things that I thought were good for the general public in our brigade. It was the first time in our village history that we were able to share things in a harmonious atmosphere, rather than fighting each other."

The Breakup

9 The village temple in Lin Brigade worshipped (or *fushi*, 'served' in local dialect) three gods: the Holy Benevolent Emperor (*rensheng digong*), Lord Chi (*chifu wangye*), and Marshall Liu (*liufu yuanshuai*). These three were Lin Village's patron deities. Another local deity, Transient Lord (*xunxing wangye*), was worshipped not just by Lin Village, but included followers in Hecu, Hongshan, and Huangcu brigades. These villages formed a ritual circle and rotated this Transient Lord among them on a yearly basis.

Villagers had virtually no knowledge of the origins or history of these local patron deities. Nor did they know why they worshipped them other than the fact that these deities would extend their spiritual power to protect them. One thing the villagers knew for sure was the birthdays of these gods and held ritual celebrations in the temple on those occasions. Those dates were marked prominently on their annual activity schedules: the twenty-sixth day of the third lunar month for Holy Benevolent Emperor's birthday, the eighteenth of the sixth lunar month for Lord Chi, the fifteenth of the eighth lunar month for Marshall Liu, and the fourteenth of the tenth lunar month for Transient Lord.

On those days villagers brought sacrifices to the village temple for these honored patron gods. Traditional dishes included whole boiled pig heads, steamed rice cakes, whole chickens, fried fish, and various fruit. Prosperity in the countryside in recent years was also reflected in sacrificial offerings. Some well-to-do villagers used beer or imported liquor in place of traditional rice wine. They burned large quantities of incense and spirit money to propitiate the deities. Villagers, especially women and older people, meditated and prayed in front of the altar, asking for continued protection from the deities. Village truck and tractor drivers came with their small silk pouches, called incense pockets (*xiangdai*), which hung in their truck cab or were put under the driver's seat for protection. Using a ceramic spoon, they carefully scooped out ashes accumulated in the incense pot in front of the altar and stuffed them into the silk pouches to revitalize their power.

Ritual Celebration

Among these four local deities, the Holy Benevolent Emperor was the most important because he was the chief patron deity among the gods. His birthday marked the biggest celebration in Lin Village. A full month before this date, which in 1985 fell on May 16 of the solar calendar, the villagers began talking and planning for this event. There was concealed excitement and heightened tension in the air. Elderly Lin Fen, the village doctor of traditional medicine, explained the mood most eloquently: "Never before in our lives have we seen so much prosperity in this village. Bless the lords! We can only reciprocate all the favors the lords have given us with the most elaborate ritual celebration that we can afford!"

Several villagers who were involved in temple activities planned the festival for three consecutive days: May 14, 15, and 16. Besides individual celebrations at the temple, these temple activists also arranged events for the entire village during these three evenings. On May 14, a feature movie would be shown in front of the temple. Then, a traditional opera troupe would be hired to perform the following two evenings. To pay for all this, the temple would collect RMB$2 per head from each villager, RMB$10 for each hand tractor, and RMB$30 for each truck in the village. Since there were more than 1,000 villagers, 70 hand tractors, and 7 trucks, revenue should be more than RMB$3,000, sufficient to cover all expenses.

The temple activists divided the village into four sections, with one activist assigned to each section to collect the "taxes," as the local people called it, for the temple. Hopping Toad Wu's son Wu Hongen was sent to Jiaomei Town, about 30 kilometers southeast, to hire the opera troupe. He was given the assignment because his mother came from Jiaomei Town, and Wu Hongen had several maternal uncles living there. He went off on his motorcycle and successfully booked the opera troupe for two nights. Likewise, Lin Qifa, the village public security head, was asked to rent a movie from a movie theater in Xiamen City. He had had many dealings in Xiamen City, and thus knew where to rent the film.

I was quite excited about this event, for it gave me the opportunity to identify the village religious activists, to explore the villagers' attitudes toward supernatural phenomena, and to study their organization of traditional public events. For the entire month prior to this festival I was busy interviewing the temple activitists about temple history, their personal involvement, and their knowledge of traditional beliefs. I was so preoccupied with my work that I didn't talk with P.S. Ye as often as I had before.

In those few meetings I had with Ye I soon noticed his hostility toward this entire event. Whenever I mentioned Holy Benevolent Emperor or the preparations for his birthday celebration, Ye would abruptly change the subject. I found out that he did pay the RMB$10 temple taxes for the five people in his family. But he used his eldest son's name in the register for the contribution, instead of his own. Then I noticed the same kind of hostility among other brigade-level cadres too. For instance, Lin Qifa, who was to rent a movie for the first evening of the celebration, conveniently claimed that he had forgotten and insisted that it was too late to arrange a movie for that night. Wu Hongen was hurriedly sent off to Jiaomei Town to rearrange the opera troupe's performance. Luckily the opera troupe had no other engagement on May 14, and was able to come a day early for one additional evening performance.

A village truck was sent to Jiaomei Town on May 13 to bring back the opera troupe. When the truckload of thirty-some people, their musical instruments, and crates of paraphernalia arrived, it stirred instant excitement in the village. Children surrounded the vacant house assigned to the troupe as its temporary residence. I was told that the troupe was paid RMB$420 per night for three nights, plus two cartons of local brand cigarettes and one catty of vegetable oil. The vegetable oil was used to wash off their makeup after the performance.

In the meantime, Black Barbarian was paid RMB$50 to build a temporary stage in front of the village temple. With the help of a few youngsters Black Barbarian tied several long bamboo poles around and over the rectangular-shaped earthen stage for a makeshift frame. He then covered the top with canvas in case of rain, and hung special lights around it.

On the first day of the celebration the village was filled with an atmosphere of jovial festivity. All work in the village stopped. Housewives were busy cooking dishes for the sacrifice and for the evening banquets. Men washed themselves and put on clean shirts and trousers. Children were sent off to village stores to buy last-minute necessities, such as a bottle of soy sauce, a carton of cigarettes, firecrackers, spirit money and incense for sacrificial burning, and the like. Village daughters who had married out to other villages returned home with their husbands and children for the banquet. Guests invited by village men for this event included their former schoolmates, comrades in military service, or business associates.

At seven o'clock that evening, I decided to go to the temple to watch activities there. It was still early, for the show wouldn't start until eight. But I thought I might be able to take photos and interview a few people there. On the way I met P.S. Ye and asked him, "Would you like to go to the temple tonight for the opera?"

"No, I am not interested," he replied harshly.

So I ignored him and followed the path to the temple yard. There, I was surprised by the number of people already gathered. There must have been more than half the villagers there. And still more were coming, carrying long wooden benches or bamboo chairs. Many vendors, probably from surrounding villages, had gathered at the other side of the temple square to sell their merchandise. Sugarcane, popsicles (called ice sticks locally), candy, bottled soft drinks, boiled peanuts, and cigarettes were hot-selling items.

A village family signaled to me and said they had an extra bench. I would be needing it, they told me, for the show would last from eight in the evening until two in the morning. I thanked them, pulled the bench under a tree, and settled myself there.

I was concentrating on making adjustments to my camera when suddenly I noticed that the crowd was growing quiet. I looked up and saw the dark silhouette of P.S. Ye walking directly toward me. He nodded at me in silence and sat quietly next to me without another word. The crowd was quiet, all gazing at Ye with curiosity, and they seemed uncertain how to react to this situation. Ding Yong, who was P.S. Ye's classmate in both primary and junior high schools and an old friend, approached with a forced, light-hearted comment. "Look who's here! Comrade Ye, this must be the closest you have been to the village temple!" While he talked he passed a cigarette to Ye.

Ye accepted the cigarette, and the act seemed to have softened the tense atmosphere. He replied sternly, "Yes, indeed, this is the first time I have come to the temple square. I am here mainly because Professor Huang is here. He is our village's honorable guest. As the responsible person of this village, I must accompany him for at least the first night of this ceremony."

To ease the tension I asked Ding Yong, "What's the name of the show tonight?"

"The Heroine Who Went to the Battlefield for Her Father," Ding replied. He explained to us the plot of the show. Even though I knew what this historical story was about, I let Ding continue his narration to divert people's attention from Ye's presence.

At eight o'clock the stage was lit and the show began. By then the entire temple yard was filled with more than a thousand people. The gathered crowd was soon absorbed in the story and paid no heed to Ye. The show was a traditional Chinese opera, combining singing and acting. The cast was all female performers, who also played male roles when needed.

While I was photographing the show, I noticed the still tense mood of Ye. He was restless, puffing one cigarette after another and moving his body constantly. I thought that his anti-religious Communist orthodoxy was tormenting him. Party doctrine told him to reject anything above and beyond material existence. He had probably publicly denounced all traditional beliefs and practices as superstitious or feudalistic. It was thus an awkward situation for him to be witnessing something that he rejected and denounced. To avoid further embarrassment, at ten o'clock I decided to leave and told Ye, "It is getting late and I want to retire. Are you leaving too?"

He hurriedly stood up and yawned. "Yes, I am tired and should go home."

I returned the bench to its owners and thanked them for its use. When I went back to the spot where I had been sitting, Ye was already gone. I was not bothered by his erratic behavior, but decided that I should talk with him the next day so that he would not be in my way during this religious festival period.

Ritual Celebration: Analysis

I went to P.S. Ye's house at seven the next morning and found him eating alone in the kitchen. His wife had probably gone to tend the pigs or do the daily laundry. It was a good opportunity to talk with him. He offered me a bowl of rice congee, but I said that I had eaten at my landlord's house. I sat across the table from him and asked directly, "Was there anything wrong with the show last night? I had the feeling that you were uncomfortable there."

With a reluctant smile, he replied, "You know I am a member of the Communist Party, and the leading cadre in this brigade. I have to take a position against superstition."

"But where was the superstition?" I inquired. "Tell me, what did you see last night at the temple court?"

"An opera," he seemed to be puzzled by my question, "titled *The Heroine Who Went to the Battle Field for Her Father*."

"That is a historical story, right? The show was not promoting superstition or feudalism. So why did you say it was superstitious?"

"Of course it was," he shot back. "Can't you see that the whole event was organized by the temple? You cannot call temple activities non-superstitious!"

"That is your perception, the standard Party line." I slowed down my argument, trying to bring in anthropological perspectives. "But if you look at the event from another angle, you will see an entirely different picture."

"Like what?" He seemed to be in no mood to compromise.

"Let's take the god's birthday celebration as an example. This is the time of year when all spring rice transplanting has been completed. Villagers have leisure time to relax. They have been doing well the past few years: making a lot of money, building nice houses, and buying good household appliances. They want to share their happiness with their family and kin. They want to reciprocate favors and help given to them by their friends and associates. They want to rekindle old social ties with their remote kin, former school mates, and business partners. What would be a better occasion than the god's birthday festival?"

"But this is still related to temple deities!" Ye stubbornly insisted.

"Why do you have to view the temple and the deities this way?" I coaxed him. "The temple and the deities are symbols. They are not real. They do not embody a doctrine or a social organization to challenge Communism or the Party. Has the theology of this folk religion ever advocated political activism? No! It only tells people to be filial to their parents, to work hard, and to anticipate rewards in this life or a next life for good deeds done now. The show we watched last night was passing on good traditional values to the audience through the story.

"Furthermore, look at the really important functions these temple activities provide for villagers." Seeing no response from him, I continued, "The temple and the deities provide the most important symbolic function for village solidarity. The village has been doing well because, as you said, it is united. Villagers are thankful. They need a rallying point to pool their collective appreciation. The temple and the deities provide just the right instruments for them to achieve this goal. Where else can they find such a focal point?"

"But what about the Party?" Ye insisted, but with a much weakened voice. "It is correct Party policy in recent years that has brought prosperity to the countryside, not those idols. They should thank the Party for all goodness in life."

"There are several problems in your viewpoint," I replied. "First of all, the villagers don't have a format in their tradition to express appreciation through political activities. Do you entertain your kin and friends by inviting them to your house for a banquet and then run a political study session? Can you send *Quotations of Chairman Mao* to your friends as a wedding gift? Political doctrines and organizations simply cannot fulfill many important social needs. It is there the temple and deities can play a role. The second problem in your view is how many people really believe they owe their current prosperity to the Party? What about all the disasters and hardships the Party brought to them? It is no wonder that villagers must turn to something traditional, such as the temple and local gods, for their social needs."

Ye had laid down his bowl and was listening with full concentration. When I finished, he lamented, "You are probably right in your assessment of the situation. Somehow I have never been able to understand why people hung around the temple or engaged in those activities. My Communist teaching never allowed me to develop the capacity to understand religion objectively. I wish my father had presented this same analysis to me to make me understand his involvement there. Had I understood the reasons for these activities better then, I wouldn't have had so many arguments with my father. I shouldn't have hastened the division of my family during the last few years of his life. I was unfilial."

With Ye's revelation, I came to understand his reluctance to be involved in temple activities. It was not just his Party indoctrination that made him abhor anything religious or supernatural. He also carried a strong sense of guilt over the conflicts he had with his father about the latter's involvement in religious activities shortly before his death. Somehow the conflicts were related to his family division. I failed to see the connection and decided to explore, "Why did you have arguments with your father, and how was that related to your family division?"

Ye seemed to realize how his ramblings had confused me. He asked me, "Do you know who the real temple activists are in our village?"

"Those five or six people who organize this god's birthday celebration now," I replied, based on my observations of the past few days.

"No," Ye said meekly. "It used to be my father, plus a few older people, such as Lin Qifa's father and Hopping Toad Wu's mother. All three died within the past two or three years. The current temple activists took on the responsibilities after their deaths."

Seeing Ye was willing to talk about the village temple, I seized the moment to ask him several questions. "When was the village temple rebuilt? Was it on the same site as the old one?"

"No," he replied to my last question first. "The original village temple was on a slope north of the village, but it was submerged after the construction of the reservoir. For the next two decades there was no village temple to house the deities. They were kept in abandoned village houses. In the past, our government policy was very much against religious worship. Furthermore, people were too poor to consider rebuilding the temple. The situation changed in the early 1980s. Villagers began to have spare money to spend. The government was less rigid about permitting people to participate in religious activities. In early 1983, my father, Lin Qifa's father, and Hopping Toad Wu's mother began to promote the idea of rebuilding the village temple. I tried to dissuade my father from taking part, but he refused to listen. He said that the gods had been treating us well by bringing prosperity to our village. We should be thankful to the deities and hence build a new temple to house them. I told him that it was all superstition. We had several heated arguments. I didn't mind if he just participated in the activities as an ordinary worshipper. But he should not take the lead in planning to rebuild the temple or organizing religious festivals. I told him that I was a Party member, and also the highest cadre in this brigade. What would happen to me if my superiors found out that the Party secretary's father was the leader of the superstitious ring in this brigade?"

"What was your father's response?" I asked.

"Not very positive. He said that I was ungrateful for all that the heavens had given us. He even suggested that if our father-son relationship was an embarrassment to me, we should consider dividing up the family. At that point I was very worried about continuing the more relaxed policy in the countryside, and wanted to distance myself from any questionable activities. Dividing up the family would at least superficially relieve me of some of the responsibility for my father's temple involvement.

"There were other reasons for me to consider dividing up the family, even though my father's temple activities were the most important one. Living conditions in my family improved drastically after I became Party secretary. With prosperity, many delayed social obligations could be fulfilled. By 1983, everyone but my youngest brother was married. They all held regular jobs in brigade or team enterprises and received steady income to help the family. My parents still farmed with the agricultural production team we belonged to and earned their work points. With all adults in the family working, our financial condition improved significantly. In that year we as a family had paid off all the debts associated with our two-story house. Since all my brothers had become independent financially and we were no longer debt ridden, it was time for family division.

Family Division

"I first discussed division with my father in early 1983, when he was fully involved in raising funds to build the village temple. He agreed with me and said, 'It is a good idea. All of you have grown up now, so you should have the opportunity to develop your own future. Since we, the old couple, can still work, you shouldn't worry about us. The only one I am concerned about is your youngest brother, A Ron, who is not married yet. Perhaps the best arrangement is for us, the old couple, to live with A Ron so that your mother can cook for him until he has his own wife to cook for him. When he gets married, each of you will contribute some money toward his wedding costs. Seeing A Ron find a good woman and get married will be my final task in life. After that, I can die in happiness.'

"With my father's permission I called a family meeting of all five brothers. It was the fifteenth or sixteenth day of the third lunar month. It is our custom here to have the family division at the midpoint, that is the fifteenth or sixteenth day, of the lunar month. The belief is that if you have the family division before the midpoint of the month, it is detrimental (*chong,* literally offending) to the first son. If the division is in the second half of the month, it is bad for the second son. Most families therefore pick the fifteenth or sixteenth day of the month for this event. Even though we have five brothers, we followed the local custom to avoid any potential mishaps. Another reason I wanted to hasten family division was to have this event completed before the village temple was built. The village temple was scheduled for completion on the twenty-third of the third lunar month. Selfishly, I thought, if I formally split with my father before the completion of temple construction, I would not be accountable for this project. My father seemed to fully understand my motivation, and cooperated.

"We had a nice, peaceful meeting to divide up family belongings. Since nobody in China owns any land, the most valuable property to be divided is the house. We agreed that my parents and youngest brother, A Ron, would live in the old house, with its three bedrooms, a living room, and a kitchen. The other four brothers divided up the new two-story building, with each one occupying a wing of one floor. The kitchen, which is located in the courtyard of the new house, is divided evenly into two sections for two of the four brothers. An additional kitchen was to be built in the courtyard for the remaining two brothers.

"Household goods that were previously shared by the entire family, such as the cooking pots, benches, water buckets, and small farm tools, were assessed in value and divided up into five piles according to their prices. Each one took whatever he felt to be most useful to him. When two of us wanted to take the same thing, we negotiated and compromised. We agreed that each of us would give RMB$10 per month to our parents for daily expenses. We also agreed that at the time of A Ron's marriage, each of the other four older brothers would contribute RMB$200 for the wedding.

"The family division process was completed in one day. We didn't have any arguments like other villagers do during their family divisions. For most others family division is often a time of bitter fighting among the sons over equity of the shares. To prevent the fighting from getting out of hand, the family often invites a paternal uncle, a respected cadre, or another senior kinsman to witness this entire process. But we didn't call upon any of our kinsmen to help. My brothers and I did it in such a smooth and polite manner that we didn't need any arbitrator. We wouldn't do anything to disgrace my father or to shame him.

"A year after our family division, A Ron married Lin Qifa's younger sister. Lin Qifa has been our brigade's public security head since 1978 and is quite popular among the Lins. This was a good match for A Ron. For his wedding, instead of the RMB$200 that we had originally agreed to give him, we, A Ron's four older brothers, gave him RMB$400 each. He had an elaborate wedding festival with over twenty tables of guests. His wedding room (*xinfang*) was lavishly decorated inside and out. My father was so proud of himself that day, I never saw him happier.

"Perhaps it was fate, or perhaps he had seen the completion of his lifelong goals. My father's prediction came true a few months after A Ron's wedding. He died in August 1984, three months after A Ron's wedding, from nostril cancer. It happened so quickly that he died a couple of months after the illness was diagnosed. I still can't bear the thought that he had passed away so quickly. Whenever I think about him, I feel sad. He worked so hard during his entire life that he had never had a moment of enjoyment. He literally worked until the last day of his life. The only luxurious thing he enjoyed was the kind of cheap cigarettes that nobody in this village today wants to smoke. He didn't drink because liquor cost too much for him. He saved every penny for us. But at the point when we became prosperous and could afford to let him live in leisure, he passed away. I hate myself for not being able to reciprocate his generosity during his lifetime.

"To prepare for my father's funeral, I went to the rocky hills south of the village and selected a good spot for his grave from where he could overlook the entire vicinity. I ordered the best marble slab as his headstone for RMB$200. To cover the dome-shaped earth tomb I used cement mixed with ocher, which makes it reddish. At the back of the tomb I had construction workers build a ditch to prevent water runoff from the hills. It was the most magnificent tomb in our village when it was completed in September 1984. The total costs for his burial, as dictated by local custom, were divided up equally among all five sons. Maybe it was fate that my father died at this juncture, for a month later the Xiamen Rural District issued a ban on all earth burials to prevent the loss of farmland. After October 1984, the villagers could only cremate their deceased. Had my father died two months later, I wouldn't even have been able to bury him properly."

I was fascinated by Ye's description of his family division, and asked him, "Is your family division process typical in this area?"

"Well," Ye pondered for a while and replied, "both yes and no. Family division takes many forms in Lin Village, but there are two predominant types that seem to be most popular here. The first one is for parents to stay on in the old house after their first son gets married and forms his own household unit. The parents, after paying off all wedding expenditures, assign a room or a segment of the house to this new couple. The parents may also give some cash, if they have savings, and household utensils to this couple for their new living quarters. From then on, this new couple manages their own income and daily expenditures as a separate family. The clearest sign of this new family's having been split off from the old one is that this couple cooks on its own hearth rather than eating with the parents and the unmarried siblings. When the second son of the parents gets married, the same procedure is repeated. The second son and his wife split from the original family and establish a new family of their own.[1] This procedure is repeated until all the sons are married and split away from home.

"The second type of family division in this area is for the old parents to hold off the division until all or most of the sons are married. This way, since each of the sons has taken his proper share of the family coffer for wedding expenses, they can better come to terms in dividing up the family. In case there is still one younger brother who is not married, the other brothers will either assign a larger share of the family wealth to him or agree to contribute a certain amount of cash to him for his wedding. After this formal division, each of the sons forms a new family."

"Why do certain families choose the first type of family division while others prefer the second method?" I asked.

"There are many factors involved in this decision." Ye seemed to be prepared for my question. "The first one is obviously related to the father's authority. If he is strong and all his sons are afraid of him, then he will be able to decide the most convenient time for division based on his personal calculation.[2] In our village, for instance, Hopping Toad Wu is known for his hot temper. When he gets angry with his sons, he just picks up a shoulder carrying pole from the ground and strikes their heads. When his second son got married, Hopping Toad decided to divide the family by literally kicking him and his older brother—also married—out of the family. After that Hopping Toad and his wife lived with their third unmarried son and their two unmarried daughters.

"The second factor affecting family division is the family's financial situation. If a family is poor, it would have problems finding spouses for the sons. In that case the family would have to stick together for as long as there were unmarried sons. The only hope was for the family as a whole to accumulate enough wealth as quickly as possible and to have proper weddings for all the sons so they would become ready for partition. But sometimes this strategy doesn't work. When the first son of the family got married, he might decide to split from the old household and set up his new unit. He favors family division because he sees no future gain in staying with the old family. Actually it would be a drain on his and his wife's income to stay in the original house to support the young, unmarried brothers. In a sense this first son, by moving out of the old family after his marriage, is abandoning his obligations toward his parents and siblings. Young couples choosing this alternative can be criticized by other villagers as 'unfilial' (*buxiao*).

"Family division doesn't imply the termination of familial relationships among all sons, or between the sons and parents, even though they have become financially independent. There are still other obligations that tie them together. The first is a ritual one the sons have toward their ancestors, including their parents, from whom they received life. For deceased ancestors, these sons must sweep and worship their tombs once every year during the Qing Ming festival, in early April. In addition, during their ancestors' death anniversaries and other major festivals, such as the traditional Chinese New Year or the ghost festival (*zhongyuan pudu*) in the middle of the seventh month, these sons also congregate to provide sacrifice for deceased ancestors. These ritual offerings normally take place in the living room of their old house, also called ancestral house, where the ancestral tablet is located.

"You must realize that our government has been taking a very negative attitude towards ancestral worship. All ancestral shrines and estates were confiscated during the Land Reform. Funeral rites and earth burials have been consistantly criticized in government publications since the Liberation. Agitation against ancestral worship reached its peak during the Four Cleanups when work teams searched village houses for things considered superstitious or feudalistic. Needless to say, activities associated with ancestral worship ceased throughout 1960s and 1970s in our village. It was only since late 1970s, after the Third Plenum, that villagers began to sweep their ancestral tombs.

"Since almost all ancestral tablets in our village were destroyed during the Four Cleanups, villagers now write their ancestors' names and birth and death dates on a sheet of red paper and hang it in the middle in the living room of the ancestral house to symbolize the ancestral tablet. If they have a photograph of an ancestor, it can be substituted for the ancestral tablet. For important ceremonial occasions, all sons bring food to their old house to worship their ancestors together. It is only after the sons have duplicated the ancestral tablet and set it in their own house or living quarters for independent ritual worship that they achieve completely independent status as new family units.

"As for living ancestors, namely, the parents or grandparents, sons are required by custom to provide basic living accommodations for them for the rest of their lives. During family division, sons determine the proportion of original family wealth they want to set aside for their parents or grandparents, and the amount of money they will contribute to the parents and grandparents each month thereafter for their food and other expenses. Parents may decide to live with only one son's family. In that case the other sons give an agreed upon sum to this son monthly for the support of the parents. When the parents die, all sons split burial costs equally. I heard that in Quanzhou Prefecture up north there is the custom of rotating the parents among all the sons for fixed periods after family division. The old couple may stay with the first son's family during the first ten days of the month, then move on to the second son for the second ten days of the month, and the third son for the third ten days. In some cases the sons, if there are only two, split up the old couple: The first son supports the father and the second son, the mother. We don't follow this practice here."

Dismantling the Collective

"Did your father's illness and subsequent death occur at approximately the same time as the dismantling of the rural collective?" I remembered that the brigade was disbanded around May or June 1984.

"Yes," Ye confirmed, "but it was purely coincidental that these two events occurred at about the same time. Our brigade was dissolved in early May 1984, only a few days after my father was diagnosed as terminally ill. In retrospect, partition of the brigade collective seemed inevitable after the government changed its rural policy in 1978. I did, however, try to prevent the inevitable by holding off pressure from both higher authorities and some villagers to do so. I had every reason to thwart or delay the dismantling of the collective system. As a collective this brigade did quite well in the early 1980s. Per capita income in our brigade has been the highest among all eighteen brigades in the Rural District since 1980. The increase was mainly from collective enterprises. You don't destroy something when it is doing well. Besides, there were those old and infirm villagers whom I wanted to protect. Under the collective system we could easily use public funds to subsidize them. What would happen to them when we dismantled the collective system?

"Many young people, including Hopping Toad's oldest son, accuse me of trying to slow the breakup process because I was afraid of losing my personal power. That was hogwash! Today, even after dismantling the brigade and team collectives, I still maintain unchallenged power in this village. What did I lose when we dismantled the brigade on May 7, 1984? Nothing! Some insist that had we divided up the brigade earlier, we might have taken even a bigger lead over the other brigades in economic development than what we have today. I can't argue against this criticism, for I don't have the ability to reverse history or change it. It was my sense of justice that played a major role in my decision to resist pressure to divide up the collective. The sad thing is that I don't think any person in this village ever understands or appreciates the meaning of justice, even though it may intimately affect his life. Peasants are so nearsighted, they can never understand anything beyond their most direct, immediate, and personal benefit. Our brigade was the last one in the entire commune to divide up, due largely to my initiative. Whether my decision was right or wrong can only be judged by history.

"The trend toward dismantling all rural collectives in China was not at all clear during the December 1978 Third Plenum of the Eleventh Party Congress. We read in newspapers about the so-called Production Responsibility System, an experiment in very poor regions of Sichuan and Anhui provinces in 1979. At that point the Production Responsibility System only implied that collectives, such as the brigade or team, contracted out certain productive work to small groups of families or even individual families. The idea was that when the peasants could clearly see that their income level was closely tied to their work, they would work harder. But in this arrangement, productive property, such as farmland and factory facilities, still belonged to the collectives and were managed by them. Collective ownership of productive property is the hallmark of socialism. If we were to dismantle collectives and abandon public ownership of productive property, then we could no longer consider ourselves socialists.

"As long as we maintain collective ownership of productive property, I have no qualms with the Production Responsibility System. I have always insisted that a person's reward from work should be directly linked to his performance. The past failure of our Communist system is that there was no direct link between work and remuneration. When high-level Party cadres made major blunders in their production plans, they were immune from any penalty. In designing and implementing totally unrealistic programs, cadres at various government offices wasted thousands and millions of dollars. What have the consequences been? Nothing. They shrugged their shoulders and claimed they had learned their lessons. Then they designed the same error-filled production plans again!

"In 1983, the Party appointed me to represent Xiamen Rural District at the Fujian Provincial People's Congress. I went to Fuzhou, the provincial capital, to attend a meeting on how to increase productive efficiency and reduce waste in our provincial government. I chatted with the director of the Provincial Planning Commission, a Zhang. He asked me how my brigade could improve production so much within such a short period of time, and wanted to know what the provincial government could learn from my experience. I said, 'It is simple. Just make the salary of responsible cadres in a provincial enterprise a certain percentage of total production. If the enterprise makes good use of capital and equipment and yields high returns, the responsible cadre's salary increases proportionately. On the other hand, if the return from this enterprise declines, so does the cadre's income. People do their best when they can directly see their personal share in it. If they waste public money while suffering no personal loss in the process, then why should they care? If you can adopt this policy across the board, in all provincial enterprises tomorrow, I can guarantee you that the waste level will be reduced and efficiency increased immediately.' He was so interested in my views that he asked me to take a ride with him in his chauffeured car around the city.

"The government began to promote this Production Responsibility System all over the nation in 1981. At that point my brigade had already developed experiments similar to this policy. In all industrial enterprises in this brigade, especially the sand brick production plants, workers received pay according to what they produced in a day. The more work accomplished, the more pay the workers received. In factory production, however, we didn't pay everyone this way because the nature of the work prevented it. For example, sand brick production requires the coordination of seven people. Two people, usually men, move sand, plaster, and coal dust with a cart to a grinder. At the grinder there is another man who shovels these ingredients into the grinder according to fixed proportions. The electric grinder then combines the ingredients into a smooth and even mixture, which are used by three workers, generally girls, to pound into square or rectangular steel molds using air-pressure hammers. Women are preferable for this job because male workers tend to be listless and have their fingers injured by the air hammers. Then there is another worker, usually a girl, who pulls the pounded bricks from the mold workers and delivers the bricks to another crew for sun drying.

"These seven people involved in a single production process are paid according to the the number of bricks produced in a day. Paying by the piece is the best method to keep workers from goofing off. But for these seven working as a team, income is shared equally. For instance, in a normal day a team of seven workers can produce almost 4,000 bricks during an eight-hour shift. The factory pays them 57 work points for every 1,000 bricks. For that day then this team earns 228 work points. If you divide those 228 work points by seven, it comes to about 32 work points for each of them that day. The worth of a point varies from year to year. At the end of a year a team calculates all its income and expenditures. After deducting all expenditures from gross income, the team's net profit is then divided by all work points earned by the team members. In a good year, such as 1984, a work point in our brigade was worth about RMB 20 cents. For a sand brick worker who earned 32 work points a day, the cash value was RMB$6.40 for that day's work. A monthly income of close to RMB$200 is not a small sum of money for young people!

"These seven workers thus form a collective work group in industrial production. Their payments are equal because of the nature of their work. Moving the sand, coal dust, and plaster to the machine, and hauling for sun drying, are the most physically exhausting jobs. They deserve good pay because they have to work under the hot sun. For the man who mixes the ingredients at the grinder and the three girls who operate the air hammers, the work may not be as tiring as the others since they stay under the shed at all times and don't move around. But their kind of work is more delicate and demands precision. They must have skill. Regardless of what they do, they must all work hard because a slowdown by one would be detrimental to the work pace of the others and hence the income of the entire team. They also have to look after each other's well-being because the entire production process depends upon good cooperation among them all. I believe that this system is a good way to increase production as well as preserve collective spirit. This method has been so successful that even today, after the breakup of collective enterprises, the managers still largely adhere to this procedure.

"In 1981 our brigade and teams began to experiment with this new Production Responsibility System in agriculture. The first experiment was called 'Uniting

Production to Contract Responsibility System' (*lianchan chengbao zhi*). Each team was divided into four or five agricultural groups (*zhu*), with between eight and ten families per group. The decision about which families should be assigned to the same group was based on several factors, including kinship ties, geographic proximity, previous relationships, and special skills needed for each group. A group was thus an operating and accounting unit below the team to carry out actual agricultural production. By reducing the size of the collective, the peasants could better see the relationship between their work and rewards.

"Production quotas assigned to the brigade, which in our case included vegetables for the city's vegetable company, pork for the national procurement office, and grain for our own consumption, would be equally divided among all five teams. Each team would then subdivide the production quota to the groups equally. Each group was required to fulfill its production quota and to sell the products to the team according to a pre-determined work-point scale. For instance, if a group sold RMB$1 worth of vegetables to the city's vegetable cooperative, this group earned four work points. In 1984, four work points equaled RMB$.80. Or, if the group produced RMB$1 worth of rice, this group earned six work points for the product."

I listened intensely to Ye's explanation of this contract system, and detected some problems. "How could you pay six work points, worth RMB$1.20 in 1984, for each RMB$1 worth of rice produced locally? And why the discrepancy between vegetable and grain production?"

"You are doing quite well to have noticed these discrepancies!" Ye replied approvingly. "Put simply, we, the brigade and team collectives, are subsidizing grain production with profits generated primarily from industrial production and secondarily from vegetable production. We have to subsidize grain production because the market value has been consistently low. The government was maintaining a tight lid on grain prices and set them at artificially low levels. Since we converted part of our land to vegetable production for the city, we can purchase certain quantities of rice from the government at official low prices. But the amount of rice our brigade purchased from the government was never sufficient for the entire brigade. We had to produce additional rice to meet our needs. Without these subsidies no one would grow rice in our brigade. In contrast to grain production, vegetable production received lower work points because the yields were higher than rice and the prices higher.

"If a work group produced vegetables, pork, or grain above the set quota in that year, it could either sell them to the collective for the cash, which would be divided up among all participating families, or distribute the products among the families in the group for their own use. The surplus could then be sold in the free market, or consumed by the family. On the other hand, if a group failed to meet its production quota, it would have to make it up by purchases from other sources, which obviously meant higher costs.

"We experimented with this policy for only one year and decided that it was too rigid. The government was then urging rural cadres to decentralize agricultural production further, down to the individual household level. The next year, 1982, we began another experiment, called 'Grain Land Responsibility System' (kou-liangtian zhi), which abolished groups beneath the teams. All agricultural laborers in a team still managed agricultural work according to the production goals set by higher authorities. They plowed the field to grow vegetables and grain. After the initial work was completed, the vegetable plots would still be managed by the team's agricultural labor crew. The crew members received work points according the nature of their work and the number of days they worked in the fields. In contrast to vegetable land, the grain land was divided up equally among all team families on a per capita basis. This grain land was to become the sole responsibility of the family it was assigned to. This family had to weed its own rice terrace, put in adequate fertilizer, and harvest its own grain. People tended their assigned grain land when they were not working in the brigade enterprises or as part of the agricultural crew.

"This Grain Land Responsibility System lasted for slightly more than one year. In 1983, the government began to push hard to implement a new 'Family Contractual Responsibility System' (jiating chengbao zerenzhi), which implies dividing up all farmland in a collective according to each family's ability and willingness to engage in agricultural production. The team determines the actual quantity of goods it intends to produce in that year, and then divides up production responsibilities among individual families along with designating a pre-determined amount of land for each family. For instance, if the team has to produce 10,000 kilos of pork to meet its government procurement quota in that year, it would assign 100 mou farmland (1 hectare = 15 mou) to fulfill this production target. If a family wants to assume the obligation of producing one-tenth of the quota, that is, 1,000 kilos of pork for the team, this family would sign a contract with the team and reserve the right to use one-tenth of the reserved land, or 10 mou. The team might also have a production quota of 100,000 kilos of vegetables in that year. It would divide up the 100,000 kilos into ten shares, or 10,000 kilos per share, with 10 mou land for each share. If a family figured that it had the human power to manage the land and to fulfill the production goal, it would sign a contract with the team. The family would receive a pre-determined number of work points for fulfilling the production quota. Any surplus produced above the required quota belonged to this family, who could dispose of it however it saw fit.

"During 1983 and early 1984, the government's agricultural policies were changing very rapidly. It became increasingly clear that the government wanted to encourage this de-collectivization (fan jitihua) process. The goal seemed to be giving back total control of agricultural production and marketing to individual peasant families. There were also rumors in late 1983 that the government intended to abolish all collectives. A few counties in southern Fujian Province responded quickly to this trend and began to adapt the 'Big Contract System' (*da baogan*), dividing up all farmland equally among all people in a collective. If a brigade has 1,000 people and 500 *mou* of farm land, it would give a half *mou* of land to each person in the brigade. A family with eight people will thus be entitled to four *mou* land. This family would sign a contract with the team for five or ten or fifteen years for the exclusive rights to use the land. The contract would stipulate the quantity of grain or pork or vegetables this family would sell to the collective per year at government-stipulated prices. Other than these required production quotas, the peasants would have complete freedom to grow what they wanted or how they chose to grow it on their land. I think the proper name for this system is not 'Big Contract System,' but rather 'divide up the land and farm individually' (*fentian dangan*).

"In early 1984, our brigade's first team adapted this new Big Contract System without first consulting me. The team head just divided up the team's land on a per capita basis. All agricultural implements were also divided. The only thing that was still in the hands of the team collective was the sand-brick factory. The team head's reason for this move was that most other brigades in this commune had already divided up collectives. Since it was the national trend, he insisted, we might as well follow it. I was furious about his reckless act. What if the other teams wanted to follow suit? I might eventually have to divide up the brigade. But as long as I could resist pressure from higher authorities or from other villagers to do so, I wanted to delay this process so that I could work out the most reasonable arrangement for all villagers. I called upon the heads of the second, third, fourth, and fifth teams and warned them not to divide up their teams without my permission. I told them that I would divide up the entire brigade when the time came.

"At that point the winds of change were already strong. There was a kind of concealed agitation, latent anxiety, and calculated expectation in the village. Many villagers, especially the infirm, widowed, and injured, were obviously worried. I remember a widow and her teenage daughter who came to see me one evening to plead their case. She said that under the collective system she and her daughter could earn work points and hence a proper living. But what would happen if the collective were divided? Since there was no man in her family, she would be unable even to plow the rice terrace given to her. How would she and her daughter make a living then? As she talked she and her daughter began to weep. What could I do? I told her that I would do my best to set up rules to protect people like her. I said the same thing to many other villagers who visited with me and pleaded for my protection.

"It became increasing clear in the spring of 1984 that a few villagers who had been involved in brigade- and team-level industrial enterprises were forming a group in favor of division. Included were Party cadres, such as the brigade chief Li Dehai, the Double-Headed Snake, and the brigade public security head Lin Qifa, and non-Party members, such as the heads of all five teams. Their rationale was easy to understand. By virtue of their direct involvement in brigade and team enterprises they had gained sufficient experience and external connections to run these enterprises as their own. They saw bigger profit margins if they could monopolize these collective enterprises. The breakup of the collectives would give them the opportunity to take control of these enterprises.

"In the meantime, ordinary villagers could also see the detrimental effects division would have on their lives. Under the collective system they or their family members were given the option of working in collective enterprises and have a good income. Even those working solely in agriculture enjoyed subsidies from industries. If these industrial establishments were taken over by a few individuals, new managers would probably hire cheaper workers from the interior of this province where wages were low, and would displace our industry workers. A privately run enterprise would not subsidize the less-profitable agriculture, a fact everyone was aware of. The standard of living for those who depended chiefly on agriculture would definitely suffer. These workers protested vigorously against breaking up the brigade and team collectives.

"An interesting coincidence in early April of 1984 brought an instructor from Xiamen University's Philosophy Department, Professor Zhou, and two of his students to our brigade to conduct a study. Their goal was to see how new economic developments in our brigade could be interpreted through Marxist philosophy. But most villagers didn't understand it. They thought that Professor Zhou and his students were members of a work team sent by the government to force partition. The entire time these three university people lived in our village, they encountered open hostility from villagers who opposed the idea of division. At that point I was under a lot of pressure, both from the higher authorities and from some villagers, to divide. I had just found out about my father's terminal illness, too. I was not helpful to Professor Zhou in his research. Nor did I make any effort to alleviate the hostility exhibited by some villagers. When they finished their project, I sent each of them a hand towel as a gift. I thought that when they packed to leave and were cursed by the villagers, they could use the towels to wipe off their perspiration.

"My final decision to break up this brigade came in late April 1984. A delegation from the National Environmental Protection Commission visited our village. I spent the whole day showing those sons of a whore around. The brigade paid for a big feast to entertain them. As they were leaving, the head of the delegation called all brigade-level cadres together and gave us a big lecture. That son of a whore accused us of thinking only about making money and paying no attention to the 'Construction of Socialist Spiritual Civilization' (*jianshe shehuizhuyi jingshen wenming*), a new political campaign just announced by the central government. He said that environmental conditions in this village were a mess. Village streets were unpaved dirt roads. Chickens and ducks were running loose. Sewage along the streets was not covered. The outhouses stank. There was no community planning for housing construction. And so on and so forth.

"I was furious. Who did they think we were? A bunch of rich overseas Chinese building a retirement compound in the countryside? Sure, to reduce the stench in the air we should stop raising chickens and hogs. We should stop collecting night soil for our crops. To eliminate the dirty outhouses we should first spend RMB$50,000 to set up a running water system in the village and then spend another RMB$50,000 to build flush toilets for every village house. You just can't believe how stupid those high-level cadres can be. They just come and criticize. They wanted us to do this and that. But where should we get the money to carry out their demands? Not only did they not provide financial help, but they drained our resources when they came to 'inspect.' After they ate our good food and smoked our special cigarettes, they slapped our faces for being filthy peasants. I really felt that I had had enough of their nonsense that day. I told myself, 'Let those idiots screw themselves. Let the brigade find its own solution. I am not going to be the guardian of their Communist ideals.'

"After the delegation from the Environmental Protection Commission left, I called brigade officials and told them that I wanted to divide up the brigade a week from that day, on May 7, 1984. In the meantime team leaders should divide up their teams. I stipulated some basic principles for division. Farmland in each team should be divided on a per capita basis to ensure equality. Farm implements should be auctioned to team members. Draft animals, chiefly cows, should also be shared by team members on an equal basis so that every household would have access to a plowing animal. At that point there were about 40 working cattle in this brigade. The division of these 40 among 1,000 villagers meant approximately 25 people sharing a cow. The team head should group four or five families, totaling about 25 people, together to share a cow. The main enterprise in each team, the sand brick factory, was to be contracted out to members of the team through competitive bidding. Whoever promised to pay the highest annual fee to the team for operating the facility would receive the contract for running the factory in that year. Contract fees collected from the sand brick factories would be used by the teams to pay land taxes, amounting to RMB$5 per *mou*, for the team members, and to pay for other social welfare benefits, such as an allowance to the 'Five Guaranteed Families' (*wubao hu*, poor families guaranteed to be provided with five basic necessities: food, clothing, shelter, medicine, and funeral expenses).

"As far as the brigade-owned collective enterprises were concerned, I told the team leaders they would be leased to the highest bidders at a brigade meeting the afternoon of May 7. Rental fees collected from brigade enterprises would be used to pay for brigade-level expenses, such as salaries of brigade officials, subsidies to the brigade primary school, social welfare expenses, and payments to the medical system. I insisted that even though the brigade collective was to be dismantled, the collective medical protection system should be maintained. The brigade would still defray expenses for preventive medicine, such as vaccines for village children, and for public sanitation, such as periodic purification of village drinking wells. Villagers would pay for their own visits to the barefoot doctors. But if they needed hospitalization in the city, the brigade would cover all transportation costs as well as 80 percent of hospital fees. I firmly believed that it was our responsibility as local cadres to provide adequate education and medical care for all villagers.

"During the week before that final brigade meeting to dispose of brigade enterprises, it was almost a chaotic free-for-all. As expected, the team leaders, mostly non-Party members, took control of team-level enterprises. A few Party cadres joined forces to control the most profitable ventures, such as Li Dehai (Double-Headed Snake), who had been brigade head since 1975, and Lin Qifa, the brigade security head since 1978. These two formed an alliance with the head of the fifth team, Hou Tong, and took over the sand brick factory of the fifth team, the biggest facility in our brigade. They also formed a partnership with a villager in the second team to outbid that team leader for control of the second team's sand brick factory. Rumor had it that Li Dehai, Lin Qifa, and Hong Tong formed a financial corporation (*caituan*) to dominate all enterprises within this brigade. After they took control of the two sand brick factories, Double-Headed Snake and Lin Qifa invited me to join their group. I declined and told them that as a top Party cadre in this brigade I would not compete with ordinary villagers to gain an unfair economic advantage.

"The political climate in Lin Village became increasingly tense as May 7 approached. There was a rumor that the newly formed financial group headed by Double-Headed Snake wanted to out-bid everyone in the village for control of most existing brigade enterprises, including the sand brick factory, the electroplating factory, the machine shop, and the saw mill. The only brigade facility they had no intention of controlling was the construction company. They figured that I was the only one who had all the proper connections to secure material for construction work. It would be futile to fight against me for control of the construction company. They probably reasoned that because had they left this financial plum for me, I would reciprocate by allowing them to take over all other brigade enterprises.

"A few brigade officials, such Hou Lingli, head of the Women's League, and Lin Chengrui, who had served as brigade clerk since 1978, were quite worried. Under the collective system, they received monthly subsidies from the brigade enterprises to augment their meager salaries. I allowed them to double as brigade enterprise's supervisor or treasurer for extra income. If the new financial corporation took over all brigade enterprises, it would definitely not pay these extra salaries. Both Hou and Lin came to ask me to stop Double-Headed Snake and his group. Another person who was in trouble was Thunderbolt Lin's step brother, Ding Yong. Ding used to be the head of the second team and was intending to bid for his team's sand-brick factory. But he was outbid by Double-Headed Snake's investment group, who used a front man from the second team to seize control of the factory. Ding Yong was quite upset, for without additional income from the sand-brick factory he would be unable to continue the construction of his new two-story house. He also asked me to lead the opposition against Double-Headed Snake's attempt to monopolize all enterprises in our village.

"On May 6, Opium Hong and Dark Skin Lin, two former brigade Party secretaries, came to see me. They expressed their concern about problems in this brigade, especially the financial group formed by Double-Headed Snake. This group's planned monopoly of all brigade enterprises would be disastrous to other villagers. The investment group would control the lives of all villagers through these enterprises. They told me they had heard that this group was ready to bid up to RMB$80,000 for all brigade enterprises, except for the construction company. They urged me to intervene. They said that if I didn't stop Double-Headed Snake's attempt, they would have no choice but to compete with the group in bidding for brigade enterprises. They said that they would be ready to bid up to RMB$80,000 for control of these enterprises. Of course, they said, they knew this act would be suicidal, for brigade enterprises would be unable to generate that much profit in a year. Something had to be done to discourage the emergence of a ruling bloc in this village other than the Party.

"I didn't sleep at all that night. Finally, by dawn, I had decided to intervene. I went to Ding Yong's house and asked him to raise RMB$5,000 cash for me for the day's meeting. The money would be used as the required 15 percent up-front money I would need if my bid was successful. Then I hid in Ding Yong's attic to sleep before the decisive meeting.

"At two o'clock the afternoon of May 7, I walked to the brigade meeting hall with Ding Yong by my side. The room was packed with villagers, most of whom were anticipating a big fight during the meeting. Indeed, the atmosphere was like a keg of dynamite about to ignite when I walked into the room. On one side of the table placed in the center of the room sat Double-Headed Snake, Lin Qifa, and several of their associates. They represented the new financial corporation. Across the table from them were Opium Hong, Dark Skin Lin, and other brigade officials who had been elbowed aside during the first round of bidding wars. Surrounding this center table were row after row of villagers, anxiously awaiting the outcome of the bidding process that would affect their lives for many years. The seat at the head of the table was vacant, apparently for me. As I was walking toward that chair, I heard a youngster murmur behind my back: 'Watch him sit in that gold armed chair (*jinjiao yi*, traditionally the emperor's chair in the court) for the last time today. Once we strip control of the brigade enterprises from his hand, this Party secretary will be nobody!'

"I sat down calmly and began my speech before the bidding. I explained the meaning of the new Production Responsibility System as established by the government's directives, and the bidding procedures we would follow to divide up brigade enterprises. Then I made some comments about the competition during the past week over the division. I said that I had heard a lot of rumors about how various groups were being formed within the brigade to fight for power. I warned them that while we were dismantling the collective, this by no means implied relinquishing Party control in the countryside. The government would not tolerate anarchy at any level. They should refrain from in-fighting like monkeys and pigs in a crowded pack. 'Regardless of whether they were monkeys or pigs,' I raised my voice and continued, 'the government could always slaughter them for meat if their behavior exceeded acceptable limits.' I used the local slang, 'When monkeys die [I will] dissect the monkeys, and when pigs die [I will] butcher the pigs' (*housi shahou, zhusi zaizhu*), merely as an analogy to show how disgusted I was with the in-fighting. But, apparently, the words fell on the wrong ears. The room was silent. The dropping of a pin would have seemed loud. Everyone was stunned by my remark about slaughtering the pigs and monkeys. They must have thought that I had intended these words to warn them about something else.

"I announced the beginning of the bidding procedure and posted my bid of RMB$20,000 annual fee for all brigade enterprises except for the construction company. I was prepared to increase my bid if Double-Headed Snake posted a higher bid than mine. But nobody dared move. They all sat in silence for the next fifteen minutes. When the allowed bidding time of fifteen minutes passed, the brigade clerk, Lin Chengrui, announced that my bid was the only one for these brigade enterprises. Frankly, it was an underbid. These enterprises could generate a profit of at least RMB$50,000 per year. After deducting RMB$20,000 for rental fees, I could have made a profit of RMB$30,000 per year. I was unprepared for this windfall. When the bidding was over and the villagers began to slip out of the meeting hall, I paid RMB$3,000 to the brigade clerk for the 15 percent down payment on my contract and left the hall. Later I heard that the construction company was leased to Wu Ming's oldest son, who had been head of it since its establishment.

"I heard that the next day Double-Headed Snake and Lin Qifa, heads of the defeated financial group, went to commune headquarters to press charges against me. They accused me of intimidating all villagers before the bidding procedure when I spoke. They alleged that I threatened to slaughter anyone who opposed me like monkeys and pigs. That was why nobody dared to bid against me. My bid was unfairly low, they said, the equivalent of taking graft from the public.

"I was called to commune Party headquarters the following day to explain all the circumstances. At that point I had already made several decisions about my contract for the brigade enterprises. With Ding Yong, Lin Chengrui, and Hou Lingli, my three allies, I discussed dividing this contract into partnerships and giving a share of the partnership to each of the former and present brigade officials, such as Opium Hong and Dark Skin Lin, and to the team leaders who were not involved in new privately contracted enterprises. My rationale was that we should take care of all those former and current officials. We could not make them return to the level of ordinary villagers when the collective organizations were dismantled. When Double-Headed Snake found out about this, he begged for a share in this partnership. Even though he wasn't qualified, I still let him split a share with Lin Qifa, so they would also benefit from this arrangement. I also gave half a share of the partnership to my fourth younger brother, who had a relatively low income from his job. In total we came up with thirteen shares so that all leading brigade officials, former and present, had a share in it. Each of these shares yielded a dividend of RMB$2,500 in 1984.

"In addition to this split, I also voluntarily raised the contract fee for the brigade enterprise by RMB$10,000 per annum. The brigade has a large operating budget. The RMB$20,000 collected from my lease would not be enough to cover all expenses. The additional RMB$10,000 contract fees that my lease contributed to the brigade administration would alleviate these problems.

"I went to commune headquarters on May 9 to report the breaking up of our brigade. I explained to them the content of my speech, and the arrangements I had made, along with a summary of my expected profits from this contract. When the commune Party leadership found out that I was not taking all profits for myself, and that my act had avoided a potentially explosive situation that might permanently split our brigade into two, they commended me for a job well done. All the charges against me were dropped."

Village Cadres

10 I had heard a lot about political campaigns during my residence in Lin Village. Based on what I learned from villagers, the very phrase "political campaign" conjured up mass rallies, public struggle sessions, and the use of brute force to carry out specific policies. Never in my wildest dreams did I expect to witness such a social drama unfold in real life, at least not during the last month of my stay in Lin Village. But then, unexpectedly, a campaign descended on the village and fundamentally changed the villagers' way of life and family structure. This particular episode, a birth control campaign, although not as brutal as earlier ones described to me by the villagers, still tremendously impressed me because of its highly dramatic effect and intensity.

Family Planning Campaign

In the middle of May 1985, rumors began to circulate among villagers that a new birth control campaign would soon be launched by the national government. The rumored new policy was to allow only one child per family in rural areas, instead of the current two-child policy. It was also claimed that all pregnant women who were carrying their second child would be taken to the rural hospital for induced abortion.

As the rumors spread, the village atmosphere became tense. Village women who were carrying their second child were especially nervous. One such example was Tiger's wife, who was already six months pregnant with their second child, and their first one was a daughter. Tiger had been counting on his wife's second pregnancy to bear him a son. Had the rumor been true, Tiger might have his family line severed because he lacked a son, the most unfortunate event for any family. During the last week of May, Tiger became very edgy. He was a good friend of P.S. Ye, and often visited him in the evenings. Several times Tiger became provoked and argued with Ye over insignificant issues. At the time, I noticed that Ye's attitude changed quite significantly too. He seemed to become more tolerant, avoiding any open confrontation with Tiger.

I tried to clear up the situation with Ye by privately asking him whether the rumors I had heard were true. Ye was unusually tight-lipped, insisting that rumors were rumors. He sometimes ignored my questions completely. But because Ye, Lin Qifa, the village security head, and Hou Lingli, head of the Women's League, were meeting frequently and secretly in the village or attending meetings at township headquarters, I sensed that the rumors were probably not completely groundless. A new campaign seemed to be brewing. Villagers were anxiously waiting.

That moment came one evening at the end of May, through the loudspeaker systems. It was Lin Qifa's terse, stern, and detached voice broadcast succinctly throughout the village: "The village government has received instructions from higher authorities to change current family planning policies. From now on, village families will be allowed to have only one child per couple. The village government has formulated the following rules to ensure compliance of all villagers with this new policy: First, any villager getting married without permission from proper authorities will be fined RMB$500. Second, from this day on, any village couple who has a second child without proper permission from the authorities will be fined RMB$800. This illegally conceived child will not be recorded on the village household registers. He (or she) will not be covered by village medical insurance, and will not be accepted by the village primary school. Without proper registration, this person will not be eligible for rationed goods. Third, all village women who have already given birth to one or more children must come to the village office for examination at 2 P.M. one week from today. Those who do not come will be fined RMB$10 per day for each day of delay. Finally, any village family who does not comply with this new policy will be cut off from the village office's regular business operations."

This announcement hit the village like a bombshell suddenly shattering a tranquil, pre-dusk moment of leisure and relaxation that most village families enjoyed before their evening meal. Even though most villagers were anticipating this announcement, they seemed to be stunned by its harshness. I was chatting with my landlord, Lin Qishan, in his living room when this new regulation was broadcast. He listened intently, and fell silent when it was over. A few moments later, he shook his head and sighed, "This is tough, very tough. Few villagers will dare to challenge this new regulation."

"You mean because of punishment for those who don't comply?" I asked.

"Yes," Lin confirmed, "especially the last point: Any family violating this new regulation will be disassociated from the village government. Frankly, the first three measures would have very little effect on the villagers. Most families now have a lot of cash. If they were allowed to have another child and thus carry on the family line, they would probably be more than willing to pay the RMB$800 fine. As far as the household registration or rationing are concerned, very few people care much about them either. The government is doing away with rationing systems. There is only rice rationing left in the countryside. Most people believe that even this will be abolished next year."

"But why would villagers worry so much about being disassociated from the village government?"

"This is so because most village families are engaged in non-farm production. For instance, there are more than 100 hand tractors in this village now. One of every two village families has a hand tractor operator, who earns at least RMB$500 per month. To buy a hand tractor, which now costs about RMB$4,500, most villagers borrow money from the government's land bank or agricultural credit cooperative. Another example is that recently seven villagers raised RMB$20,000 to set up a heavy machine shop in the village. Half of their investment funds came from government loans and credits. To apply for such loans a family must have the village government's stamp of approval. Without that, financial institutions will not consider any individual loan applications. The village government thus controls the villagers' investment plans. Unless a village family is content with farming on its meager contract land, which most villagers do not consider adequate now, it will have to deal with the village government in one way or another. That is why the last measure will ensure villagers' compliance with this new policy."

I wasn't convinced by Lin Qishan's explanation, and decided to verify it with P.S. Ye. As I walked to Ye's house, the sun was setting on the horizon, with a small pinkish-red glow cast behind the village's darkened silhouette. At Ye's house I found a dramatic event occurring. Ye was sitting in a rattan chair in his dimly lit dining room, with his head tilting up toward the ceiling, as if ignoring something. An old woman with silver hair and traditional black blouse and pants was kneeling in front of him. Her palms were pressed together, half raised in front of her as if she were praying. She was mumbling something inaudible to me.

Seeing my presence, Ye became embarrassed and tried to dismiss the old woman, "Go, go away! This is government policy and I had nothing to do with it."

As I drew closer, I recognized the woman as Tiger's mother. She made no move but insisted, "Just let my son have this second child! You and Tiger are cousins. How can you be so cruel to see his family line discontinued? Spare him this time and I will be willing to become a cow or a horse to serve you in my next life!"

Ye cast a desperate look at me and said to her: "What can I do? I can only promise you I will try my best to save Tiger. But there is no guarantee. But if you don't leave now, I will let the township office's birth control work team go directly to your house!"

The threat of the work team apparently had the desired effect. Tiger's mother promptedly rose and said, "I am leaving now. Just don't send the work team over. You promise me that you will take care of Tiger, right?"

"Right!" Ye waved his hand impatiently for the woman to leave.

After she left the room, Ye's facial muscles relaxed and he signaled for me to sit down. I took a chair across the table from him and said, "So, all the rumors about this new birth control policy were true!"

"Yes," Ye replied. "But I couldn't tell you anything before because I didn't want to create unnecessary panic in our village."

"How do you think villagers will respond to this new policy?" I tried to steer the conversation to test Lin Qishan's view that economic punishment was the most effective enforcement weapon.

"To be honest with you, all villagers hate it," Ye answered without hesitation. He then confidently predicted, "But they will all eventually comply with this new policy."

"How can you be so sure?" I insisted.

"For two reasons," Ye replied carefully, as if he had been preparing for the question. "First of all, this is not the first time we have had birth control regulations in our village. The first time was the most difficult, just like when you put a yoke on an ox's back for the first time. It will resist and struggle. But once the yoke is accepted by the ox, you can tighten it repeatedly, even to the point of choking it to death. Peasants are like oxen. Once they accept something as inevitable, you can continue to tighten the screw. They will complain at first, but will come to terms with reality. The second reason I am confident the villagers will comply with this new regulation is that we threatened to ostracize any family who dares to challenge this new rule from the village's financial activities. Investment in private enterprises is the biggest concern of all village families now. Without the village government's approval, no village family could possibly borrow money from government banks or credit associations."

So Lin Qishan was correct after all, I told myself. I also found Ye's analogy between this birth control policy imposed on peasants and that of putting a yoke on an ox interesting. "When was the first time that birth control plans were implemented in Lin Village?" I asked.

"It started in the early 1970s.[1] In 1974, the government began to promote a three-child family policy in the countryside. It was definitely the most difficult one. At that time there was strong resistance to this restriction in the countryside. Not only were the peasants against it, many rural cadres also refused to follow this policy. Work teams were sent down periodically from the commune office to check and enforce this campaign. Women found to be in their fourth pregnancy were dragged to the commune hospital for induced abortion. After the delivery of a third child a woman was fitted with an IUD [intrauterine device] or had a tubal ligation. Those who accepted tubal ligation voluntarily were awarded some cash or gifts. Party cadres who failed to comply with this new regulation or refused to enforce it were promptly fired from their posts. Once the peasants realized that the government was determined to carry out this policy, they grudgingly accepted it.

"This three-child policy lasted for about three years, until 1977. After that, the government reduced the number from three to two per family. Not only were newlyweds allowed to have only two children, but they had to wait for at least three years between children. At that time there was still strong resistance in our village against this policy change. It was my most difficult task during my years in public service. Under this new policy, after the birth of the first child, a woman would have an IUD implanted at the commune hospital until two years after the first delivery. The IUD would then be removed for the second conception. If the woman conceived before this two-year waiting period, she would be required to have an abortion. If the family refused to obey the regulation and had a second child too soon, the brigade would fine this family RMB$10 for each month this second child was born ahead of schedule. At that point most village families were still poor, and RMB$10 was a stiff fine."

"What would happen to a woman after giving birth to the second child?" I asked.

"Four months after the delivery of the second child, the woman would be taken to the commune hospital for a tubal ligation. This was far more reliable than an IUD, which is not 100 percent foolproof. It could also be removed easily. So, after fulfilling the quota of two children, the women underwent surgery. In 1982, the government imposed further restrictions by extending the interval between the first and second child from three to four years. Many villagers were disgruntled about this new policy, but resistance was minimum. They seemed to realize that there was nothing they could do, so they accepted it with resignation. This two-child family policy lasted until now, when the government imposed this one-child-per-family policy in rural areas."

"Now, who actually formulates these policies? Is it the national government that issues a policy for the entire country, or the local government making its own rules? Somehow I have the feeling that the punishment adopted in Lin Village was formulated by the local government," I prompted Ye.

"You are both right and wrong, as usual," Ye replied in his half-teasing tone. "The national government only sets guidelines for birth control. For instance, the national government may set a growth rate target of eleven per thousand for the next year, and ask the provincial government to comply with the goal. The provincial authorities, upon receiving this goal, then figure out how many births can occur in this province during the following year. They then established rules for the entire province to meet this goal. In Fujian Province, for instance, the provincial government stipulated during the current campaign that all rural families can now have only one child per family. But under certain conditions a couple is allowed to have their second child. One condition is that the average farmland per person in an area exceeds 50 *mou* or more. Only a few counties in the western part of the province, where there are a lot of mountains and few residents, meet this condition. Another condition is allowing the miners to have a second child because the accidental death rate among coal miners is high. A high birthrate allows coal mining communities to replenish the labor force needed for mining. The third condition for an exemption is if both the husband and wife were only children. They are then allowed to have two children so that each family will have an heir to carry on the family line. Even if one or both children are girls, the family can keep the girl at home and bring in a husband for her to carry on the family line. These specific, detailed regulations are formulated by the provincial government based on actual conditions in the province.

"While the provincial government sets the rules, it is left to the local governments at the township and village level to meet the goals. In our case, the village government decided what the most effective measures were to enforce this new ruling. In our village, business investment is the biggest concern among village families. We can threaten people with cutting off their business ties. But in a poor village where there are few business activities, this stipulation would be ineffective. Different localities have to develop different strategies in order to carry out the policy."

I seemed to remember that urban residents in China had adopted the one-child policy a long time ago, and didn't seem to resist it as strongly as the country people. I asked Ye, "Was it true that city residents adopted this one-child policy much earlier? How come this policy was so readily accepted by city people?"

"Cities in China adopted a one-child family policy in 1979." Ye scratched his head as if in search of the proper answer. "City people can easily adopt the one-child-per-family policy for practical reasons. First of all, city people generally don't have enough living space. For instance, the average living space for residents in Xiamen City is about two square meters per person. It is already very crowded. Besides, all city residents work in government offices or enterprises. By the time they retire, the elderly can live on their retirement pensions, which amount to 70 to 80 percent of their regular wage. They don't have to rely on their children to support them in old age.

"The situation in the countryside is completely different. Our living space is not restricted. The average housing space in our village now is about twenty square meters per person. Most city families don't even have that much space for the entire family. In addition, we peasants live on our labor. We have no retirement pension to draw on when we grow old. Who is going to support me if not one of my sons? We peasants are not prejudiced against girls or women. But, the fact is that girls are generally married out to another family when they grow up. You need to have at least one son to stay on with the family.

"In other words, unless the government can develop a comprehensive pension system for peasants, until then I feel the government should allow a peasant family to have two children. Even if you have two girls, you can still marry out one daughter and keep one home. The girl who stays home can take in a husband from another family that has two sons. This way we can solve the problem of old-age support."

"How is the family planning policy carried out in Lin Village?" I changed the subject a bit. "Who actually enforces it?"

"I normally stay aloof from this birth control business," Ye lit a cigarette and answered. "I allow the head of the Women's League, Hou Lingli, to deal with this problem. She keeps records on all village women about the number of children, IUD implants, and tubal ligations. Because Hou is in charge of the village-wide family planning program, she also takes care of village men who are willing to undergo a vasectomy. It is amusing to see Hou accompanying men to the commune hospital for the operation. Sometimes a newly transferred nurse or doctor, who doesn't know Hou's official responsibility, might ask her, 'Are you related to this man? Are you his wife? Why do you come with him if you are not related?' She says she is often embarrassed by these questions. There are only seven men who have had vasectomies in this village. Vasectomy is not popular here because men believe the operation could make them impotent. These seven men have had a vasectomy either because they are dedicated Party members who responded to the call of the government to act as other people's models, or because their wives were in poor health and thus unsuitable for tubal ligation. Villagers believe that any cut in the body means the loss of essential bodily essence (*qi*). Both vasectomy and tubal ligation are considered detrimental to a person's health. That is one additional reason why villagers hate this birth control policy."

"But why can't the government promote pills or condoms, which are not as harmful to the body?" I asked about possible alternatives.

"The government doesn't believe the peasants would use contraceptive devices voluntarily," Ye responded. "This would be like inviting a wolf to guard the sheepfold. Peasants would do anything possible to have an additional child. Even when a woman has an IUD, she might have this device removed by an illegal midwife. I heard that in this area there is a midwife who comes to our village periodically to perform this service for RMB$10 per person. That is why we need to round up all the women in the brigade once in a while for checkups to make sure their IUDs are in place. Of course tubal ligation is the safest method preventing unwanted births. But the government is reluctant to perform it liberally for practical considerations. A woman may have given birth to the maximum number of children she is allowed. But one of the children may die. When that happens the woman is entitled to have another child. Tubal ligation is very difficult to reverse, thus making it difficult for the woman to become pregnant again."

It was now quite late at night. I said goodbye to Ye and returned to my apartment.

Implementing the Policy

The week following the announcement of this new one-child family policy, horrible stories circulated among villagers about how this campaign was being conducted in other villages. I was told, for instance, in Hongshan Village, a work team headed by a deputy township mayor and a handful of cadres from the township office arrived with a van on the first day of June. Upon hearing of the arrival of the work team, several families with pregnant women fled, mostly to the women's birthplaces in other counties. A few families hid their pregnant women under the bed and locked the door as if no one was home.

The work team forced its way into the homes. If they found a woman hiding inside, they took her for a pregnancy test. All those with positive results were taken to the township hospital for abortion. If the entire family had fled, the work team would take household valuables—such as a television set, a sewing machine, or a bicycle—to the township headquarters. It would then leave word for the owner that if this family didn't come to claim these valuables in person at township headquarters within three days, the township office would simply confiscate all goods. For poor families that didn't have anything of value, the work team dismantled their house doors or windows as collateral.

On June 6, the day the birth control work team was to come to Lin Village, the village was unusually calm and quiet. All activity in the village ceased and villagers anxiously awaited their fate. A shiny blue van arrived at the village office at 9 A.M., carrying a deputy township mayor and three township office cadres, who formed the most dreaded work team. P.S. Ye and other village officials greeted them at the office and immediately had a closed-door meeting with them for the entire morning.

Lunch was a banquet prepared by Hopping Toad Wu, apparently out of the village coffer. I was invited by Ye to join the meal and sat next to Deputy Mayor Ho. During the meal I had the chance to talk with Ho about this campaign. He told me that the entire township (formerly the commune) had eighteen villages (formerly brigades), and was divided into five zones for this campaign. There were five deputy mayors at the township office, and each of them was in charge of a zone with three or four township officials that formed the work team. Each work team thus had three to four villages under its jurisdiction to implement this birth control campaign. Deputy Mayor Ho's zone included Hongshan, Lin, Mudhole, and Hilltop villages. He also confirmed that he had had a great deal of difficulty in Hongshan Village. His work team members had to crawl over a few house walls to gain entry to the houses. Yes, the rumors had been true. Sometimes they found pregnant women hiding inside. For those who fled, the work team took their valuables or house doors. He jokingly told me that if I went to the township warehouse now, I would find a lot of television sets and front doors. It took six full days to complete this campaign in Hongshan Village.

"But," Deputy Mayor Ho said confidently, "I don't think I will have any problem here in this village. P.S. Ye is an effective cadre, and villagers follow his lead."

It was half past one after lunch, and there were already many villagers gathered around the office, mostly women. Ye asked Hou Lingli to check through the list and found that all twenty-seven women who had already had one child but who had not been sterilized were there. Deputy Mayor Ho winked at me as if to remind me of his prediction.

The work team divided the women into two groups, and took them by van to the township hospital in Jiangtou for checkups. When the second group of women departed, I saw Tiger's mother come out of the crowd and walk straight to Ye. She pointed her finger at him and cried, "You said that you would do your best to protect my daughter-in-law. But how come now she is taken to the township hospital? You son of a whore! You should die an accidental death!"

Ye's face turned green but he didn't respond. He then turned to me and told me that he would go to the hospital with the work team to be able to continue their discussion as the van returned. Realizing that I was not invited to join them, I excused myself and went back to my apartment.

That evening I heard fragmented reports from villagers that a few women who were taken to the hospital were forced to have abortions. But other than that, everything else seemed to work out fine. The work team accomplished its task late that night and went back to Jiangtou Town.

Ye's Analysis

The next morning I went to Ye's house to find out how he had handled the work team and why this campaign was so successfully carried out. He seemed to be anticipating my visit and readily apologized to me. "Sorry I couldn't let you attend our meeting yesterday. You probably know that, recently, the U.S. government has been making a big issue in the United Nations out of our country's family planning practices. Since you are from the United States, the township government has specific instructions not to involve you in this campaign."

"I don't want to get involved in this campaign," I lied, realizing I had no choice. "As long as you can tell me how it is carried out, I am satisfied."

"That sounds fine with me," Ye assured. "Tell me what you want to know."

"What kind of arrangements did you work out with the work team during the meetings?" I asked. "And how did you decide which women should have an abortion?"

"This is a complex issue," Ye replied slowly. "When the new policy was announced last week, there were several women in this village who were already pregnant and who, under the former two-child family policy, were entitled to have their second child. They have waited for four years after their first delivery and are legal under the old regulations. These cases have to be honored, otherwise

I will lose my reputation. There were also several women who were pregnant for the second time but have not waited long enough. The interval between the first and second pregnancy is less than four years. These are unauthorized pregnancies under the old rule, and have to be treated differently.

"The first thing we did in the closed-door meeting with the work team yesterday was to clarify our situation with the township office. We found out that for 1985, the township has a target population growth rate of eleven per thousand. Our village has slightly over 1,000 people, so that means we can have a net growth of eleven people. Now, we also have an average death rate of ten per thousand per annum in our village. This means that our village is entitled to have twenty-one births in 1985. Thus, twenty-one births is the quota for 1985. We drafted a contract with the work team, stating that the number of births in our brigade in this year will not exceed this quota. Failure to observe this contract will subject this village to a fine of RMB$5,000.

"Once this was determined, we began to discuss specific cases. There were ten marriages in the village in early 1985, which means that we have to reserve ten births to these ten couples. There were another five pregnant women who, under the former two-child family policy, were entitled to have their second child. We thus had to subtract five births from the remaining eleven for them. This left only six births this village could have for the remainder of 1985. We noticed that there were at least eleven women who were not supposed to become pregnant but were. We had to select for abortion five out of these eleven unauthorized conceptions to meet this quota.

"Besides these eleven unauthorized pregnant women, there were another sixteen who had IUDs, and hence not supposed to be pregnant. I told the work team that I would turn all twenty-seven women over to the commune hospital for checkups. We wanted to use our six-births quota for all those more than six months pregnant. I argued that it is too dangerous for women more than six months pregnant to have abortion. If there were more women in this category than our quota, the village would pay this RMB$5,000 fine to the township. The village would in turn fine those women whose pregnancies were illegal. For all women whose pregnancy were below five months, they would undergo induced abortion at the commune hospital immediately."

"How did Tiger's wife fit in this scheme?" I asked.

"She was in the unauthorized pregnancy category, for her daughter is only two years old. But she is definitely more than six months pregnant. I figured that this was the only way I could save her. The work team agreed with my suggestion and took all women to the hospital. Of the original eleven unauthorized pregnancies, including Tiger's wife, ten of them were already above six months. Only one, whose surname is Ma, was five months pregnant and was ordered to have an abortion. Among the remaining sixteen women who didn't appear to be pregnant, the hospital found out that six of them were also pregnant. They were also ordered to have abortions immediately. Another five who had had the

IUDs removed had them reinserted at the hospital. In the end we had exceeded our quota by four births this year. Our village will pay the RMB$5,000 fine to the township government, but we saved four babies. I consider that a great accomplishment."

"Did all the women ordered to have abortions accepted it willingly?" I asked.

"More or less," Ye replied. "The only trouble I had yesterday was with the Ma woman, who was five months pregnant and was asked to have an abortion. She refused to go to the abortion room. She insisted that I had a personal vendetta against her and singled her out for punishment. Why would she be the only one out of the original eleven that was required to have an abortion, she demanded? It was because she was not originally from this village. Brigade officials dared only to pick on outsiders, she claimed.

"I was furious about her accusations. I instructed Lin Qifa, the brigade security head, to tell Ma, 'If you don't like the abortion procedure in the hospital, secretary Ye will have a better treatment for you when we return to the village. He will send the brigade militia to drag you to the brigade office. He knows which spot on your stomach to kick to make you abort!' My warning apparently worked. I heard this Ma woman went sheepishly to the abortion room. After her operation I asked Hou Lingli to send her RMB$60 from the brigade treasury as nutrition money, plus half an ounce of jinseng root to restore her health. But do you know what? That whore didn't appreciate what I did for her! She sent her husband to the township office last night to charge me with intimidation. She said that I wanted to kick the baby out of her stomach. Knowing that I was only pretending to be mean, the township officials just ignored her."

As we were talking, Tiger's mother appeared in Ye's courtyard. She had a broad smile on her face, but approached the door step in a sinuous manner. She said apologetically to Ye, "Please forgive me for what I said yesterday afternoon. I didn't mean it. I knew that you would do everything you could for Tiger. I will burn incense and pray for you in our temple."

"Never mind what you'd said!" Ye impatiently waved her away. "As long as you stop cursing me either to my face or behind my back, I am satisfied."

"I will never do that again," the old lady murmured and left in the same swift manner that she came.

Ye as Mediator

I was amused by this entire episode and half-jokingly asked Ye, "Do you receive this sort of treatment from villagers all the time? I thought you were the village boss. Tiger's mother seemed to have no reservations when she pissed on you in public!"

"What can I do in a situation like that?" Ye shrugged and smiled reluctantly. "Peasants are never appreciative. They always expect you to do everything for them, but never consider what they can do for the public good. Actually Tiger's mother is better than most villagers. She at least realized that she had mistreated me and came to apologize. Most other villagers would just piss on you and forget about the whole event after you meet their demands."

"So, what is the reward for being a local-level official in this village?" I solicited his opinion.

"Well, that is a question I have been asking myself constantly," Ye replied. "Serving as a leading Party cadre in a Chinese village is not an easy job. One has to cope constantly with conflicting interests and pressures. On the one hand, we have to follow directives issued from higher authorities to accomplish this or that. We have to comply with these demands because the Party always takes it as a serious challenge to its authority if a local cadre disobeys such orders. The Party has all sorts of stern measures to discipline disloyal cadres. On the other hand, when executing Party orders, especially unpopular ones such as birth control policies, we inevitably offend disgruntled villagers, and then we have to spend the rest of our lives with them. Resistance from the villagers makes our tasks doubly difficult.

"I find myself in a no-win position between the national government and the rural populace. The government views us, the rural cadres, through doubting eyes. We are first seen as an extension of the bureaucracy. We, the village cadres, are ultimately responsible for carrying out government policies. But, in the meantime, the government has also been suspicious about rural cadres having been co-opted by their kinsmen and community, and hence think we are corrupt. Similarly, villagers look at us ambivalently. On the one hand they feel we should represent them in dialogue with the government, especially when the government wants to enforce unpopular policies. We should channel the peasants' views and feelings to the government. When the government imposes unpopular practices, villagers feel the rural cadres should resist those policies on their behalf. But then villagers also believe that we are ready to betray their interests and side with the government since it is from the government that we have authority. No matter what we do, we are criticized. My principle of administration, based on past experiences, is to be protective of the villagers' interests as much as possible. When carrying out actual government directives, I try not to go to extremes. Moderation is always the safest conduct, as my father always told me. In our day-to-day activities rural cadres have to be very careful to take a middle of the road approach in everything we must deal with.

"Take farming as an example. In May 1984 when we partitioned the brigade collective, there were slightly more than 1,000 people in this village. The total farmland we have is 700 *mou*. In the breakup process each person received approximately 0.7 *mou*. In my family, with my wife Baozhu, myself, and three children, we received 3.5 *mou* of land as our private contract land. Even though I don't care much about farming in the first place, I have no choice but to farm this contract land as part of my duty. When I started to farm my own land I realized the dilemma I would face. If my land appeared to be poorly farmed with below average yields, the villagers would definitely point their fingers at me and say, 'Look at the poor field that son of a whore has! Of course he really can't farm! The Party secretary has been living off the sweat and blood of us, the poor peasants, for the past few years. Of course he doesn't know how to farm!' If I work hard and have a good harvest, the villagers criticize me from another angle: 'Of course the Party secretary can do a good job! He has all the proper external connections to obtain additional chemical fertilizer and pesticide for his farm.' You are damned if you do, and damned if you don't! That's the basic dilemma village cadres face. Thus, when I farm my land, I carefully keep a middle-ground approach for staying close to the average in the brigade."

"Surely some villagers will be very critical of you as a public official. Every political system or political figure faces the same problem," I assured him. "But you still have all the power to affect the villagers' lives. Do they feel compelled to promote good relations with you because of that?"

"Of course some do. But you have to be very careful in drawing the line between their support of you in executing a policy and their currying favor with you through illegal means. As a top Party cadre in this village I have been very careful to maintain my integrity. One common mistake many Party cadres commit is to take things that don't belong to them. For example, during the last Chinese New Year in February 1985, Hopping Toad Wu's son Wu Hongen came to visit me. He sent me a can of biscuits. When I opened the can I found a red envelope containing RMB$1,000 in it. I immediately called him over and returned the money to him. Not that I don't like money. I could have definitely used the money to buy a color television that my children have always wanted to have. But what would happen if I took that money? The next time Wu Hongen made a mistake, I would be unable to stand up and criticize him. Why should he give me that money if not for buying my favor? You receive something that is not rightfully yours, you will have to reciprocate with something more valuable in return.

"Many villagers brought me gifts, especially cartons of imported cigarettes, Good Companions. When they did, I would pay them the current market price. I would tell them that I enjoyed Good Companions myself. I thanked them for taking the trouble to buy the cigarettes for me. I would also tell them that since I didn't know how much they actually paid, I would just reimburse them the current market price.

"A month ago the foreman of the brigade construction company brought me a portable stereo system. He said that he would lend it to me. If I liked it, he said, he would sell it to me for RMB$300. You know how much it costs in Xiamen's friendship stores? At least RMB$1,000! This fellow was smart. He knows that I don't take bribes. What he was doing was not bribing, but selling something to me at a discount price. I told him that I don't listen to music, and therefore have no use for this stereo. He then made another offer: 'What about a motorcycle? A three-year-old, second-hand Yamaha 100 cc for RMB$1,000?'

Frankly, I was quite tempted. I had been thinking about buying a Yamaha motorcycle for some time. I also thought about the popular saying among Party cadres: '[If one] has authority but does not use it, it expires and is invalidated' (*yoquan buyong, yuqi zhuofei*). But I remembered that my father had always told me not to take things that were not my proper share. Besides, I hate people who are greedy. How could I allow myself to be something that I dislike?

"With all political power concentrated in the hands of the brigade Party secretary, his opportunity for corruption is tremendous. This can be easily concealed too. For instance, in 1983, after my family division, I decided to move out of the two-story building that I shared with my three brothers. I wanted to build a new house of my own. I purchased stone slabs, cement, bricks, and steel from my friends at reasonable prices. A few workers at the brigade's construction company volunteered to build the house for me. But I declined their offers and hired instead migratory workers from Huian County. In doing so I avoid any potential implications of corruption. The only workers I hired from the brigade construction team were carpenters for the roof and windows. At first they refused to accept payment for their works, but I insisted. Then they suggested a price lower than the regular fee charged by ordinary workers. I paid them according to their suggestion and told them that I considered their favor based on our friendship and because we live in the same village. There would be no future favors that I owed them as brigade Party secretary. I asked each of them to write a receipt for my own record. In doing so I was keeping myself away from future unnecessary obligations because of their work for me. I finished my house in early 1985 at a total cost of about RMB$15,000, much cheaper than comparable houses in the village."

I pondered over what Ye had said and raised a question: "You mean you don't take graft more because of your conscience than because of an institutional mechanism to prevent you from doing so? What about your superiors? Are the cadres in township offices supposed to be watching over your shoulder?"

"Theoretically, yes," Ye replied neatly. "In reality, however, brigade-level cadres have a lot of autonomy as long as they implement the policy directives issued from the top. Village-level officials are all Party members. If a villager brings charges against a village cadre to the township office, who do the township authorities listen to first? Of course the village cadre. Township officials and village officials are all Party members, so Party loyalty supersedes official obligations. This allows local cadres to abuse their power. In fact, most of this township's eighteen brigade Party secretaries are very corrupt. They use their authority to channel public funds. During the recent breakup of rural collectives, many brigade-level cadres made a fortune. The best-known person in this respect is Huang Jincheng, who is the Party secretary of Hecu brigade. I figure that Huang Jincheng must have over half a million dollars under his name now. Huang Jincheng's case is an interesting one and it illustrates the fundamental problem in our political system.

"Huang Jincheng came to power in his brigade during the Cultural Revolution. Hecu Village directly faces the offshore island, the Little Quemoy, occupied by Nationalist bandits. Because of its frontline location, Hecu is directly under the jurisdiction of the army division commander. Huang has been very good in cultivating a relationship with the military. He was recommended by the former division commander to become Hecu's brigade head in 1968, then promoted to brigade Party secretary in the late 1970s. Because he has the support of the military, nobody at the township level dares confront him for his wrongdoings. If you saw that little bastard in person, you would never believe he could be vicious. He is basically a short, stupid, illiterate country idiot, but he pretends to be someone of power and broad knowledge. He carries a pistol all the time, seemingly to show his self-importance. Whenever he has an argument with people, either in his brigade or at the commune office, he pulls out his pistol, lays it in front of his opponent and says, 'What are you going to do with me? You think you are better than I am? Show me what you have!' This is a very effective way to intimidate people.

"Let me give you a few examples to show how corrupt Huang is. Hecu brigade has a fishing fleet that fishes along the coast. Whenever the fleet returns, Huang sends his subordinates to check the catch and pick out the best items, such as oysters and crabs, for his family use. This is minor compared with his abuses of brigade funds. A few years ago, Huang had the brigade purchase three Liberation brand trucks with public funds, and then leased two of them to his two sons for minimal rental fees. As a result, each of his two sons is making more than RMB$10,000 per year. When his two sons reached marriageable age, Huang Jincheng sent out his subordinates to scout for the prettiest girls in his brigade. When a girl was identified, Huang sent a subordinate over to the girl's house to propose. The messenger would tell the girl's parents, 'Huang Jincheng wants your daughter to marry his son. If your daughter marries Huang's son, she will be transferred to a light, clerical job away from the farm.' And that he did. After the marriage, Huang's first daughter-in-law was assigned to the brigade textile factory as its treasurer. His second daughter-in-law got a job in the brigade administrative office.

"Probably Huang's most outrageous act was when the government appropriated a piece of reclaimed land along the Hecu coast. The RMB$200,000 compensation the government paid to this brigade was quietly stashed away by Huang. This particular incident involves my brigade, too. When Hecu brigade built this reclaimed land in the early 1970s, our brigade sent a work team to help in its construction, without compensation. We should therefore now receive a share of this government compensation.

"After Hecu brigade dismantled its collective in 1983, Huang Jincheng invested in the construction of a textile mill in his village. You know how he got construction workers for his textile mill? He ordered the teachers in his brigade's primary school to engage in 'voluntary labor work' (*yiwu laodong*) on a rotating basis.

The teachers grumbled, but nobody dared to challenge Huang's order. When the former district deputy Party secretary, a man named Pan, heard about Huang's abuses in Hecu, he was furious and swore that he would remove Huang from that position. Pan declared that either he would fire Huang as Hecu brigade Party secretary, or Pan himself would resign from his post as district deputy Party secretary. Since the district administration is two steps above the brigade, so you might think that Pan would succeed in removing Huang Jincheng from his brigade Party secretary post. But that turned out not to be the case. When Pan brought the charges against Huang Jincheng to his superiors, Pan was immediately transferred to a factory in Quanzhou City.

"To some extent I think Huang Jincheng's behavior is even worse than the warlords or landlords before the Liberation. How does Huang Jincheng maintain his power? Apparently, military support has been crucial. Even Xiamen City's Party secretary wouldn't dare offend the army division commander. Besides that, Huang Jincheng knows how to protect himself. For instance, when the Fujian Provincial People's Congress held its annual meeting in Fuzhou City in April 1985, Huang collected the best oysters he could find from his brigade fishing fleet and delivered them to Fuzhou by special car and fed the representatives. Of course he would not say that he sent these oysters. He claimed that he was sending the oysters on behalf of the people of Hecu to congratulate the successful opening of the provincial congress. There is a Chinese saying: 'Once you eat from someone, you will have a soft mouth toward that person; once you take from someone, you will have tender hands toward that person.' How could the provincial representatives and officials act against Huang Jincheng after feasting on the nice oysters he sent them? Whenever government officials or newspaper reporters visit Hecu brigade, Huang prepares the best food and wine to entertain them. Even though he spends brigade funds, Huang Jincheng is the one who will be remembered for all the niceties. That is how a corrupt local official like Huang maintains power for so long."

"What you are saying is that a village Party secretary generally has unchecked power within his reign," I commented. "If this official does not have conscience or personal integrity, he can easily abuse his power and then cover it up, like this Huang Jincheng. But I have the feeling that Huang is an exceptional case among all village Party secretaries in this township. Do you agree?"

Ye nodded his head in agreement. I contunued, "If Huang is indeed a special case, what factors prevent a village cadre from becoming another Huang Jincheng?"

Ye thought for a moment and replied, "There are two considerations that have more or less prevented rural cadres from becoming completely corrupt. One is the central government's political campaigns. Some previous campaigns were aimed at rural cadres. You don't know when the next campaign will come. To avoid being the object of struggle sessions, you should not mistreat the local people.

"The second factor that serves to minimize abuses by rural cadres is that not all rural cadres will be promoted out of the countryside. If you are to stay in the village for the rest of your life, you should be more careful in dealing with your villagers while you have power. Even if the villagers do not retaliate now, they may do something against your children in the future.

"When you consider these two factors, you can understand why sometimes the local cadres are willing to modify or even tacitly resist unpopular government policies to suit local conditions. One method is stonewalling a specific policy. When the government directive arrives, you set up a committee to 'study' it. Then you claim to have selected a couple of experimental model cases to evaluate the actual effects of this policy. In the meantime you look at other brigades to see how and what are they doing. If this policy is indeed unpopular, you take it back to the committee for further 'study.' So you can drag your feet for at least several months. When you are required to actually implement this policy, you can also water it down by creating a few loopholes.

"One such example in our brigade is fishing in the reservoir. This man-made lake belongs to the commune, and the commune administration has an office, headed by Dark Skin Lin now, to supervise the stocking of and fishing in this lake. Many people in the vicinity steal fish from this reservoir. My estimate is that at least two-thirds of the fish in the reservoir are stolen each year. Only one-third of it is being caught by the commune office. So the commune office ordered all villages surrounding the lake to step up night patrols to prevent theft and to arrest those who steal fish from this lake. When I received this order, I set up a committee to investigate the most effective way to implement this policy. Then I reported to Dark Skin Lin that our brigade would increase patrols around our lake shore at night. This, of course, is all on paper; I actually did nothing. Why should I? People in other brigades steal fish from the reservoir, too. If I carried out this order seriously, I could definitely stop some of the stealing in our brigade. But that would only increase opportunities for other brigades. Why should I cut back on a source of nutrition for my villagers for the benefit of other brigades?"

Ye's Programs

I had known all along that P.S. Ye had misgivings about the situation in rural China. He disagreed with many of the heavy-handed policies the national government established in the countryside. He regarded the Party and many of its beliefs as contradictions of peasant cultural traditions. But in the meantime Ye appeared to be a dedicated Communist, upholding the ideal of working for the common good. His unwavering commitment to justice and to the disadvantaged, such as the aged and infirm in Lin Village, made him an outstanding example of the dedicated Chinese Communist necessary to remake human nature. How could a person like Ye reconcile the conflicting roles he played as a social critic and as a Party loyalist? I wondered. Under the current policy of decentralization, his position as a Party functionary had been significantly undermined and his power substantially trimmed. What kind of future prospects did he have? What type of personal adjustments must he make to cope with this new situation? I put these questions to Ye a few days before my departure from the village. He gave me some very straightforward answers.

"After the breakup of our brigade in May 1984, I began to work on an investment plan. I predicted that the profit margin of sand brick manufacturing in our brigade would decline. Other brigades in the vicinity had seen our success and had established similar production facilities. There are more than fifty sand brick factories across the island now. With this increased competition, sand brick prices will soon bottom out. Another problem with sand bricks is the need for coal dust in the mixture. Since more buildings in Xiamen City will be skyscrapers, the sand bricks, containing incompletely burned coal dust, will become a fire hazard. I speculated there would eventually be a ban on using sand bricks in tall buildings. Under this circumstance, I supposed, the traditional kiln-fired red bricks would be in great demand.

"I began to discuss with the manager of a ceramic floor tile factory in Xiamen City about building a new, mechanized red brick kiln in our village. This kiln is far more efficient than traditional kilns. It takes the traditional brick kiln at least four weeks to produce one kilnful of bricks: one week for the earth brick molds to be stacked inside the kiln, the second week for them to be fired with slow but constant fire, the third week for the fired bricks to cool off, and the fourth week for the fired bricks to be brought out. The new mechanized red brick kiln uses a different procedure. Coal dust is mixed with clay when the earth brick molds are made. Then, the earth molds are driven through the kiln and fired by electrically generated heat. When the heat is high enough, it induces the coal dust in the mold to burn. At the other end of the kiln appear finished red bricks. The entire process takes only twenty-four hours.

"Nobody knows where this new mechanized red brick manufacturing technology has come from. Some say that it was invented in Yugoslavia and brought back to China by one of the students sent there in the early 1980s. Others believe it was developed in Malaysia recently and brought back by an overseas Chinese. Anyhow, the manager of Xiamen City's ceramic floor tile company knew about it and discussed with me the possibility of setting up a factory in our village. I thought it was a good idea and began to discuss this venture with other villagers in early 1984.

"Around June of 1984 I called the first meeting of all potential investors in our village. My plan was to have eight shares costing RMB$10,000 each. I invited most brigade-level Party cadres to join me. At that point the government was still ambivalent about how large a private enterprise could be. If we included most of the village's leading Party cadres in this enterprise, we could call it a collective enterprise and hence circumvent government regulations. The two former

Party secretaries, Opium Hong and Dark Skin Lin, decided to join, as well as Lin Chengrui, the brigade clerk who later was appointed brigade head, and Hou Lingli, head of the Women's League. Ding Yong, Thunderbolt Lin's stepbrother, who worked closely with me during the breakup of the brigade, also participated. There were two people I had to invite, but didn't really want to, Li Dehai, the brigade head, nicknamed Double-Headed Snake, and Lin Qifa, brigade security head. I still can't forgive them for their plot to take over all brigade enterprises during the breakup.

"I first approached Double-Headed Snake and asked if he would be interested in putting RMB$10,000 into my new enterprise. Even though, at that point, Double-Headed Snake must have had at least RMB$20,000 in the bank, he didn't dare to invest. Even though he is the richest person in this brigade, he is still a typical nearsighted, illiterate peasant: He holds tight to the small gold pot under his pillow and knows nothing about investment. I was delighted when Double-Headed Snake told me that since he was involved in a sand brick factory he had no spare money for this new venture.

"My next task was to make a gesture to invite Lin Qifa to join this venture, while letting him know that I really didn't want him to. I went to his house the day before our first meeting, knowing in advance that he wasn't home. Only Lin Qifa's wife Jiang Jinhua, Thunderbolt Lin's stepsister, was there. I casually told her that I was planning to organize a new enterprise and would have our first meeting the next day. I told her that if Lin Qifa was interested in joining us, he could come to our meeting. Apparently Lin Qifa understood when he realized I had conveyed the offer through his wife, a woman. He didn't join us.

"The investment in this mechanized red brick kiln has been a great success. Among the eight investors, one is the manager of the ceramic floor tile company in Xiamen City. Another one, surnamed Huang, is a skilled worker from Fuqing County in northern Fujian who will be serving as the manager of the new plant. Huang hired about fifty workers from his home village to work here. People in northern Fujian are poor and are willing to work for a minimum wage. The remaining six shares are owned by our villagers. We began to produce red bricks in November 1984. Sales have been brisk. We could hardly keep production up with market demands. In 1984, even though the production period was only about one month, we generated close to RMB$20,000 net profit. When Double-Headed Snake heard about our huge profit, he came to beg me to let him buy one or even half a share in this enterprise. I told him that when we needed cash for constructing the plant and the manpower to start the enterprise, he refused to join us. Now that we had everything set and began to enjoy the profit, he wanted to have a cut in it. Sorry, I told him, but no deal.

"The year 1984 was the best of my life. From my share in the brigade enterprises contracted under my name, I received RMB$2,500 as my year-end dividend. In addition, the mechanized red brick kiln paid RMB$2,000 profit for my share. With that money, I paid off all my debts. And I was not the only one making good money that year. Almost all other villagers were successful during 1984. A village man who operates a hand tractor to transport bricks can easily make RMB$400–500 per month, twice the amount a university professor is making. Even the widow who came with her daughter to plead for my protection before the breakup told me that she was making a lot of money by growing vegetables on her contract land and selling them in Xiamen's free market. Every evening this woman carries the vegetables from her field and washes them for next morning's market. The daughter hauls the two basketsful of vegetables on her bicycle and rides down to Xiamen. The widow told me that she is making about RMB$200 to $300 per month, much better than before the division.

"As you can see, general economic conditions in our village have improved significantly since the division in May 1984. I can't think of a single family who has become poorer now after the breakup than they were under the collective system. There is one thing, however, that worries me: Even though general living conditions among all villagers seem to have improved since the division, the gap between rich and poor families has also increased. I estimate there are about one dozen village families in our brigade making more than RMB$10,000 per year. But on the other hand, the bottom-level families are making only about RMB$1,000. This increased disparity within the village may create problems in the future, and I am concerned about it."

"Why can some people benefit from this new policy and become prosperous, while others do not?" I asked. "Can you characterize those who have been successful?"

"Yes," Ye replied succinctly. "Based on my observations, several types of people in our village are now doing far better than the others. The first group includes high-level cadres who have good external connections to develop new enterprises. These cadres are also doing well because they know more about current policy trends. They can take advantage of this new situation because they have better business timing. In our village this includes me; Double-Headed Snake, the former brigade head; Lin Qifa, the brigade security head; and Lin Chengrui, the current brigade head. The second type of people who benefit most from current reforms are army veterans who learned special skills during their service. Most of the truck drivers in Lin Village learned their trade while serving in the military. A diligent truck driver in our village makes about RMB$1,000 per month now. People in this category include Lin Qishan and Hou Tong. The third type of people who make a lot of money under the current private ownership system are those with higher education and professional skills, such as medical doctors, accountants, and salesmen. People who don't fit into any of these categories are making some progress, but not as dramatic as those with specific skills.

"One ridiculous thing happened when our brigade became known as a successful unit. Suddenly, every government office in Xiamen Rural District discovered we owed it money. Two weeks ago, a man from the Rural District's tax office came to our village. I wasn't around that day. This tax man talked to Lin Chengrui, the new brigade head, and told him that our brigade owed RMB$8,000 to his office in back taxes. He told Lin to get a check ready for that amount so he could collect it the following week. When I returned that evening Lin reported this incident to me. Lin was preparing to draft this check. I yelled at him, 'You stupid son-of-a-whore! How could you give away our RMB$8,000 so easily? Why do you think we should pay the money? Just because this tax man said so? Let me handle him when he comes next week!'

"The following week this tax man indeed came. Before he even opened his mouth, I confronted him, 'You wanted to collect back taxes from our brigade, ha! Let me tell you what, before we pay this RMB$8,000 to the government, I want you to first clear up a debt the government owes us. Here is the bill: First, for the past thirty-six years, the government never paid us a single dime to support the aged, the injured, martyrs' families, and servicemen's families in our brigade. The total costs amount to RMB$50,000, plus interest. Second, during the past fifteen years, since the government didn't hire enough teachers for our primary school, we had to hire two additional teachers with funds from our own budget. We figure the government owes us RMB$15,000 for these two teachers' salaries. And for the public health system that we have here . . .' Before I finished reading my list that son-of-a-whore ran away and never dared return again.

"I have gained a reputation in this area as one who speaks his mind directly. I found out that this is the best way to deal with government officials. Let me tell you about a recent experience. I was elected as a representative to the Xiamen City People's Assembly in 1984. At our first meeting, chaired by Deputy City Mayor Zhang Ketong, we discussed the problems of our people watching television programs broadcast by the Nationalists. Television signals are sent from Taiwan to the Quemoy Islands. Since we are so close to Quemoy, people can easily pick up Taiwan's programs. Before 1983, the government was very stern about people watching Taiwan programs. Anyone caught was fined RMB$100 for the television set and another RMB$40 for each person in the audience. But most people here love Taiwan's programs because they sometimes have programs in Minnan dialect and because they are interesting programs. After 1984, control over watching Taiwan's programs became relaxed and almost everyone on Xiamen Island tuned in to Taiwan's stations.

"In our City Assembly meeting Deputy Mayor Zhang called this problem an epidemic. He declared that poisonous corruptive elements from the Nationalist bandits had been transmitted to our area through television programs. He urged us to take strong measures to prevent the growth of this epidemic. He even indicated that he had contemplated spending RMB$600,000 to set up an electronic jamming station in the Xiamen area to interrupt television signals from Quemoy. After his speech I responded. I told him I couldn't believe he was so stupid that he did not see the real problems we were facing here. People turned away from our own television programs to watch those from Taiwan because our programs were of poor quality. Why waste RMB$600,000 to build a jamming station? Why not spend the money to improve the quality of our own programs? Deputy Mayor Zhang was stunned by my harsh remarks and didn't know how to respond. He just let the entire issue drop and never raised it again.

"In late 1984, the Xiamen City government asked the township Party secretary if I would like to be deputy chairman of the City Assembly. This would be a full-time job, and I would be able to move my household registration to the city. Had this offer come to me five or ten years earlier, I would probably have jumped at it. What else could I expect in life if not the opportunity to be elevated from the status of a rural cadre to a national cadre? Plus the opportunity to move to the city!

"When the township Party secretary asked me, I turned him down. I told him, 'I am not interested in becoming a government official (*guan*). Here in the village I represent the people (*min*). As long as I stand on the side of the people, I am safe. Tell me, how much do you make per month now as the top Party cadre in the township? RMB$90 per month! You know how much I spend for my imported Good Companion cigarettes per month? At least RMB$150. As a national cadre, you are prohibited by the government from investing in private enterprises. If I take the job in Xiamen's City Assembly, I will be as poor as you. Forget it, comrade, I am not interested.'

"Maybe I will one day regret this decision. But with so many ups and downs in my life, I don't know how to decide what is best for me or what my goal in life is anymore. Sometimes I wonder what has happened in the countryside in the past few years to cause such a dramatic turnaround. Before, all country cadres were eager to become national cadres. Furthermore, ordinary villagers felt honored to be invited to join the Party. But now no villager wants to be recruited. For example, in 1978 when I became brigade Party secretary, there were thirty-one Party members in this village. Now there are still thirty-one. The central government urged us to recruit young and capable people as new Party cadres, but I have failed in all my attempts to persuade anyone to join. People like Hou Tong, the very capable head of the fifth team, or Ding Yong, my close associate, have all declined my invitation to become Party members. Hou Tong put it in the most eloquent manner when he said to me, 'Why should I join the Party? To pay my monthly Party dues? To turn myself in for vasectomy or to turn my wife in for tubal ligation when the Party has a birth control campaign? No way. I am not joining this Party.'

"It is understandable that peasants now have a very negative view of the Party. They talk about Communist ideals with cynicism. They even make puns to ridicule the government. For instance, they turned Xiamen City People's Government (*xiamen renmin shizhengfu*) with a minor twist of the tongue in the local dialect into 'Xiamen city people feeding the government' (*xiamen renmin sizhengfu*). Another popular pun is 'the dictatorship of the proletariat' (*wuchan jieji zhuanzheng*), which in local dialect sounds like 'proletariat always carry rationing coupons' (*wuchan jieji quanzheng*). Whenever there is an unpopular policy that the villagers don't like, they come to me and curse the Party in front of me. I tell them, 'Don't curse me! I don't like these new regulations any more than you do. But since the government has the power and we don't, we'd better follow the rules.'

"I can understand peasants' cynicism toward Communism. There is a fundamental flaw in Communist theory that can be seen very clearly in practice. Communism states that all people are the same with equal abilities and similar needs. Accordingly, then, we should give up all our personal ambitions and interests and strive for the public good. But every peasant knows that these assumptions are wrong. Some people can learn fast while others are slow. There are some farmers who can cut rice straw much faster than others. There are also people who take every opportunity to sneak away from work, and who like nothing more than the fruits of other people's labor. The bottom line is, Why should more capable or dedicated people work hard for those who are less capable or just plain lazy? After a few years of experimenting the peasants realized the whole idea was unrealistic and turned away from it. That is why we have problems recruiting Party members in the countryside.

"Maybe in the long run it is beneficial to have less government presence in the countryside. It seems the peasants are doing quite well under the more relaxed policy of Deng Xiaoping. If you just make a quick comparison between the countryside and the city, you will see the difference in the speed of change. City reform started in October 1984. But have you seen any tangible changes in Xiamen? Probably very few. On the contrary, even before the national government held its Third Plenum of the Eleventh Party Congress in 1978, the countryside was agitating for change. When the new agrarian policy was announced, peasants urged local cadres to change. Peasants in a sense were ready to change as soon as the new policy was announced.

"There are two ways to look at the different ways the city and countryside are changing. On the one hand, peasants in China today are still at the bottom of the social hierarchy. Peasants are only one notch higher than the common criminals in labor reform camps. Why? Just look at actual conditions. If a person in the city or a high-level government official commits a real crime, this person is sent to a labor reform camp as punishment. If a city resident or a government official commits a lesser crime, he is sent down (*xiafang*) to the countryside to live with us. Living in the countryside with peasants is a punishment, from the government's viewpoint! So we peasants are condemned. We have nothing to lose and are therefore ready to accept changes.

"Now, if we look at city people on the other hand, we see that they have too much at stake to risk new ideas and changes. They enjoy government subsidies for food, housing, and retirement pensions. They have job guarantees. When inflation flared up in early 1985, the government immediately gave RMB$2 per person each month to city residents as a subsidy to counteract pork price increases. But have we peasants ever received any such subsidies? Never. It is therefore understandable why city residents are reluctant to accept change.

"My real hope now is for the current policy to continue for a few more years. By 1986, most of our villagers will be able to retire the loans they took out in 1984 during the breakup. By then we can definitely make even more dramatic improvements, since our investments will not be restricted by our loan obligations. For the villagers to expand their vision and to learn new investment opportunities, I am thinking about organizing a tour group from our brigade to the Shengzheng Special Economic Zone. There the villagers can definitely see what a modern city looks like. A tour to the stores there will make them realize what kind of household goods are used in a modern family. We can channel our investments into production facilities producing goods to meet our future needs. Maybe in a couple of years when travel restrictions are relaxed, I will have the chance to visit Hong Kong. Or even go to the United States to see you. Who knows?"

Notes

Chapter 1: Prologue

1. Several works on the subject of geomancy are available in English. They are Maurice Freedman 1964, 1968; Emily Ahern 1973; and Sarah Rossbach 1983. For the relationship between cosmic forces and health in the Chinese context, see Marjorie Topley 1975, Huang Shu-min 1979, and Authur Kleinman 1980.

Chapter 2: Family History

1. The term "feudal" or "feudalistic" is used loosely in China. Most commonly it is used in a historical sense to denote the time before the "Liberation"—the Communist victory in 1949. Used in this way, the dynastic periods in China prior to 1949, and all practices associated with them, literally, the whole Chinese cultural legacy, are included as feudal or feudalistic. The term carries an explicitly negative connotation. But when the Chinese Communists used this label for actual practices, they tended to be more selective in its coverage. The criterion for this discretionary use of the term normally follows the orthodox Marxian theory of human history or directions of political wind at that moment. Generally speaking, we can say that traditional religious practices such as ancestral cults and shamanism are consistently condemned as feudalistic, as well as arranged marriage, patriarchal authority, bound feet, concubinage, and so on. One exception to this category is traditional Chinese medicine.

2. Southeast and south China are known for this type of single-surname lineage village. For more discussion see Maurice Freedman 1958, 1966; Huang Shu-min 1980.

3. Chinese peasants follow a lunar calendar, which uses the rotation of the moon to designate days of a month. Roughly speaking, the Chinese New Year begins in February.

4. The farmland unit used in China is called a *mou*. One hectare equals 15 *mou*, while one acre is about 5.7 *mou*.

5. The importance of maternal kinsmen in the traditional Chinese social context is discussed extensively by Bernard Gallin 1960, and Bernard Gallin and Rita Gallin 1985.

Chapter 3: The Liberation

1. Gambling is strictly illegal in China, and the Chinese government has taken strong measures to suppress it. But in the countryside, apparently, this heavy-handed approach has not been very effective. See Chapter 7 for more discussion on gambling in Lin Village.

2. The Chinese government launched land reform across China in 1951. Peasants were classified as landlords, rich peasants, middle peasants, poor peasants, and tenants/workers, according to Mao's original investigation in Hunan Province. See Mao Zedong 1965. Several writings dealing with this political campaign are available in the West: William Hinton 1966, Chen Yuan-tsung 1980. Both works provide vivid accounts of the authors' personal experiences during this period.

3. Even though during the immediate post-Liberation period the Chinese Communists recruited mainly tenants and poor peasants for the Party, this pattern soon changed to favor middle peasants. A similar account of the new "elite" position of the middle peasants in the countryside is seen in Peggy Printz and Paul Steinle 1977.

Chapter 4: Hunger, Hunger

1. Rice can be cooked either dry or watery—much like porridge in the West. The watery version is called congee.

2. The Great Leap Forward, a part of the Three Red Flags movement, officially lasted from 1958 through 1960.

3. This fraudulent practice apparently had its unintended victim—the Chinese government. Studies showed that the Chinese government, unaware of the extent of fabrication in grain production records during the initial period of the Great Leap Forward, increased grain export in 1959 and 1960, thus further aggravating the famine. See Alan Piazza, 1986.

4. The use of rice chaff and brown sugar to cure edema is also reported in Keng Ling 1972: 228.

5. In-depth analyses of Chinese rural collective organizations can be found in William Parish and Martin Whyte 1978.

6. See for example Victor Nee 1985 and Stevan Harrell 1985.

Chapter 5: Joining the Act

1. To build a school to meet the demands of a local unit, such as a village, a factory, or a government office, is a common practice in China. This kind of school is called "civilian-run school" (*minban xuexiao*) as opposed to "public school" (*gongli xuexiao*). The state normally does not provide operating funds or teachers for civilian-run schools. Teachers of civilian run schools are called "civilian school teachers" (*minban jiaoshi*).

2. The best discussion of the impact of political campaigns in rural China is Anita Chan, Richard Madsen, and Jonathan Unger 1984.

3. An insightful discussion of the roles of "work teams" used by the Chinese government in political campaigns is Victor Nee and David Mozingo 1983.

Chapter 6: Return Home

1. When the May Sixteenth Document was issued, it was declared written by Chairman Mao. It was only after Lin Biao's death that the Chinese government announced that this document was actually drafted by Lin and issued under Mao's name.

2. Breaking Down the Four Olds includes: old thoughts, old culture, old custom, and old habits. This phrase was first coined by Mao in his "Speech at Yen-an Literature Discussion." See Mao Zedong 1965.

3. The formal name of the United Revolution is Xiamen Municipality Revolution-to-the-End United Command; and Fostering Revolution is August 29th Xiamen Commune. A vivid discussion of factional fighting between these two is available in Keng Ling 1972.

4. The date of this battle, August 23, 1967, which P.S. Ye told me, is different from Keng Ling's recollection, which indicates August 19, 1967. I have been unable to determine which of the two is correct.

Chapter 7: Security Head

1. The Chinese government has now claimed that the Cultural Revolution extended from 1966 through 1976, with the downfall of the Gang of Four as its termination point. For practical reasons it is more reasonable to consider the Red Guards period of 1966–1969 as the Cultural Revolution era.

2. Reverse *yang*, or *daoyang*, is a traditional Chinese belief related to the sudden burst of male sexual energy. If treated improperly, the penis of the affected man will shrink back to the abdomen; impotency results.

Chapter 8: Prosperous Years

1. Sworn Brotherhood is a traditional Chinese practice whereby unrelated boys entered into quasi-kinship relationships through a ritual process. On this topic, see Bernard Gallin and Rita Gallin 1977 and David Jordan 1985.

2. The term *guanxi*, or personal connections, is regarded by the government as a serious problem in China. It raises serious questions about equity in the new economic reform when individuals with connections often circumvent laws and regulations. It is apparent here that P.S. Ye looked upon personal connections as his real political asset.

Chapter 9: The Breakup

1. For an in-depth discussion of family division in rural China, see Myron Cohen 1976, 1978.

2. The personality of the household head in determining the family division process is clearly explained in Margery Wolf 1968.

Chapter 10: Village Cadres

1. A discussion on the method and magnitude of China's birth control campaign can be found in Stephen Moser 1983.

Bibliography

Ahern, Emily M.
 1973 The Cult of the Dead in a Chinese Village. Stanford: Stanford University Press.
Anderson, Eugene N.
 1988 The Food of China. New Haven: Yale University Press.
Bernstein, Richard
 1982 From the Center of the Earth: The Search for the Truth About China. Boston: Little, Brown.
Bianco, Lucien
 1971 Origins of the Chinese Revolution, 1915–1949. Stanford: Stanford University Press.
Buck, Pearl
 1949 The Good Earth. New York: John Day Company.
Butterfield, Fox
 1982 China, Alive in the Bitter Sea. New York: Times Books.
Chan, Anita, Richard Madsen, and Jonathan Unger
 1984 Chen Village: The Present History of a Peasant Community in Mao's China. Berkeley, Los Angeles, and London: University of California Press.
Chen Yuan-tsung
 1980 The Dragon's Village: An Autobiographical Novel of Revolutionary China. Middlesex, England: Penguin Books.
Chesneaux, Jean
 1973 Peasant Revolts in China: 1840–1949. New York: W.W. Norton & Company, Inc.
Cohen, Myron L.
 1976 House United, House Divided: The Chinese Family in Taiwan. New York and London: Columbia University Press.
 1978 Developmental Process in the Chinese Domestic Group. In Arthur Wolf, ed. Studies in Chinese Society. Stanford: Stanford University Press.
Elvin, Mark
 1973 The Pattern of the Chinese Past. Stanford: Stanford University Press.
Fairbank, John King
 1979 The United States and China (4th ed.) Cambridge: Harvard University Press.
Freedman, Maurice
 1958 Lineage Organization in Southeastern China. London: Athlone.

1964   Chinese Geomancy: Some Observations in Hong Kong (mimeo). Paper prepared
        for Seminar on Cognitive and Value Systems in Chinese Society, Bermuda,
        January 24–25, 1964. Collected in G. William Skinner, ed. The Study of
        Chinese Society: Essays by Maurice Freedman (1979). Stanford: Stanford
        University Press.
1966   Chinese Lineage and Society: Fujian and Kwangtung. London: Athlone.
1968   Geomancy. Proceedings of the Royal Anthropological Institute of Great Britian
        and Ireland, 1968: 5–15. Collected in G. William Skinner, ed. The Study
        of Chinese Society: Essays by Maurice Freedman (1979). Stanford: Stanford
        University Press.

Gallin, Bernard
1960   Matrilateral and Affinal Relationships of a Taiwanese Village. *American An-
        thropologist*, Vol. 66, No. 4: 632–42.

Gallin, Bernard, and Rita Gallin
1977   Socialpolitical Power and Sworn Brother Groups in Chinese Society: A Taiwanese
        Case. In Raymond D. Fogelson and Richard N. Adams, eds. The Anthropology
        of Power: Ethnographic Studies from Asia, Oceania, and the New World.
        New York: Academic Press.
1985   Matrilateral and Affinal Relationships in a Changing Chinese Society. In Hsieh
        Jih-chang and Chuang Ying-chuang, eds. The Chinese Family and Its Ritual
        Behavior. Taipei: Institute of Ethnology, Academia Sinica, Monograph Series
        D, No. 15.

Harrell, Stevan
1985   Why the Chinese Work So Hard. In *Modern China*, Vol. 11, No. 2.

Hinton, William
1966   Fanshen: A Documentary of Revolution in a Chinese Village. New York:
        Vintage Books.

Ho, Ping-ti
1955   The Introduction of American Food Plants into China. *American Anthropologist*
        Vol. 57, No. 2: 191–201.

Hsiao, Kung-chuan
1960   Rural China. Seattle: University of Washington Press.

Hsu, Francis L.K.
1948   Under the Ancestor's Shadow: Chinese Culture and Personality. London:
        Routledge & Kegan Paul.

Huang, Shu-min
1979   Changing Taiwanese Peasants' Concept of Time: Its Impact on Agricultural
        Production. In *Iowa State Journal of Research*, Vol. 54, No. 2, pp.191–
        200.
1980   The Development of Regionalism in Ta-chia, Taiwan: A Non-kinship View of
        Chinese Rural Social Organization. In *Ethnohistory*, Vol. 27, No. 2, pp.
        243–266.
1981   Agricultural Degradation: Changing Community Systems in Rural Taiwan.
        Washington D.C.: University Press of America.
1987   The Strategy of Prosperity in a Chinese Village. *Journal of Developing Societies*,
        Vol. 3, No. 2, pp. 119–136.

1988   Transforming China's Collective Health Care System: A Village Study. *Social Science and Medicine*, Vol. 27, No. 9, pp. 879–888.

Jordan, David K.
1985   Sworn Brothers: A Study in Chinese Ritual Kinship. In Hsieh Jih-chang and Chuang Ying-chang, eds. The Chinese Family and Its Ritual Behavior. Taipei: Institute of Ethnology, Academia Sinica, Monograph Series B, No. 15.

Keng, Ling
1972   The Revenge of Heaven: Journal of a Young Chinese. New York: G.P. Putnam's Sons.

Kleinman, Arthur
1980   Patients and Healers in the Context of Culture: An Exploration of the Borderland Between Anthropology, Medicine, and Psychiatry. Berkeley, Los Angeles, and London: University of California Press.

Lattimore, Owen and Eleanor
1944   China, A Short History. New York: W.W. Norton & Co.

Legge, James
ND   The Four Books: Confucian Analects, the Great Learning, the Doctrine of the Mean, and the Work of Mencius. Shanghai: The Chinese Book Company.

Leys, Simon
1974   Chinese Shadows. New York: The Viking Press.
1985   The Burning Forest: Essays on Chinese Culture and Politics. New York: New Republic Books.

Mao Zedong
1965   Selected Works. Peking: Foreign Languages Press.

Moser, Stephen
1983   Broken Earth: The Rural Chinese. New York: The Free Press.

Nee, Victor
1985   Peasant Household Individualism. In William Parish, ed. Chinese Rural Development: The Great Transformation. Armonk, N.Y.: M.E. Sharpe.

Nee, Victor, and David Mozingo, eds.
1983   State and Society in Contemporary China. Ithaca, New York: Cornell University Press.

Parish, William L., and Martin K. Whyte
1978   Village and Family in Contemporary China. Chicago & London: The University of Chicago Press.

Perkins, Dwight
1969   Agricultural Development in China, 1368–1968. Chicago: Aldine Press.

Piazza, Alan
1986   Food Consumption and Nutritional Status in the PRC. Boulder: Westview Press.

Potter, Sulamith Heins
1983   The Position of Peasants in Modern China's Social Order. *Modern China*, Vol. 9, No. 4.

Printz, Peggy, and Paul Steinle
1977   Commune: Life in Rural China. New York: Dodd, Mead & Company.

Rossbach, Sarah
    1983   Feng Shui: The Chinese Art of Placement. New York: E.P. Dutton, Inc.
Shue, Vivienne
    1980   Peasant China in Transition: The Dynamics of Development Toward Socialism,
            1949–56. Berkeley, Los Angeles, and London: University of California Press.
Topley, Marjorie
    1975   Chinese Traditional Etiology and Methods of Cure in Hong Kong. In Charles
            Leslie, ed. Asian Medical Systems: A Comparative Study. Berkeley, Los
            Angeles, and London: University of California Press.
Wolf, Margery
    1968   The House of Lim. New York: Appleton-Century-Crofts.
    1985   Revolution Postponed: Women in Contemporary China. Stanford: Stanford
            University Press.

Glossary of Chinese Characters

Anhai Town　　安海鎮

Anxi County　　安溪縣

Bantou Town　　扳头鎮

buxiao　　不孝

caituan　　財团

Changtai County　　長泰縣

chaoyin, ganmei　　超英趕美

Chen Baozhu　　陳宝珠

chifu wangye　　池府王爺

chizu　　吃祖

Chu Lian　　促联

chong　　冲

chou zhumushui　　抽猪母税

da baogan　　大包干

daofang　　倒房

daotouzai   倒头栽
daoyang   倒阳
Dazhai   大寨
Ding Yong   丁勇
dizhetou   低著头
dizhupo   地主婆

erzeng, yijiang   二增一降

fan jitihua   反集体化
fang   房
fengshui   風水
fentian dangan   分田单干
Frontline Commune   前沿公社
Fujian   福逊
Fuqing County   福清杲
fushi   服侍

Gao Dalou (Black Barbarian)   高大楼
Ge Lian   革联
gongchan feng   共产風
gongji jin   公极金
gongli xuexiao   公立学校

gongshou 共首

gongyi jin 公益金

gongzuodui 工作队

guan 官

guanxi xue 关系学

Guankou Town 灌口镇

guojia ganbu 国家干部

Haicang Township 海仓镇

han 寒

Hecu Brigade 何厝大队

Hilltop Village 山顶村

Hong Ahui 洪阿辉

Hong San 洪三

Hongshan Brigade 洪山大队

Hou Hannan 侯汉男

Hou Lingli 侯灵丽

Hou Qiang 侯溪

Hou Tong 侯桐

housi shahou, zhusi zaizhu 猴死杀猴，猪死宰猪

huai fenzi 坏分子

Huang Bingfu 黄秉富

Huang Jincheng 黄金城

huibao 回报

Huian County 惠安果

ida, ergong 一大二公

iku, sitian 忆苦思甜

jiating chengbao zerenzhi 家庭承包责任制

jianshe shehuizhuyi jingshen wenming
建设社会主义精神文明

Jiangtou Township 江头镇

jiaoji fei 交际费

Jiaomei Township 角美镇

jiefang pai 解放牌

Jimei Township 集美镇

jinjiao yi 金交椅

kouliangtian zhi 口粮田制

kurouji 苦肉计

kuogan huiyi 扩干会议

laobaixing 老百姓

Li Ai 李矮

Lianban Village 蓬板村

lianchan chengbao zhi 联产承包制

Li Dehai (Double Headed Snake) 李徒海

lishi fangeming 厂史反革命

Lin Boting (Chubby Lin) 林柏亭

Lin Chenghu (Tiger) 林承虎

Lin Chengrui 林承瑞

Lin Da 林大

Lin Fen 林汾

Lin Fucheng (Tuxedo Lin) 林福成

Lin Leshan (Thunderbolt Lin) 林樂山

Lin Leshui (Playboy) 林樂水

Lin Lihou 林立后

Lin Qifa (Stocky Lin) 林其发

Lin Qishan 林其山

Lin Tie 林铁

Lin Xiang (Dark Skin Lin) 林祥

Lin Xiulan 林秀兰

liufu yuanshuai 刘府元師

Liu Shaoqi 刘少奇

Longhai County 龙海果

Longyan County 龙岩果

Lujiang Mansion 鹭江大厅

luobo 蘿卜

majiang 麻將

maozi 帽子

menkou gong 门口公

min 民

minban jiaoshi 民办教师

minban xuexiao 民办学校

minbing yingzhang 民兵营長

Minnan 闽南

minzhu jizhongzhi 民主集中制

Mingxi County 明溪县

mou 畝

mouchan qianjing 畝户千斤

Mudhole Village 土窟村

Nanan County 南安县

nannu guanxi 男女关系

Nanyang 南洋

nongcun ganbu 农村干部

nuxu zhuo 女婿桌

pideng fanji youqingfeng 批鄧反击右倾風

pilin, pikong 批林批孔

pinnong xiehui 贫农协会

posijiu 破四旧

qi 气

qiangda chutouniao 枪打出头鸟

qingli jieji duiwu 清理阶级队伍

Qingliu County 清流界

Qing Ming 清明

Quanzhou Prefecture 泉州府

Quemoy 金门

rensheng digong 仁圣帝公

sanchaohong 三朝红

sanfen jiucaigen, shengguo suangongfen

三分韭菜根, 胜过祁工分

santong 三同

shaji jinghou 杀鸡警猴

shejiao zongtuan 社教总团

shehui zhuyi jiaoyu 社会主义教育

siqing yundong 四清运动

Taoyuan Commune 桃园公社

Taoyuan jingyan 桃园经验

tiding 提定

tiangong 天公

tianshi, dili, renhe 天时、地利、人和

tiechi 铁齿

Tongan County 同安果

tongji 童乩

tongxue 同学

tongzhizhe 统治者

Wan Li 万立

Wang Guangmei 王光美

Wang Wenshan 王文山

Wang Xiuhua 王秀花

wubao hu 五保户

wuchan jieji quanzheng 无产阶级全记

wuchan jieji zhuanzheng 无产阶级专政

wucan caibaocai, wancan baocai bao baocai

午饮菜包菜，晚饭包菜包包菜

Wu Hanlin (Mustached Wu) 吴汉林

Wu Hongen 吴宏恩,

Wu Ming 吴明

Wu Liang (Hopping Toad) 吴良

Wutong Village 五涌村

wuxing 五行

xiafang 下放

Xiamen City 厦门市

xiamen renmin shizhengfu 厦门人民市政府

xiamen renmin sizhengfu 厦门人民饲政府

xiang 乡

xiangdai 香袋

xianggui minyue 乡规民约

xinfang 新房

Xinglin 杏林

Xu Village 许村

xunxing wangye 巡行王爷

yang 阳

Ye Fei 叶飞

Ye Jaide 叶加德

Ye Qinghui 叶清辉

Ye Wende (P.S. Ye) 叶文德

yiwu laodong 义务劳动

yoquan buyong, yuqi zhuofei

有权不用,逾期作废

Zhang Lingzhu (The Witch) 张铃珠

Zhang Ketong 张可同

zhaozhui 招赘

zhibao zhuren 治保主任

zhongyuan pudu 中元普渡

zhu 紐

zhugong 猪公

Index